COLLABORATION IN THE HOL

Also by Martin Dean

AUSTRIAN POLICY DURING THE FRENCH REVOLUTIONARY
WARS, 1796–99

Collaboration in the Holocaust

Crimes of the Local Police in Belorussia and Ukraine, 1941–44

Martin Dean

Applied Research Scholar
Center for Advanced Holocaust Studies
United States Holocaust Memorial Museum
Washington, DC

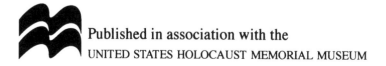

Published in association with the
UNITED STATES HOLOCAUST MEMORIAL MUSEUM

First published 2000 by
MACMILLAN PRESS LTD
Houndmills, Basingstoke, Hampshire RG21 6XS
and London
Companies and representatives
throughout the world

ISBN 0–333–68892–9 hardcover
ISBN 0–333–68893–7 paperback

A catalogue record for this book is available
from the British Library.

This book is printed on paper suitable for recycling and made from fully managed and sustained forest sources.

10   9   8   7   6   5   4   3   2   1
09   08   07   06   05   04   03   02   01   00

Printed and bound in Great Britain by
Antony Rowe Ltd, Chippenham, Wiltshire

Published in the United States of America by
ST. MARTIN'S PRESS, INC.,
Scholarly and Reference Division
175 Fifth Avenue, New York, N.Y. 10010

ISBN 0–312–22056–1

Contents

List of Photographs and Maps

Photographs

1 Jewish work column in Mogilev
Source: *BA* Koblenz 138-1083-25.

2 Handover to the civil administration in Minsk, 30 August 1941
Source: *BA-MA* Freiburg RH 22/225.

3 Gendarmerie of the Mir post in uniform, 1942
Source: *Niedersächsisches Staatsarchiv in Oldenbourg*, Best. 140-5 acc. 38/1997.

4 Schutzmannschaftsposten Sarig, Kiev district, 1942
Source: *BA* Koblenz, 73-46-41.

5 Jewish women and children guarded by local police prior to mass shooting, Sdolbunov district, Ukraine, October 1942
Source: USHMM W/S # 17877.

6 Jewish corpses from the mass shooting, Sdolbunov district, October 1942
Source: USHMM W/S # 17879.

7 Deportation of local inhabitants to Germany, 1942–43
Source: *BA* Koblenz 146-1542-10a.

8 Anti-partisan action near Minsk, 1943
Source: *BA* Koblenz 70-43-52.

Maps

1 Polish eastern territories in 1939
2 *Generalkommissariat Weißruthenien* in 1942
3 *Reichskommissariat* Ukraine: *Generalbezirke* Volhynia-Podolia, Zhitomir, Kiev and Nikolayev, 1942

List of Tables

Introduction

A definition of terror is when most crimes are committed by the police. In Belorussia and Ukraine this nightmare came true under German occupation: according to German book-keeping, more than a million Jews were shot by Himmler's police forces and their local collaborators in the east between 1941 and 1943.[1] Using considerable new evidence this book will examine how this little understood aspect of the Holocaust was implemented by local forces on the ground.

The main focus of attention will not be the German units of the Security and Order Police, already familiar to students of Himmler's police structure. Instead research has been concentrated on the local police collaborators on duty in every Belorussian and Ukrainian town. Known to the Germans as the '*Schutzmannschaft*', they were recruited from volunteers at the start of the occupation. These men played an indispensable role in the killing process. In terms of police manpower involved in the atrocities in these areas, they outnumbered their Nazi German colleagues.

The method of killing by mass shooting and the participation of men from the local population gives the Holocaust a unique character in these eastern territories. It differs considerably fom the impersonal mechanization of Nazi genocide, seen as characteristic of the Polish 'death camps'. Only a few kilometres from Sobibor and Treblinka, local policemen assisted in the mass shooting of their neighbours within earshot of their own homes. These massacres culminated in scenes of singular brutality, which could not be kept secret from the local population. Indeed many Christians profited directly from the slaughter.

Whilst the events of the Holocaust provide the central concern, an effort has been made to examine the activities of the local police within the full context of Nazi occupation policies. In the east, the Holocaust did not take place in isolation, but formed an integral part of the dynamic relations between the occupying forces and the local population. As Bernhard Chiari has argued, local police service consisted primarily of routine guard duties and, increasingly from 1942 onwards, direct participation in the bitterly fought partisan struggle.[2] The implementation of anti-Jewish policies was only one of several tasks they had to fulfil. Questions regarding the nature and motivation of these collaborationist units can only be answered within the overall framework of the conflict behind the Front.

Wartime events will be examined in more or less chronological order, to reflect how the different aspects of Nazi policy impacted upon each other. For instance the initial development of partisan resistance was closely related to the German treatment of Soviet prisoners of war. Occasional breaks will be made in the narrative to permit particular aspects, such as local police organization and German economic exploitation, to be analysed in greater depth.

The opening chapter briefly examines the Soviet occupation of eastern Poland in 1939–41 (see Map 1), in order to set the scene prior to the German invasion. Soviet behaviour not only fuelled local anti-communist resentment, to the detriment of the Jews, but provided a foretaste of the terror to come for Poles and Jews alike.

'Operation Barbarossa' is described in Chapter 2 on the basis of contemporary German reports and the recollections of local inhabitants; the development of Nazi genocide in the east came in a series of intensifying steps. Initial restrictions against the Jews and 'intelligentsia' actions were followed from August 1941 by a 'First Wave' of mass killings, as Himmler extended the group of victims to include women and children and brought in further units to support the *Einsatzgruppen* operations. A detailed case study of the *SS* Cavalry Brigade in the Pripyet marshes will demonstrate how the initial transition to genocide operated in practice.

By the autumn of 1941 all four *Einsatzgruppen* were engaged in the mass shooting of Jews. This 'First Wave' of killings is outlined in Chapter 3. The role of the local police was generally a supporting one alongside units of the Order Police, *Waffen SS* and *Wehrmacht*, which also particpated in the slaughter. In some local massacres, however, such as those in Mir, Jody and Borisov in Belorussia, local policemen played a particularly active role. This is illustrated by detailed court testimony given recently regarding the massacre on 9 November 1941 in Mir. Harsh measures against Soviet prisoners of war also served as a warning to the entire population as to what they could expect from German rule.

Over the winter of 1941–42 the German Order Police incorporated the local police volunteers into Himmler's police structure as uniformed *Schutzmannschaften*. With this now more reliable instrument in each locality, German police leaders cleared the remaining ghettoes of Belorussia and Ukraine during the course of 1942–43. In Chapter 4 the organization of the local police will be examined closely. Particular attention will be given to the background, recruitment and duties of the *Schutzmänner* on the basis of extensive new sources.

The events of the 'Second Wave' killings are not well-known, partly due to the shortage of contemporary German documentation. In the former Polish areas, however, the death toll was greater during this 'Second Wave' than during the '*Einsatzgruppen*' killings of 1941.[3] Chapter 5 will concentrate on the implementation of the ghetto 'liquidations' in 1942 and 1943. Examples are taken from the Zhitomir and Nikolayev regions in Ukraine, as well as Slonim and Nesvizh in Belorussia. An overview will also be given of the pattern of killings around Glubokoye (east of Vilnius) to the north and in the region of Volhynia-Podolia. Particular attention will be paid to the active role of the local police in these final 'liquidation' actions and especially in the subsequent tracking down of Jews in hiding. The Nazis placed considerable reliance on the loyalty and initiative of local police collaborators during this phase of the Holocaust.

German economic exploitation is examined in Chapter 6, primarily for its effects on the population as a whole. Requisitions, deportations and forced labour were all enforced with local police support. These measures contributed to the development of partisan warfare from the summer of 1942, which in turn influenced the prospects for Jewish survival and resistance in the forests. Interpretations of German administration in the east, concentrating on the plans for reform discussed at the higher levels, should be contrasted with the reality of exploitation, corruption and even demoralization in the local offices.

In Chapter 7 the brutal reprisals against partisan families conducted by the police are set against the realities of Soviet partisan tactics and the complexities of the rival nationalist partisan organizations. The actions of local policemen towards victims other than Jews must be taken into account in assessing their behaviour. The experiences of Jewish partisans in the forest are also assessed. Open conflicts between Ukrainians, Poles and Lithuanians towards the end of the occupation demonstrate another form of 'ethnic cleansing', which developed in the 'power vacuum' left by declining German influence in 1943. Civilians bore the brunt of the casualties in these bitter partisan struggles.

As a postscript in Chapter 8, the escape routes and post-war fates of local policemen are contrasted with the experiences of Jewish survivors. In the turmoil of post-war resettlement, perpetrators and victims often took similar paths after the war. Unfortunately the rivalries of the Cold War denied justice to both victims and perpetrators. Finally the nature and significance of local police collaboration in the Holocaust is summarized in the conclusion.

The geographical area of this study is bounded effectively by those regions of Belorussia (_Generalbezirk Weißruthenien_) and Ukraine (_Generalbezirke_ Volhynia-Podolia, Zhitomir, Kiev and Nikolayev), which were brought under German civil administration by the end of 1941 (see Maps 2 and 3).[4] Together these regions had a population in excess of 10 million inhabitants, of which approximately 7 per cent were Jews. Much of this area was Polish territory until 1939; certain differences can be observed between the attitude of the population in the former Polish areas and those who had experienced some 20 years of Sovietization. In this study most of the detailed research has been conducted in the former Polish areas. However, a few examples have also been taken from the former Soviet areas for comparison.

The research has consisted primarily of a number of local case studies, which lay down several patch-work squares over this vast territory. Considerable use has been made of personal eye-witness testimony, mainly from post-war legal investigations: the history of local collaborators can only now be written, with the aid of their own trial records. The triangle of perpetrators, victims and bystanders has been completed where possible, in order to present a kaleidoscopic picture of events, seen from several perspectives at once.

The opening of the Soviet archives since 1989 has provided a wealth of new captured German documentation, especially with regard to the German administration and police forces. The collections in Moscow, Minsk, Brest and Zhitomir have been used extensively, as well as the excellent resources now on microfilm at the US Holocaust Memorial Museum. Reference has been made to the relevant secondary literature to assist in explaining the overall framework of the occupation.

In presenting the story an effort has been made to permit the sources to speak for themselves within the framework of a closely argued narrative. Given the nature of the subject and the sources used, the methodology can perhaps best be described as 'forensic history': explaining the processes involved through a meticulous presentation of the evidence from local investigations. It is in the wealth of detail opened up by numerous personal descriptions that the reliability of the sources can be tested. Particular emphasis has been placed on exploiting a broad range of contrasting material. Conflicting accounts have been directly compared, testing each against the totality of evidence available.

In some respects my research reflects the criminal investigations from which much of the information has been derived. The study of history is inherently a branch of detective work, following promising leads in the archives, in order to establish the relevant facts. By recounting in detail the crimes committed by the local police, it is possible to analyse the structure and nature of this organization. A profile can be drawn up of the men serving within the police ranks. Recruitment, motives and even post-war fates are examined by studying testimonies and data assembled for numerous local collaborators. As the last legal proceedings draw to an inevitable close, it is time for history to evaluate the part played by the *Schutzmänner* in the Holocaust from the considerable sources now available.

The extensive use of historical testimonies collected primarily for legal purposes raises certain questions of methodology. In most instances the full names of both witnesses and perpetrators have necessarily been concealed. Much new evidence from communist investigations has been examined and subjected to careful comparison with the other available sources. With regard to the statements by eye-witnesses, there is in most cases little doubt that the events described actually took place. Certain systematic errors can be detected, however, for which allowances have to be made: for example, details regarding dates and numbers are sometimes inaccurate due to memory lapses or mistakes made in the transcription of the statement. Many witnesses clearly lacked specific knowledge about the particular units involved and are unable to identify the perpetrators clearly. Nevertheless it is often remarkable how much detail can be recalled, even more than 50 years after the event.

Naturally the evidence of perpetrators must be treated with particular care and can only be used reliably when corroborated independently, or for matters not related to questions of personal guilt or innocence. The motives of the perpetrators can only be assessed from a sensitive analysis of all available sources. Ultimately it is not possible to know precisely what was going on in the minds of the killers; the conclusions of historians on such matters must be regarded cautiously as informed speculation rather than facts.

For many understandable reasons the history of the collaborationist local police in the occupied Soviet Union has been largely neglected hitherto. Whilst doggedly prosecuting all collaborators as traitors at home, the Soviet government was reluctant to acknowledge publicly the scale and extent of collaboration with the German invaders. Émigré historians, for similar if opposite motives, have preferred to play down the active collaboration of individuals in German police atrocities, stressing instead the frustrated aims of nationalist groups for independence. Local participation in the Holocaust in countries such as Lithuania and Ukraine remains a sensitive issue, demanding carefully chosen words from those holding the highest offices of state.[5] In view of the importance of the topic, one of the aims of this work is to fill what remains a large gap in the literature, using a very broad base of source material.

Our current understanding of the Holocaust still owes an enormous debt to the seminal work of Raul Hilberg, who provided the first detailed history of the Holocaust on the basis of captured German documentation.[6] In recent years his ground-breaking research has been carried forward by many scholars, most notably Christopher Browning, who has made a series of significant contributions on the subject.[7] As the recent pioneering studies of the German historians Dieter Pohl and Thomas Sandkühler for the regions of Lublin and Galicia in the General Government have shown, the implementation of genocide on the local level was often a complex process involving both personal initiatives and pragmatic considerations.[8] A number of young German scholars are currently piecing together many of the remaining fragments on the basis of the new material now available from the Soviet and German archives.[9]

Of most importance to this study have been the detailed local testimonies available for several locations in Belorussia and Ukraine. These permit a perception of the implementation of policy on the ground which was not previously possible. Existing studies of German occupation policy in the east, such as the classic work of Alexander Dallin or the analysis of reform attempts by Timothy Mulligan, have concentrated on high-level policy.[10] The records they examined consisted mainly of the correspondence of senior figures in the local administration with their superiors in Berlin. It is only recently, through the innovative research of Bernhard Chiari for Belorussia, that a more detailed analysis of the everyday experiences of the local population has been attempted.[11] The personal recollections of individuals give the traumatic experiences of the war a more immediate impact.

Essential to a full understanding of the Holocaust is also the viewpoint of the victims. The stories of the survivors are doubly important, not only as vital evidence of what happened, but in order to understand their unique perspective: many felt themselves to be virtually isolated from the population as a whole. Some of the foremost accounts have been written by people who themselves survived Nazi persecution: most notably the excellent studies by Shmuel Spector for Volhynia, but also vital contributions by Shalom Cholawsky and Hersh Smolar for Belorussia. The books of Necama Tec on Oswald Rufeisen and the Bielski partisans have provided a particular inspiration through their sophisticated analysis of local events on the basis of oral testimony.[12]

The considerable reliance of Himmler on local participation in the Holocaust and the overall significance of the 'Second Wave' of total 'liquidations' in 1942–43 are both important aspects, which have been much underestimated by Holocaust historians in the past. In 1942 and 1943 German police organizations and their collaborators killed in excess of half a million Jews, mostly by shooting, within the 1940 borders of the Soviet Union. By providing detailed information on both the organization and timing of the Holocaust, this book will provide further impetus to the growing historical debate on how the Holocaust was implemented in the east.

In view of the inevitable problems involved, it should be noted that the statistics presented are given as an accurate representation of the information found in the available sources. Demographic data and reports on the number of victims for any particular action, however, are in most cases only estimates. The figures are intended to give an impression of the scale of the events described, but should be treated with a degree of caution. A precisely accurate figure is unfortunately not to be expected.

Ultimately, the history of local collaboration in the Holocaust cannot be written in terms of the number of victims; it consists rather of the cumulative experiences of numerous individuals. How did they react under the terrifying circumstances of Nazi genocide and partisan war? Using their own words, this book attempts to present the viewpoint of ordinary people living in the villages, many of whom experienced the horrors of the Holocaust and the realities of police brutality in their own front yard.

Notes

1. R. Headland, *Messages of Murder*, p. 105 gives a minimum figure of 1 152 000 on the basis of German reports for the period up to December 1942.
2. B. Chiari, *'Deutsche Herrschaft'*, pp. 181–9.
3. See Table A.5 in the Appendix.
4. An anglicized version of the Russian name has been used for most places purely for reasons of convenience. The term Belorussia has been retained, rather than the modern Belarus, which dates only from very recent usage. The term 'eastern Poland' refers to the inter-war Polish borders and is used purely historically.
5. See, for example, F. Golczewski, *'Entgegen dem Klischee'*.
6. R. Hilberg, *The Destruction of the European Jews*.
7. See for example, C. Browning, *The Path to Genocide*; C. Browning, *Ordinary Men*; and C. Browning, *Fateful Months*.
8. T. Sandkühler, *'Endlösung' in Galizien*; D. Pohl, *Nationalsozialistische Judenverfolgung*; D. Pohl, *Von der 'Judenpolitik' zum Judenmord: Der Distrikt Lublin des Generalgouvernements 1939–44*.
9. See, especially the forthcoming dissertations of C. Gerlach (*Einsatzgruppe B*), A. Angrick (*Einsatzgruppe D*) and C. Dieckmann (Lithuania).
10. A. Dallin, *German Rule in Russia*; T. P. Mulligan, *The Politics of Illusion and Empire*.
11. B. Chiari, *'Deutsche Herrschaft'*.
12. S. Spector, *The Holocaust of Volhynian Jews, 1941–44*; H. Smolar, *The Minsk Ghetto*; S. Cholawski, *Soldiers from the Ghetto*; S. Cholawsky, *The Jews of Bielorussia during World War II*; N. Tec, *In the Lion's Den*; N. Tec, *Defiance: The Bielski Partisans*.

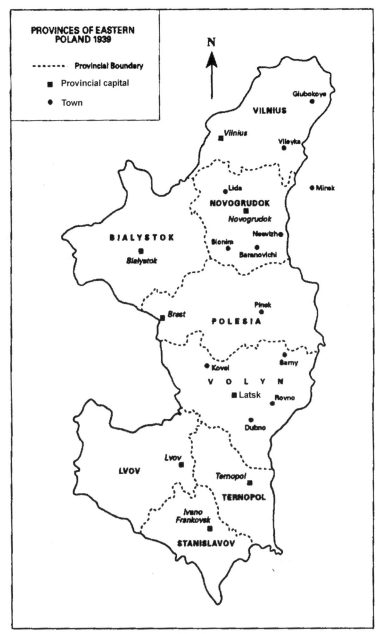

Map 1

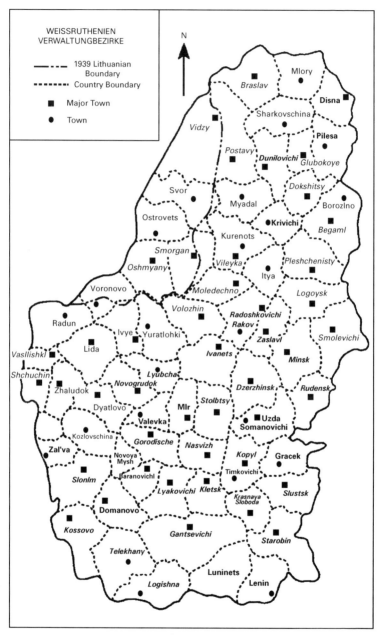

Map 2

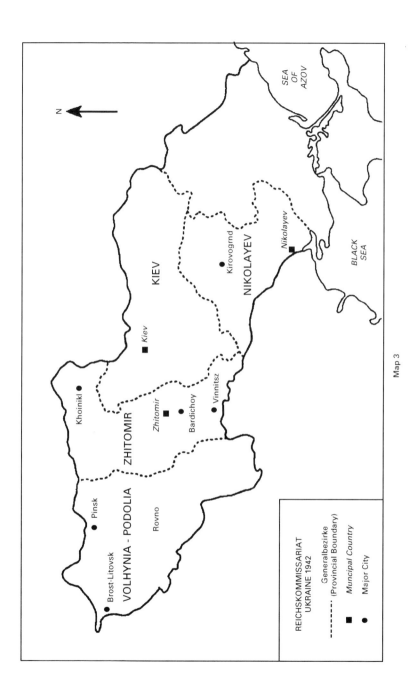

SEA OF AZOV

BLACK SEA

Nikolayev ■

Kirovognd ●

NIKOLAYEV

KIEV

Kiev ■

Khoiniki ●

ZHITOMIR

Zhitomir ■

Bardichoy ●

Vinnitsz ●

Pinsk ●

Rovno

VOLHYNIA - PODOLIA

Brost-Litovsk ●

N

REICHSKOMMISSARIAT
UKRAINE 1942

- - - - - Generalbezirke
(Provincial Boundary)

■ Muncipal Country

● Major City

Map 3

xvii

Acknowledgements

The number of persons who have supported my research over the years is legion, such that it is possible here to mention but a few. My thanks, however, go to all who have given me their assistance and encouragement, most notably to Dorothée Berendes, my wife. I am particularly indebted to Alisdair Macleod and Bernhard Chiari, who worked the 'coal face' in the Belorussian archives at my behest. Christopher Browning, Konrad Kwiet and Jonathon Steinberg have inspired and tutored me through their examples as leading scholars in the field. I am grateful also to Peter Black, Bernhard Chiari, Hans-Heinrich Wilhelm and Jack Kagan for their advice and criticism regarding earlier drafts of my manuscript. The views expressed here are, however, purely my own; any errors or ommissions are my own personal responsibility.

A very special thanks must go to Pearl Resnick and the US Holocaust Memorial Museum for their generosity, which has given me the opportunity to produce this work. I am also deeply indebted to my genial and unstinting former colleagues at the Metropolitan Police War Crimes Unit and the Australian Special Investigations Unit, most notably John Ralston, Michael Griffiths and David Lloyd. A number of major archives have eased my path through the mountains of paper. The late Alfred Streim at the Central Office in Ludwigsburg was always a tower of strength and sanity, whose warmth and wisdom is greatly missed. Dr Stanislaw Kaniewski and his colleagues at the Polish Institute for National Remembrance, and also Ivan Ivanovich Sukhoverkh and the staff of the Belorussian Procuracy, became friends and comrades over years of close co-operation.

For their considerable assistance during my usually hectic archival visits around the world I would like to express my gratitude to Anna Terebun in Brest, Tatyana Franz in Zhitomir, Natalya Redkozubova in Minsk, B.F.H. Meyer, formerly of the military archive in Freiburg, Suzanne Pivcova in Prague, Josef Henke and Reinhold Bauer in Koblenz, David Marwell and Aaron Kornblum in Washington, Adam Witko in Hayes and my colleagues Stefan Kühmeyer and Ludwig Norz in Berlin.

Finally a most heartfelt thank you goes to Bob Waite for his warm friendship and support. There has been literally a cast of thousands without whom this work would not have been possible; I remain indebted to them all.

MARTIN DEAN

List of Abbreviations

AK	*Armija Krajowa*	
	Polish Underground Home Army	
BdS	*Befehlshaber der Sicherheitspolizei*	
	Senior Commander of the Security Police	
BSO	Belorussian Self-Help Organization	
DP	Displaced Person	
FK	*Feldkommandantur*	
	Field Command post	
Gestapo	*Geheime Staatspolizei*	
	Secret State Police	
GFP	*Geheime Feldpolizei*	
	Secret Field Police (*Wehrmacht*)	
HSSPF	*Höhere SS-und Polizei Führer*	
	Higher SS and Police Leader	
KdG	*Kommandeur der Gendarmerie*	
	Rural Police Commander	
KdO	*Kommandeur der Ordnungspolizei*	
	Commander of the Order Police	
KdS	*Kommandeur der Sicherheitspolizei*	
	Commander of the Security Police	
Kripo	*Kriminalpolizei*	
	Criminal Police	
NCO	Non-commissioned officer	
NKVD	Soviet State Security Police	
	(Forerunner of the *KGB*)	
OD	*Ordnungsdienst* (Order Service)	
	Local militia (military administration)	
OK	*Ortskommandantur*	
	Local Command post	
OKH	Germany Army High Command	
OKW	German Armed Forces High Command	
OUN	Organization of Ukrainian Nationalists	
Pol. Bn.	Police Battalion (Order Police)	
Pol. Rgt.	Police Regiment (Order Police)	
PoWs	Prisoners of War	
RFSS	*Reichsführer SS* (Heinrich Himmler)	
	Head of SS and German Police	

RM	*Reichsmark*	
	German currency	
RSHA	*Reichssicherheitshauptamt*	
	Reich Main Security Office	
SA	*Sturmabteilung*	
	Stormtroopers of the Nazi Party	
SD	*Sicherheitsdienst*	
	Security Service of the *SS* (intelligence)	
SS	*Schutzstaffel* (protection squads)	
	Elite bodyguard of Nazi Party built up by Himmler into own empire within the Party	
SSPF	*SS- und Polizei Führer*	
	SS and Police Leader	
UPA	Ukrainian Resistance Army	

1 The Soviet Occupation of Eastern Poland, 1939–41

On 17 September 1939 the Red Army advanced cautiously into the eastern half of Poland. It was an unusual invasion as some inhabitants initially thought that the Soviet troops had come to help them fight the Germans.[1] Advancing Soviet forces rapidly disabused them, however, by installing their own authority in the occupied areas. The public justification for the Soviet advance was the need to restore order and protect the kindred Belorussian and Ukrainian peoples after the collapse of the Polish state.[2] In fact Stalin was merely securing his prize of eastern Poland as negotiated under the secret terms of the Molotov–Ribbentrop Pact.

Limited resistance was offered to the Red Army by the scattered Polish border troops up to 25 September 1939.[3] Their will to resist, however, had already been broken by the force of the preceding German onslaught. The hopeless dilemma of the Polish forces, confronted with the reality of a fourth partition, is recalled by a former soldier:

> In September [1939] a Major arrived...he gathered all the soldiers and told them that from the west we are being invaded by the Germans and from the east by the Russians, that we do not know who to fight against, and he told us to go where we wanted.[4]

The soldier went home to join his family. In eastern Poland, the takeover was grudgingly accepted as the *fait accompli* the Soviets had intended.

With remarkable haste the Soviet authorities set about formally annexing the occupied areas. On 22 October 1939 carefully orchestrated 'elections' were held for People's Assemblies in both the Ukrainian and Belorussian sectors of Soviet-occupied Poland. In preparation, extensive propaganda was organized by activists from the Soviet interior assisted by local teachers. Attendance at the numerous propaganda meetings was generally compulsory. On the day itself reluctant voters were often escorted to the polls with the assistance of militiamen. The *NKVD* (Soviet State Security Police) did not hesitate to use open intimidation to ensure that candidates proposed by the Soviet authorities received the expected 'overwhelming' support. Voter turnout was over 90 per cent everywhere and few dared even to spoil their ballot papers in the prevailing oppressive climate.[5]

On 1 November 1939 the Supreme Soviet in Moscow approved the petition of the Assembly of the western Ukraine for incorporation into the Ukrainian Soviet Republic. Approval for the petition of western Belorussia to be included in the Belorussian Soviet Republic came the following day.[6] These decisions were ratified by the Belorussian and Ukrainian Supreme Soviets in Minsk and Kiev in mid-November.

The Soviet forces encountered a mixed reception amongst the local population in eastern Poland. Some Belorussians initially welcomed the arrival of the Red Army. In spite of brutal *NKVD* purges against 'disobedient' Belorussian communist activists in the late 1930s, they hoped for an improvement in their social and cultural position compared with Polish rule. The Polish authorities had restricted Belorussian education and also persecuted some nationalists.[7] Thus a combination of hope and fear encouraged Belorussians to demonstrate support for the new order. In many towns triumphal arches and enthusiastic crowds were organized to greet the Red Army as it arrived. In particular, the integration of western Belorussia within the Belorussian Soviet Socialist Republic fulfilled hopes for a unitary Belorussian national state, albeit under the aegis of Soviet domination.

The rigid nature of that domination, even for Belorussian communists, is revealed in extracts from a letter by W. P. Laskowicz addressed to the First Secretary of the Belorussian Communist Party:

> The joy felt on the part of the whole nation as a result of liberation was followed as early as the second day by the declaration that all revolutionaries, members of the *KPZB* (Communist Party of western Belorussia), *Komsomol* members, who had only just been released from Polish prisons, were enemies; the *KPZB* was considered to be a party founded by Polish military intelligence. Greater madness could not have been expected. Our struggle, our sufferings, our dreams for a happy future were mocked and spat upon. I'll say more: many *KPZB* members were arrested, and all the rest found themselves under constant surveillance . . . Our enemies laughed at these idiotic events.[8]

The mass of the Belorussian peasantry lacked a strong national identity, many in Polesia being described only as 'local'.[9] For them the economic changes brought by the Soviet regime were of the greatest significance.

Responses in Ukraine were equally mixed. Ukrainian peasants had their own expression for those who periodically came to their country, usually to exploit its resources. They called them *zajdy*, or those who 'strolled in'. It was undoubtedly prudent to welcome them warmly, in the hope of ameliorating their behaviour.[10] Nevertheless, rumours about the great famine and the purges in the 1930s in Soviet Ukraine may have tempered their enthusiasm.[11] As with the Belorussians, amongst the first to suffer were Ukrainian communists. In 1938 the Comintern had ordered the dissolution of the Communist Party of western Ukraine (*KPZU*) for nationalist deviations.[12] The enthusiasm of fervent nationalists in Galicia for the creation of a united Ukraine was also tempered by the means of its achievement through the Red

Army. Nevertheless, at this time, the Ukrainians offered no organized resistance to the Soviet takeover.

The Poles were a major target for Soviet repression. They had formed a dominant minority in eastern Poland and held most of the leading positions in state and society prior to the Soviet invasion. In areas just to the east of the demarcation line with Nazi Germany, members of the Polish administration, including the police, retreated west, attempting to reach the relative safety of Romania.[13]

Upon their arrival, the Soviet authorities began arresting Poles who had held posts of responsibility, such as politicians, officials, schoolteachers and lawyers, and interned all Polish soldiers as prisoners of war (PoWs) in a series of camps.[14] Polish Army officers and former policemen were then screened out by interrogation. The outlook for these men was bleak: they were soon deported to the Soviet Union where many were subsequently killed, most notably some 4000 army officers at Katyn, near Smolensk.[15] The PoWs were also classified by nationality and some Belorussians and Ukrainians were released.

In the initial chaos it was possible for a few PoWs to escape, although many prefered to await official discharge papers, rather than run the gauntlet of Soviet bureaucracy without them. As winter approached, however, the prison camps became more permanent and expectations of a rapid release were disappointed. Instead the Soviets put their captives to work on construction projects. Many were held under harsh conditions until the German invasion, when the attempt was made to evacuate them east into the Soviet Union.[16]

Local communist sympathizers, including some Jews among them, initially welcomed the Soviets with joy. They assisted the new regime by forming local militias and helping with the establishment of a provisional administration. The militias took part in disarming and arresting the Polish police, arousing anger amongst Poles. Yet the arrival of Soviet officials and policemen from the east in November 1939 caused many local communist activists, including Jews, to be dismissed from their positions of responsibility.[17]

By the appointment of its own people, the Soviet regime intended tightening its grip on the newly occupied areas. Elections were also used for this purpose. They did not provide any democratic legitimation, as one Jewish survivor recalls: 'The local council elections were also rigged, the Russians put their own selected people on the council, for instance there was a blacksmith who was a poorly educated Jew, a simple man who was just put into the council to do their will.'[18] The experience of voter registration and close scrutiny of voting was perceived as a means for identifying political opponents.[19]

Following the arrest of the Polish police, the Soviets utilized the newly created local militias to enforce their policies. Apart from local communists, even some former criminals received postings in the militia.[20] For many it was particularly surprising to see Jews serving as policemen on the streets.[21] For some Poles, who had lost their former pre-eminence, this was a particular provocation and added fuel to the latent anti-Semitism of the inter-war period. Overall control of the militia, however, lay firmly in trusted hands.

Most feared were the *NKVD* officers who came from the east and were distinguished by the red piping on their uniforms. They were responsible for dealing with enemies of the regime. Amongst their tasks was supervision of the militia and the running of the numerous and overcrowded prisons.[22] These prisons were used primarily for the purposes of interrogation rather than the punishment of persons already sentenced:

> the institution of prison is conceived of, primarily, as a sort of isolation ward in which the process of investigation of the prisoner's case is carried on. This investigation may continue for over a period of weeks, or months, or even of years. The investigating judges alone decide upon each prisoner's individual regimes...[they are] transferred continually from cell to cell, solitary or savagely overcrowded or plain punitive according to the amount of pressure required to break down resistance in each case. Detention in prison generally, the prison regime itself, and the use of punitive cells...have all lost their initial functions, and now serve simply as means of exerting pressure during the conduct of investigations.[23]

Typical of the strong executive power exerted by the Soviet authorities was the clearing of villages close to the border area.[24] This was done in order to create a security zone. A local inhabitant from near Brest-Litovsk recalls: 'our village was situated on the bank of the river Bug. The Soviets moved us from there to former ethnic German houses further east.'[25] People were ordered to abandon their homes and thereafter the buildings were destroyed.[26]

The main effect of Soviet occupation, however, was more sinister. Traditionally the Russian response to nationalist resistance in Poland had been deportation to Siberia.[27] Soon after the Soviet annexation of the Polish eastern territories a series of mass deportations started, which inspired fear throughout the occupied area.

Three main waves of deportations to the east were conducted by the Soviet authorities during the first half of 1940.[28] In February two main targets for arrests by the *NKVD* were Polish 'military settlers' and those who worked as foresters in the countryside. These were added to Polish civil servants, officials and policemen from the towns, some of whom had been arrested previously.[29] Some 220 000 persons were deported to work, mainly on *Gulag* (Soviet punitive labour camp) projects clearing forests in the east of the Soviet Union. One reason for these particular arrests may have been to reduce the risk of Polish partisan resistance in the large forested areas of eastern Poland.[30] The absence of these men no doubt influenced the course of the subsequent partisan struggle during the German occupation.

A few Poles managed to avoid deportation by changing their place of residence. A family which was living near Volkovysk escaped to stay with friends in Baranovichi, having received a tip-off that they were on the list to be deported in February 1940.[31] Similarly, cases are known where Poles were released from captivity and permitted to return to their families in Soviet-occupied Poland.[32] These contradictory examples demonstrate the arbitrary nature of much that took place. 'The manner in which arrests were carried out was characteristic. In the houses in which they took place, not only the men whom the police had actually come to fetch were arrested, but everybody who happened to be in these houses at the same time.'[33]

On 13 April 1940 the families of a number of selected groups were taken for deportation. Their men had been arrested previously and the families were now deported, as they were viewed as potential enemies of the regime. The groups included Polish Army officers and non-commissioned officers (NCOs), policemen, landowners, businessmen, officials, teachers, lawyers and political activists, including former communists. Apart from the Polish intelligentsia, many Jews and even some of the more wealthy Belorussian and Ukrainian peasants were included in this batch. The destinations of the families were civilian residential localities in Kazakhstan, where they were employed in a variety of jobs. Conditions were harsh and a number of those deported, especially children, died on the journeys or subsequently in exile.

Estimates put the number of those affected in this massive wave of deportations at around 320 000. The families did not hear anything of their menfolk whilst in Kazakhstan. Given the nature of Soviet bureaucracy, and especially the prevailing strict travel restrictions, it was almost impossible for them to escape back to the west.[34]

In accordance with an agreement signed between Germany and the Soviet Union on 28 September 1939, about 128 000 ethnic Germans (*Volksdeutsche*) were 'repatriated' from the Soviet-occupied zone. This huge population transfer was completed rapidly within the two months leading up to 9 February 1940.[35] A few ethnic Germans remained in eastern Poland, but were subsequently viewed with some suspicion by the Germans, having failed to relocate at this first opportunity.[36]

In the autumn of 1939 it is estimated that more than 300 000 refugees from western Poland, most of them Jewish, found themselves in the Soviet zone of occupation once Poland was partitioned.[37] They were cramped into limited housing space, as they also had to compete with the host of newly arrived communist officials from the east for limited facilities. In 1940 these refugees were forced to choose between adopting Soviet nationality and staying in the occupied zone, or being 'repatriated' to the German side. Reference was even made in official posters to the repatriation agreement with Germany mentioned above, which in fact only referred to those of German ethnicity.

The Soviet authorities had no intention of repatriating these refugees. Instead they chose to punish with exile those who failed this deceitful test of loyalty. A Jewish survivor from Slonim recalls the way in which this was carried out:

> A number of the Jewish refugees from Poland expressed a wish to return to Poland to collect their winter clothing. The Soviets encouraged them to do so. When they came forward their names were put on a list. The Soviets then deported them to Kazakhstan and did not permit them to return to their homes.[38]

Some 240 000 refugees from western Poland were deported by the Soviets at this time, the vast majority during a third wave of deportations on 29 June 1940. About 60 per cent of them are thought to have been Jews. One estimate is that, of those deported, about 10 per cent perished on the journey and many more undoubtedly died in the *Gulag* camps in northern Russia and Siberia. Ironically, the survival rate for these Jews was nevertheless much higher than those who remained behind to be caught by the German killing units.[39]

A fourth wave of deportations from the Baltic states and western Belorussia took place between 13 and 21 June 1941, following the Soviet annexation of the Baltic states in the summer of 1940. An estimated 300 000 persons were affected on this occasion, although the measures were more chaotic in view of the ensuing German invasion on 22 June 1941.[40]

The policy of deportations was in effect a geographical solution to the pacification of the area. It can to a limited extent be compared with forcible population transfers carried out by the Germans in western Poland at the same time. The main groups affected were those committed in some way to the Polish cause, those with relatives abroad, those viewed as 'capitalists' (including merchants and landowners), foreign nationals (mainly refugees) and those who already had relatives in prison and labour camps. All were seen as in some way a threat to the Soviet regime. This policy more than any other was quintessential to the way Soviet rule was viewed by the mass of the local population. According to Polish sources, about 10 per cent of the overall population of eastern Poland (13.5 million) was deported to the east and was not expected to return.[41]

In eastern Poland the Jews lived primarily in the medium-sized towns or *shtetl*, where they often formed a local majority. They worked mainly to service the agricultural population of the surrounding countryside as tradesmen and artisans. The Jewish community was usually concentrated around the central market place, which formed the focal point for their commercial activities.[42] During the late 1930s the Jewish population of Poland suffered from the anti-Semitic economic policies of the Polish government. The Jews were burdened with additional taxes and regulations, such as that which required them to close their shops on Sundays (in addition to Saturdays).[43] There was even an official policy preparing for the emigration of Poland's Jews.[44]

For the Jewish communities of eastern Poland the Soviet occupation entailed many changes. Some Jews were initially relieved to see the Soviet troops, as they were greatly concerned by the German advance. One Jewish girl expressed the belief that the Soviets 'would bring stability, peace, culture and food'.[45] In her home town of Slonim 'thousands lined the streets to greet the approach of the "rescuers"'.[46]

Surprisingly the Red Army is described by local inhabitants as comparatively disciplined and well-behaved, in contrast to the poor reputation of the old Tsarist Army. Jewish witnesses portray them as polite and friendly: 'when the Russians first came, everyone was happy. In the beginning, the Soviets were generous, handing out cigarettes and money.'[47] Most importantly they paid for goods with money supplied to them in advance. It would appear that they had been carefully briefed on how to behave towards the local population.[48]

With regard to employment and social status many Jews experienced an improvement under Soviet rule. They were more or less treated equally alongside Poles, Belorussians and Ukrainians. As one survivor explained: 'it may be said that in general the Jews had better times under the Russians, because they had equal opportunity and rights in all areas, a situation which did not exist during the Polish regime'.[49] For younger Jews, the new opportunities in work and education encouraged many to accommodate themselves to the Soviet order. Only a few maintained underground Zionist activity and their allegiance to the Hebrew language.[50] The Zionist underground attempted to smuggle members across the border to Lithuania or Romania.[51] The border police captured many, who then joined the list of candidates for deportation. Few of those who made it to Lithuania or Romania completed the further hazardous journey on to Palestine.

The Soviets viewed all conquered peoples as a possible threat, to be forcibly incorporated into the communist system. With regard to the Jews, who were not granted the status of a nation in Soviet ideology, the aim was to assimilate them as soon as possible, by uprooting Jewish communal and religious organizations. In many places their collapse was almost 'spontaneous': 'with the entry of the Red Army nobody dared to call a meeting of an organization or an institution. All community or national contacts from that day on went underground.'[52] Likewise the Jews considered it wise to attend communist meetings and march with the demonstrations.[53]

Soviet political and economic changes severely affected the Jewish population. By contrast to the already Sovietized Jews of Minsk, 80 per cent of whom worked in factories or the administration in 1939, in eastern Poland over 80 per cent of Jews still worked as traders or craftsmen,[54] so that restrictions on travel rendered traditional trading occupations impossible. Some shopkeepers retained their jobs, but were converted to salaried officials of the state. Businesses and other property were confiscated and those viewed as capitalists subject to discrimination and deportation. One man recalls being 'forced to leave his government job merely because he was the son of a merchant according to his passport'.[55] Others were not permitted to remain in the cities, and were moved to smaller towns and villages away from the frontier zone.[56]

Jewish craftsmen fared somewhat better as their handworker status fitted more easily into the categories acceptable to Soviet ideology. The most common Jewish craftspeople in eastern Poland included tailors, shoemakers, hatters, carpenters, housepainters and blacksmiths. These trades were not nationalized, but forced to form co-operatives (*artels*) along Soviet lines. The *artels* were effectively run by the state authorities, who appointed the management and set both prices and wages. The effect of these changes for the mostly Jewish craftsmen was to make them salaried employees with a fixed, if lowly, income.[57]

The most visible sign of change in the *shtetl* was the decline of religious observance on Saturdays (*shabat*) and the religious holidays. Sovietization encouraged the abandonment of traditional dress or even smart clothes, which might attract the unwanted attentions of the militia. People were afraid to meet and talk to each other in the streets. All this added to the prevailing oppression, drabness and shabbiness, which was the hallmark of communist eastern Europe.[58]

Judaism was formally tolerated in line with 'Stalin's Constitution' and the Soviet authorities did not interfere directly with Jewish religious practices.[59] Nevertheless organized religion was constantly under pressure to limit its activities: for instance, rabbis were heavily taxed and religious education driven underground. Press articles often carried an anti-religious tone and official working hours made no allowances for traditional religious observance.[60]

The majority of Jews in eastern Poland had succeeded in retaining their cultural identity, speaking Yiddish or Hebrew as their native tongue. Under the Soviets, teaching in Hebrew was forbidden and even the number of schools teaching in Yiddish declined as the occupation went on. The most frequent argument used by parents for the abandonment of Yiddish was that it would be of no use at institutions of further education within the Soviet Union.[61] For many Jews it was the loss of their culture which hurt the most: 'See what they have done to us. The *Kehillah* is no more, the *Talmud Torah* is gone. Synagogues, we have none; no schools, no holidays, no *chalutzim*, no *Eretz Israel*, nothing, nothing. We are going towards nothing at all.'[62]

The eastern part of Poland was a poor and relatively backward economic region. In the remote areas of Volhynia, Polesia and much of western Belorussia, timber was the main natural resource; communications were primitive and there had been little industrial development. Nevertheless, the soldiers of the Red Army were astonished at the wealth of food, clothes and consumer goods openly for sale compared with the bare shop windows back in the Soviet Union. The favourable exchange rate of one *złoty* to one rouble enabled the 'easterners' to empty the shops legally in rapid time. Particularly attractive items were fountain pens and watches, almost unheard of at home.[63]

Thus the usual symptoms of the command economy soon made an appearance. The combination of fixed prices and a shortage of goods naturally encouraged people to resort to barter and black-market operations, in which the Soviets themselves proved most experienced. Queuing became ubiquitous: 'in the streets, there were lines for bread, for soap, for sugar, for everything. People would come early just to find that others had arrived even earlier.'[64]

On 1 January 1940 the *złoty* was abolished with almost no prior warning. Only 300 *złoty* could be exchanged into roubles at one to one, thereby wiping out the bank savings of most people.[65] Combined with the low level of wages paid by state employment and the effects of expropriation, this meant considerable impoverishment for much of the population. People were forced to spend what savings they had and sell off objects of value. For those deported to the east, even the most worthless Polish trinket might buy them a crust of bread or useful tool to help them survive.[66]

Not all who experienced the Soviet occupation remember it entirely in negative terms. A Jewish survivor from Kletsk records in retrospect: 'there was no unemployment. The rich lost their fortunes, but on the other hand the poor were satisfied with the new regime which had improved their lot.'[67] For some poor artisans the security of a steady income and cheap bread may have been an improvement on the cut-throat competition prior to the war.

Soviet rule began with the nationalization of industry and stores, and the implementation of an eight-hour working day. Private enterprise was effectively throttled by high taxes and numerous regulations.[68] Nevertheless, after the initial dislocations caused by the change of economic system, unemployment fell as jobs became available in the state-run industries and administration.

The spoliation of Polish goods was also conducted on an official level by the authorities. Entire factories, loose tiles, and even door knobs were confiscated and shipped to the USSR, usually in a most wasteful fashion. The impression made on the local inhabitants was one of shabbiness and decay. In the view of one Ukrainian inhabitant: 'everyone lived, ate, and dressed worse than before'. At the same time the Red Army requisitioned and plundered what it needed in terms of food and transport for its own use. This was mainly extracted from the large estates, but small peasants were also affected.[69]

Some of the refugees from western Poland, banished from the cities, were enticed to migrate into the Soviet Union by official offers of work, especially in the Donbas mining region. However, the stories of unemployment, hunger and inhospitable conditions (brought back by the few that managed to return) underlined the primitiveness of Soviet life, even compared with eastern Poland. The effects of such stories actually encouraged some Jews to opt for a return to German occupation.[70]

In western Ukraine land reform and collectivization were key issues. In eastern Galicia and Volhynia over 80 per cent of the large landowners were Polish. On 28 October 1939 the People's Assembly of western Ukraine announced the confiscation of the lands of great landowners, monasteries and state officials. Some land was redistributed to small peasants. The majority of confiscated land remained in the hands of the state and was later used to establish state farms, in which 'unemployed' agricultural workers were given jobs. After a cautious start, a large number of collective farms were established during 1940–41.[71] Given the variegated ethnic mixture in the occupied lands, the Soviets exploited economic policies in an effort to divide and rule the local peoples.

At the time of the Soviet occupation, the roughly 13 million inhabitants of eastern Poland were made up of about one-third Poles and one-third Ukrainians. Apart from a few Lithuanians, Germans and Russians, the remaining third of the population was divided more or less equally between Jews, Belorussians and the Orthodox inhabitants of Polesia, known as 'locals'.[72] Given their minority position in this part of Poland, the Poles had undertaken a number of measures prior to 1939 to strengthen their position. Polish settlement was encouraged by subsidized government loans. In particular, Polish ex-combatants from the Russo-Polish War of 1920–21 were encouraged to settle in the east. Furthermore, many Poles were brought in to take up jobs in the administration, schools and public services. Above all 'Polonization' was pursued through education policies, with Polish being legally required as the language of instruction for most subjects.

Discrimination against non-Polish minorities in terms of state employment, economic life and schooling was, however, accompanied by lively social and political activity within all communities. Open ethnic violence was limited to terrorist attacks by the Ukrainian nationalists (OUN) in the 1930s, which provoked forceful state repression by the Polish police and army.[73] Nevertheless the relations between ethnic communities in the east are frequently described as having been 'good' or 'normal', even if there was little social contact between Christians and Jews other than at school or in business. Active anti-Semitic abuse was confined to a small, albeit vociferous, minority.[74]

At the time of the Soviet invasion in September 1939 the breakdown of law and order resulted in a few incidents of ethnic conflict. Poles were killed by peasant vigilante groups and improvised militias in several areas. The Soviets openly encouraged the peasants to take revenge against their Polish land-lords in the early days of the Soviet occupation. At Gorodeya, near Nesvizh, 'Commissar' Danilov reportedly proclaimed to a local audience: 'if someone has a grudge against somebody else, he can do with him what he wants – take his property or even life'. At the same time Polish border units in retreat, often assisted by civilians, fought brief 'battles' to punish disloyal groups of Belorussians, Ukrainians, 'locals' and Jews. Their own fate when captured by the Red Army was often sealed by summary justice.[75]

The Soviet Union, drawing on the Tsarist experience in breaking national-ist resistance, employed tried and trusted methods to eradicate the Polish state once more. Soviet officials arrested Polish leaders in the army, police and administration, to be deported or shot. The families of those arrested were also dispersed to the often fatal 'cold storage' of forced labour in the east. Given only a few minutes to pack, many died on the journey in over-loaded cattle trucks with insufficient food and water, freezing in winter and dehydrating in summer. Infants suffered a very heavy toll in these inhumane conditions.

Nevertheless efforts to deprive the Polish deportees of their national identity still met with fierce resistance. Many instances are recorded of the deportees breaking into patriotic song as their trains left the stations. Chil-dren forbidden to speak their native tongue took particular pleasure in this continuing act of defiance.[76] Back in Poland the rapid disbandment of all political parties and labour organizations encouraged the formation of a Polish underground movement.

The Soviets counted on winning support from the other minorities by promoting their interests at the expense of the formerly dominant Poles. Whilst the Polish leadership cadre was being rounded up for deportation, Ukrainians and Belorussians were being promoted to unaccustomed posi-tions of responsibility. This can be seen clearly in the pre-selected lists of candidates for the October 1939 elections. In Lvov, for example, practically all delegates were Ukrainians, demonstrating the eclipse of the considerable Polish population.[77] Initial land reforms were exploited in the same way to gain the confidence of the local peasantry at the expense of Polish landlords (*pans*). In the southern provinces, the first months of Soviet occupation saw a period of Ukrainianization, as Ukrainian schools were opened and Ukrai-nian langauge newspapers appeared.[78]

The Soviet takeover greatly reduced the number of schools teaching in the Polish language. Instead, teaching in Ukrainian, Russian or Belorussian was greatly encouraged, although a few Yiddish schools also survived.[79] These changes caused headaches for the remaining teachers who might have to learn the new language rapidly themselves, before teaching it to the children. The assault of the communists against religion was also concentrated upon the more receptive younger generation. All schools were secularized and religious instruction replaced by strongly anti-religious propaganda.[80]

The press in the occupied territories was also closely censored. The few Yiddish newspapers produced, for example, were forbidden to mention German atrocities against the Jews on account of the Hitler–Stalin Pact. Many books were removed from libraries and acceptable Soviet works were in short supply.[81] During the run-up to elections, an army of propagandists preached on the benefits of Soviet rule at endless lectures and meetings, where attendance was compulsory.[82] Red banners and portraits of Stalin displaced Polish eagles and flags as ubiquitous symbols of a Soviet state that intended to leave no reminders of the system it had replaced.

In the face of this totalitarian claim to power, the local population generally acquiesced in the rapid changes which ensued. At the same time, the Soviet system also sought the complicity of part of the local population. For instance, avaricious neighbours were encouraged to denounce others by the prospect of a share in the property of those banished as a result.[83] As Jan Gross has argued, this harnessing of private resentments by the state demonstrated both the power and limitations of totalitarianism. Whilst underlining the ability of the state to dispose of its citizens as it wished, it also opened the door to arbitrariness, corruption and the pursuit of private interests.[84] For his part, Stalin stopped short of confronting the Ukrainians simultaneously with the Poles, as his first aim was to consolidate his grip on the new territories. Given the specific local conditions, collectivization was deemed a suitable means of political control over a vast rural area that was not seen as loyal to the Soviet regime.[85]

Acquiescence did not, however, mean approval of the changed circumstances. Despite the new opportunities for advancement offered to Ukrainians and Belorussians, a mutual disillusionment developed between the Soviet authorities and local nationalist sympathizers. Both Ukrainian and Belorussian underground organizations looked to Germany for support in the inevitable struggle with the Soviets.[86] Equally the Soviets sometimes found themselves forced to fall back on Polish schoolteachers and lawyers for administrative posts, as qualified alternative personnel was not available. Thus the ground was already laid for the similar conflicts and alliances that would be played out during the German occupation which followed.

It is impossible to understand the events of the German occupation without examining the effects of the brief period of Soviet rule. For the mixed populations of eastern Poland the arrival of the Red Army in the autumn of 1939 meant political repression, deportations and significant economic change. Policies which had confirmed Polish political dominance in the 1930s were reversed and the Polish elite became the main target for *NKVD* persecution.

Soviet policies aimed at strengthening their centralized grip over a largely rural population. The *NKVD* sought to eliminate any group which might pose a threat to Soviet rule. Thus local communists, Belorussian and Ukrainian nationalists, or Jewish political activists were also included on their lists. The totalitarian claim of communism to be the only legitimate political organization was imposed by force.

The impact of political repression, combined with the withering effects of Soviet economic reforms, caused many local inhabitants to greet the Germans as liberators in 1941. In truth they would have welcomed anyone who promised to free them from the recently applied Soviet yoke. Radical Ukrainian nationalists had worked closely with the Germans in exile and many Ukrainians recalled German assistance during their brief period of independence in 1918.

It is difficult to estimate how much anti-Semitism was exacerbated by the Soviet occupation. There is no doubt that Nazi and nationalist propaganda made great play of the presence of Jews within leading positions of the communist hierarchy. Detailed analysis shows, however, that few local Jews obtained positions of power under Soviet rule.[87] Nevertheless, the perception among many non-Jews, reinforced by their own prejudices, was that the Jews supported and profited most from the Soviet system.

Limited subjective evidence regarding actual anti-Semitism under Soviet rule reveals no great change from Polish times. Government discrimination against the Jews decreased, as Jews were for the first time able to hold positions of responsibility in the community as a whole. Nevertheless, it was precisely the sight of a few Jews in the police and administration which rankled amongst Poles, Ukrainians and Belorussians, for whom this was previously unthinkable.[88] People who lost jobs or suffered persecution under the Soviets were most likely to be susceptible to the logic of Nazi propaganda, which depicted communists and Jews as virtually interchangable. Certainly it was those harbouring strong anti-Soviet resentments who soon came to the fore under German rule.

Undoubtedly the economic and political upheavals of 1939–41 disrupted local relations between ethnic communities, which stored up hatred for the greater conflagration to come. At the same time it is fair to say that without the presence of the Nazis with their radical ideology, a systematic programme of genocide would have been unthinkable. Nevertheless, it was relatively easy for the Nazis to recruit people locally who were prepared to carry out their terrible policies for a variety of different motives.

Of particular interest is a comparison of the methods adopted by the *NKVD* in controlling their newly occupied territories with those employed by the Germans. In 1939 both totalitarian systems aimed at crushing possible resistance from the remnants of the Polish state. The methods employed were remarkably similar in focusing on the Polish elite and subjecting its members to arrest, deportation and murder.[89]

The main difference between the two systems was reflected in their respective ideologies. Whereas the Germans were obsessed with the concept of race and defined their enemies accordingly, the Soviets were less concerned with national or ethnic differences. For the *NKVD*, landowners and capitalists were also high on their list of sworn enemies. National groups were only of interest to the Soviets insofar as they were likely to resist Soviet rule.

The mass deportation of over one million persons from eastern Poland clearly demonstrates the arbitrary nature of Soviet repression. It was a geographical solution to political control, designed to isolate and demoralize potential opponents in the newly occupied areas, whilst also providing much-needed labour in the east. A few people managed to escape the net, sometimes merely because they were not at home at the time of the round-up. Nevertheless, the impact of such large-scale measures was to intimidate the entire population and disrupt the plans of those actively organizing resistance. For Soviet citizens under Stalin, it was a fact of life that you could be arrested and deported from one day to the next without any apparent explanation.

Another feature of note was the treatment of the families of those arrested. These too were deported by the *NKVD* to work in remote areas with little prospect of escape.[90] The logic was that close relatives of prisoners were likely to harbour long-standing resentments; many died from the privations involved in transport to, and life in, so-called 'free exile'.

Here too the Germans were later to follow policies with a similar rigorous logic. Jewish children were exterminated on racial grounds; and as the partisan war escalated, it came to involve mutual reprisals against the families of collaborators and partisans, as both sides invoked the hereditary principle in defining their enemies. It is interesting to note that it was customary, even before 1941, for the totalitarian Soviet state to take action against the families of its avowed opponents.[91]

In several respects the subsequent German occupation adapted the methods developed by the Soviets during their brief period of rule: for instance, the Soviet collectivized farms were largely left intact by the Germans, as this was believed to be the best means to ensure supplies for the army.[92] Both regimes also sought to exploit national rivalries between Poles, Ukrainians and Belorussians to assert their own authority through the traditional imperial policy of divide and rule.

The trauma of Soviet mass deportations, even for those who remained behind, left deep scars which still influenced all ethnic groups during the

German occupation. For the Jews, German 'selections' were initially seen as ominous, but not necessarily fatal, in the light of similar Soviet round-ups. The effect of German labour transports into the *Reich*, however, was too reminiscent of Soviet deportations to work as a voluntary policy; as a compulsory measure it was a propaganda disaster.[93] In spite of working conditions generally more civilized than in Siberia, the local population anticipated a concentration camp rather than a modern factory or a well-stocked farm when contemplating the prospect of deportation. This measure, together with indiscriminate murderous reprisal actions, would drive even potential allies into the arms of the partisans. One is reminded that the arrogant and dismissive racial ideology of the Germans with respect to the indigenous peoples proved pyschologically more oppressive than the Soviet version, which (officially at least) proclaimed all citizens to be equal, regardless of ethnicity.

The effects of Soviet occupation on the Jewish communities are also of significance for the even greater trials which followed. Pinchuk's interpretation of the Soviet occupation for the *shtetl* Jews of eastern Poland stresses the loss of community in the face of rapid social change. This left Jews isolated and alone when confronting the Nazis. A Jew from Grodno complained: 'Everyone was living for himself. The Jews maintained very little contact with each other. It was as if all friendships were frozen, as if people suddenly lost confidence in each other. One could feel a sense of reservation everywhere.'[94]

Certainly it was the family more than the wider community which remained the focal point for Jews in the Nazi ghettoes. Concern for weaker family members was one reason for remaining together rather than risking escape.

Jews were deprived of information regarding the Nazi treatment of their people as a result of Soviet censorship. The Hitler–Stalin Pact meant it was forbidden for Jewish journalists to write about Germany's anti-Semitic policies. Thus some Jews were unprepared for the full horrors of Nazi occupation and did not attempt to flee. Older Jews even recalled the correct behaviour of German soldiers during the First World War, in contrast to the indiscipline of the Tsarist Russian Army.[95]

Prior to the German invasion, some Jews in eastern Poland opted to return to the Nazi-occupied zone due to the hardships of Soviet rule. Few were permitted to leave in this direction, especially as the Germans were eager to deport their own Jews to the east. A familiar story typifies the Jewish plight at this time:

At Biala Podlaska, the first station on the German side of the border, the train carrying refugees from the east encountered the train moving west. 'When Jews coming from Brisk [Brest] saw Jews going there, they shouted:

"You are insane, where are you going?" Those coming from Warsaw answered with equal astonishment: "You are insane, where are you going?"[96]

Apocryphal or not, this gallows humour demonstrates well the difficulties Jews encountered in assessing exactly which of the two systems posed the greater threat to their lives, at a time when the Germans had not yet taken the final steps towards genocide. It is indeed a strange irony that it was precisely the harsh Soviet policies of deportations and military conscription which did much to preserve Polish Jews from the fate of their brethren in the Nazi Holocaust.[97]

2 'Operation Barbarossa'

On 22 June 1941, early in the morning the Germans attacked our territory. There were lots of gun shots. Many Russian soldiers were killed...these were border guards...Many houses were destroyed but the majority remained standing. The Russians retreated and by 10am that same morning the Germans had taken over this area.[1]

This was how one local Belorussian recalled the opening of 'Operation Barbarossa'. The German invasion of the Soviet Union began with a surprise attack. During the night hundreds of German aircraft could be heard overhead roaring towards their targets in the east.[2] Between 3.00 and 3.15am an overwhelming artillery bombardment opened up across the River Bug.[3] Shortly afterwards German armoured forces and infantry crossed the Soviet frontier.

The German forces were confident of victory. In a Daily Order issued at the time of the invasion, Divisional Commander Lieutenant General Johann Pflugbeil of the 221st Security Division invoked the recent astonishing triumphs of the *Wehrmacht* to inspire his men:

> Until now, there has been no opponent either in the east or the west who has been able to withstand our will to victory and our attacking thrusts. So we will also defeat every opponent in the coming struggle, until the final victory of Germany has been secured.[4]

This arrogant assurance of success among the Germans contrasted starkly with the shock and surprise experienced on the Soviet side. The massed waves of German aircraft destroyed some 1200 Soviet planes, mostly on the ground, during the first day of the conflict.[5] Despite clear warnings from many sources, Stalin chose to ignore them and the Red Army was taken largely by surprise.[6] It could offer only scattered resistance and was sent reeling backwards from the start. For example, in the sector of the German VII Army Corps, the initial attack went according to plan, without encountering serious opposition. Daily targets were achieved by midday on 22 June.[7]

In Moscow, Stalin spent the first 24 hours in continuous session with the *Politburo*, awaiting definite news from the Front. Reports of enemy air attacks arriving from all sectors soon confirmed the seriousness of the situation. It was left to Molotov to break the news to the nation in a radio speech. Orders were issued for an immediate counter-attack; but the Red Army was too scattered and stunned to respond effectively.[8]

The citizens of the Soviet Union had been led to believe the Red Army would quickly throw back any aggressor. A war on Soviet soil was seen as unthinkable. On the evening of 22 June the greatest relief was brought by news that Great Britain would stand by the Soviet Union in her struggle against Hitler's Germany.[9] In many western areas, however, the immediate task was now to prepare the evacuation of key personnel, files and equipment before the imminent arrival of the Germans.

Despite limited Soviet resistance, the destructive effects of the German onslaught were considerable. For example, the village of Chersk, just to the east of the River Bug, was subjected to a severe artillery bombardment in which some 30 houses burned down on the first day of the war.[10] In this central sector German armoured forces pushed deep behind Soviet lines, by-passing and isolating strongpoints such as the historic fortress of Brest-Litovsk.[11]

One of the first active measures taken by the Soviet government on 22 June was to decree the mobilization of reservists born between 1905 and 1918 in nearly all military districts.[12] In the western districts, however, the rapid German advance soon disrupted these efforts. A resident of Baranovichi, over 100km east of the frontier, has described his demoralizing experiences:

> I was mobilized from the very first day of the war. All day and all night people were being mobilized. On the Monday evening we were ordered to take a couple of hours' rest and return on Tuesday. When we returned on Tuesday the Military Committee didn't exist any longer. It had left during the night. I wanted to run away, but it was already obvious that we were surrounded.[13]

Residents in Slonim recall a similar scene, as those called up for 24 June returned home once they saw that their Russian officers had abandoned them.[14] Given that these western territories had only recently been incorporated, the local population was unable and often unwilling to resist the invasion, especially in the absence of effective leadership from the communist officials brought in from the east.

As the Germans advanced, the towns and villages of western Belorussia experienced direct contact with the invaders. Advancing some 50–60km per day, the first German soldiers arrived in Slonim on 24 June. Here locals recall vividly the damage from bombing:

> My family house had been bombed and burned to the ground on the day before. I took my child and looked for somewhere to hide, it was then that I saw the first Germans. They were from the *Wehrmacht*. There was a lot of damage caused in the town from the bombing and the subsequent fires. This was because all the houses were made of wood.[15]

On 27 June 1941 elements of 18th *Panzer* Division entered the picturesque town of Nesvizh at around 9.00pm. This was slightly later than planned, as they had initially lost their way due to incorrect route marking. According to a female resident their arrival was virtually uncontested: 'there was no battle for Nesvizh, the Soviets simply retreated and the Germans marched in'.[16] In the wake of the German arrival, there was some looting of the state-owned shops by the local population in the town.[17]

By the evening of 27 June advanced German units had entered Minsk, some 300km from the frontier, beyond the old Polish border.[18] Further north, most of Lithuania was occupied by 30 June. On that day in the Latvian capital, Riga, German units of XXVI Army Corps were preparing to cross the River Dvina.[19] In the Baltic states the locals welcomed the Germans as liberators; the Red Army and its collaborators were concerned mainly with escaping. Only on the Southern Front was initial progress less rapid. Here Army Group South faced the main concentration of Soviet forces, deployed to protect the industrial heartland of Ukraine.[20]

During these first few days, intimations of the brutal nature of the developing struggle were already becoming visible. Behind the front lines on the Lithuanian–German border, units of the Secret State Police (*Gestapo*) from Tilsit began shooting Jewish civilians and communists on 24 June.[21] Prior to the invasion, Hitler's orders had set aside the provisions of international law. In particular, brutal treatment of PoWs and the civilian population, especially the Jews, would ensure that the war would continue behind the Front after German front-line troops had passed through.

From its conception Hitler viewed the war against the Soviet Union as a struggle to the death between two diametrically opposed ideologies.[22] In this respect German conduct of the war would be quite different from the campaigns in the west or even Poland. Hitler's aim was not only to defeat the enemy, but to seek his physical destruction. Respect for the internationally accepted 'laws of war' was cast aside. In orders issued by the *Wehrmacht* prior to the invasion, German soldiers were freed from punishment for measures taken against hostile civilians. Soviet political Commissars were slated for execution if captured. Above all the Soviet opponent was depicted as barbarous, Asiatic, treacherous and ruthless in supposed justification for these extreme measures.

The so-called *Gerichtsbarkeitserlaß* (military jurisdiction order) issued on 13 May 1941 permitted the summary execution of suspect elements and the enforcement of collective reprisals.[23] In his covering letter on 21 May, the German Army Commander, Walter von Brauchitsch, noted that this order was only intended for cases of genuine resistance. Nevertheless, in stressing that the main task of the troops was the struggle with the armed forces of the enemy, he also ceded to mobile units of the Security Police and *SD* (*Einsatzgruppen*) the conduct of 'cleansing' operations in the army's rear.[24] (*SD* stands for *Sicherheitsdienst*, who were the Security Service of the *Schutzstaffel*, or *SS*.)

Written orders to the *Einsatzgruppen* at the start of the invasion do not mention the complete elimination of all Jews;[25] nevertheless the ambiguous terminology employed left scope for extreme measures from the start. This prepared the way for a subsequent systematic radicalization. Mention was made, for instance, in the initial *Einsatzgruppen* orders that Jews in state and Party positions were to be executed, as well other radical elements. At the same time local pogroms were to be orchestrated unobtrusively by the *Einsatzgruppen*. Bolsheviks and Jews (rather than the Polish intelligentsia) were to be the main targets for these initial 'cleansing actions'.[26]

The military discussions and orders of this period demonstrate that the German Army shared much of Hitler's ideological perception of the war as a crusade against a supposed Judaeo-Bolshevik conspiracy. The military historian, Jürgen Förster, has interpreted these orders as the declaration of a *Vernichtungskrieg* (or 'war of destruction') against the Soviet Union.[27] The aim was literally to destroy an enemy comprised of racially inferior peoples, in order to create living space for German settlement in the east. The German leadership viewed the bombing of cities and the starvation of the civilian population as war aims in themselves.[28]

This destructive energy was directed in particular against the Jews. At the start of the German invasion, the collapse of Soviet authority was often followed by local progroms. In the former Polish district of Volhynia, Shmuel Spector has identified over 20 places where the local Ukrainian population carried out pogroms against the Jews at this time. In some cases the persecution began even before the Germans had arrived. Although the motive was often the acquisition of Jewish property, over half of the incidents recorded involved acts of murder, sometimes on a large scale. For instance, in Tuchin 70 Jews were killed and a large number were wounded, including women and children.[29]

A typical example took place in the town of Gnivan, near Vinnitsa in Soviet Ukraine, in July 1941. Here the Germans and Ukrainians humiliated the local Jews: they rounded them up, locked them in a room and made them dance. 'After the dances they forced them to beat each other and those who wouldn't beat their friend, brother or father were beaten by the Germans with rifle butts.'[30]

Similar pogroms took place in Lithuania, where local nationalist 'partisans' played an active role. *Einsatzgruppe A* estimated that self-protection organizations 'liquidated' over 20 000 communists and Jews in the Baltic states before these formations were dissolved and incorporated into a civil auxiliary police.[31] The discovery of slaughtered prisoners in some *NKVD* jails inflamed anti-Semitism amongst the local population.[32] According to an *Einsatzgruppen* report, in Lvov the population roughly herded together around 1000 Jews and delivered them to the prison which was occupied by the *Wehrmacht*. The Jews were employed to remove the bodies of the *NKVD* victims from the jail, before the Ukrainian militia murdered most of them in turn. In Sambor, also in Galicia, some 50 Jews were murdered by an enraged mob.[33]

Dr Walther Stahlecker, the commander of *Einsatzgruppe A*, confirmed in his report that it was deliberate policy to incite pogroms in the first days of German rule. These pogroms gave the appearance of popular support for the measures against the Jews. Care was to be taken, however, to ensure that Germans were not seen to be co-ordinating these actions.[34] Not all attempts to inspire pogroms met with success. Some people were still afraid that the Russians would return.[35] Evidence regarding pogroms in Belorussia has so far only been found for the former Polish areas.[36] Amongst local Belorussians there were fewer organized nationalist activists to support German measures.

These initial pogroms took place under German military administration. While soldiers were sometimes seen to be actively participating in the actions, on other occasions the *Wehrmacht* stepped in to restore order, bringing the pogroms to a halt. Spector cites such an instance in the town of Dubrovitsa on the basis of Jewish sources. It was not in the interest of the temporary military administration to permit violent disturbances. These could get out of hand or allow military discipline to collapse.[37]

The first aim of the military administration was to restore order and protect the army's lines of communication. This was supervised by a series of Field and Local Commandants' posts (*FK*s and *OK*s) in the major towns. They started by appointing reliable mayors in all settlements and the requisite number of auxiliary police. In Belorussia it was intended to employ Belorussians as far as possible and only to use Poles when there was no alternative.[38] In the Mir *rayon* (sub-district), near Baranovichi, the Germans formed a local police force within a couple of weeks of their arrival. The police was made up primarily of Belorussians, although some Poles and local Tartars were also represented. Initial recruitment was on a voluntary basis.[39]

The successes of the initial German '*Blitzkrieg*' in the northern and central sectors had been spectacular. In the first few weeks the Germans captured hundreds of thousands of Red Army soldiers. Many others threw away their rifles and put on civilian clothes in order to avoid capture. At this time most of these men were not partisans, as they sought only to get home or find work with local people in order to survive.[40] In spite of Stalin's appeals for resistance, there was little fighting spirit amongst the demoralized soldiers or the local populace, who were often relieved to see the Soviets depart.

Large numbers of former Soviet personnel behind the front lines posed considerable security problems for the German rear area forces. As a result the Germans conducted frequent checks to see if non-locals were present amongst the population. A local inhabitant from Slonim has described this procedure:

After a couple of nights the Russians attacked Slonim from the forest. The Germans then ordered all the men to go to the sports stadium where I remained for one week. We were not given any food, only water. I was questioned by people who were working with a priest whose job it was to find out amongst the people in the stadium those who were actually from Slonim. I had identification which proved I was from Slonim and was allowed to go home.[41]

The fate of those who were not released is indicated by the *Einsatzgruppen* reports. In Minsk a civilian prison camp was established by the first troops to march through. Nearly all the male inhabitants of the town (about 40 000) were taken there. The camp was then screened by units of *Einsatzgruppe B* assisted by the Secret Field Police (*Geheime Feldpolizei* or *GFP*) of the *Wehrmacht*. The Germans then released some of the men who were able to prove their identity. According to one *Einsatzgruppen* report, however, more than 1050 Jews were 'liquidated' along with a number of criminals, functionaries and 'Asiatics'.[42]

The Soviet authorities made concerted attempts to evacuate key personnel and equipment once it was clear that an area was going to fall into German hands. For example, in Slonim, large numbers of civilians were evacuated to the east by the *NKVD*. Many departed from Slonim on foot the very day that the Germans arrived.[43] Soviet officials from the east, essential workers and their families received priority for the limited evacuation facilities.[44]

Historians have wondered why more Jews did not attempt to flee before the advancing German troops. In considerable disarray at the start of the German invasion, the Soviet authorities pursued no consistent policy with regard to the Jews. In some areas the Jews were encouraged to retreat, whereas elsewhere they were hindered on their journey, especially at the old border of the Soviet Union.[45] A few examples demonstrate the sort of difficulties encountered:

Jewish youths from Nesvizh who arrived at the old Soviet border, about ten km from their township, on the fourth day of the war, were ordered to turn back so as 'not to create a panic at a time when the Germans are being pushed back'. When the youths refused, the sentries threatened them at gun-point. Only a handful managed to slip across the border.[46]

Groups of Jewish refugees from Novogrudok, attempting to flee with what luggage they could carry, were also forced to turn back within hours. Only through persistence did some manage to cross the former Soviet frontier, after the guards had fled.[47]

Many Jews had learned about the harsh treatment to be expected at the hands of the Germans from refugees who had escaped western Poland. Generally it was only the younger people and those closely linked to the

Soviet authorities who sought to flee. Understandably others feared for the health of children and elderly parents if they were to take to the road.

Among the Jews who left home, difficulties were encountered owing to the rapid German advance. Deep encircling pincer movements of armoured units and continuous bombing of communication centres and transport facilities hindered the flight of the civilian population.[48] Dov Levin has estimated that due to the rapid German advance only about 70 000 Jews managed to escape eastwards from the former Polish areas of the Soviet Union. Nevertheless, this remained a higher proportion than amongst the population in general.[49] Further east, where the Soviets had had more time to prepare the evacuations, a greater portion of both men and material could be saved, especially from the larger cities with good communications. This also applied to the Jews, more of whom fled from these areas.[50]

The Soviet evacuations were both spontaneous and official. Usually official evacuations of factory workers and collective farmers were carried out by rail, while others who sought to flee made their own way on foot. The reality did not always match up to the propaganda image of carefully prepared feeding stations and shelter. For example, a woman who was evacuated with her 14-year-old boy from Kiev to Sal'sk, about 80 miles south-east of Rostov-on-Don, in the summer of 1941 had to endure an exhausting journey of some four weeks.[51]

During his speech which openly declared partisan warfare on 3 July 1941, Stalin also announced a policy of scorched earth in retreat:

> the enemy must not be left...a single pound of grain...The collective farmers must drive off all their cattle and turn over their grain to the safe keeping of the state authorities for transportation to the rear. All valuable property, including...grain...that cannot be withdrawn, must be destroyed without fail.[52]

In a further broadcast, Moscow radio announced on 8 July 1941: 'wherever Hitler advances, he will find nothing but desert and scorched earth'.[53]

As part of this plan, Soviet destruction battalions remained behind on the retreat to destroy anything that might be of value to the Germans. By late July, within the pre-1939 borders of the Soviet Union, these measures were beginning to prove effective. On arrival in Vitebsk *Einsatzgruppe B* reported that:

> The power station has been destroyed, fresh water is in short supply, and industry, primarily textiles, has been annihilated. One textile factory formerly employed 15 000 people...In the rural district surrounding Vitebsk the Russians have deployed destruction squads which systematically destroy vital installations and entire towns. These squads comprise 10–15 men and operate in conjunction with *Komsomol* members...Shortly

before the Soviets abandoned Vitebsk, a large number of leading industrial figures and workers were evacuated to other areas by train. It appears that the Soviets are concentrating industrial workers in the Volga region in order to build up an industry there or to strengthen existing industries with skilled workers.[54]

In Ukraine the slower rate of advance gave the Soviets the opportunity to try to save more from the western areas. In the Kirovograd, Nikolayev and Odessa regions, however, areas that were not occupied until early or mid-August, a large part of the Machine Tractor Stations' stocks still fell to the enemy. The evacuation from the south-western Ukraine became a chaotic race conducted by tractor drivers and evacuating animal herds trying to cross the Dnepr river before being cut off by the German advance. For Ukraine only about 40 per cent (20 000 out of 50 000 tractors) were successfully evacuated, which proved to be a similar proportion to that for Belorussia (4000 out of 9000).[55] Nevertheless the lessons learned in these initial evacuations proved useful. Subsequently the Soviet authorities were able to save much valuable manpower and equipment from the industrial heartland of southern and eastern Ukraine.

The effects of these Soviet policies served to exacerbate the economic problems already caused by the war. The work of the collective farms was badly disrupted by requisitioning and looting, which in turn had a serious effect on the supply situation. Above all, food was very short in the cities because many farmers from the surrounding districts stopped bringing in supplies. They refused Russian money and only accepted German currency or barter goods.[56] The Soviet policy on retreat was for existing stocks of food to be evacuated, distributed to the people, or destroyed.[57] In Zhitomir the Russians destroyed all food supplies before leaving the city. Here, according to German reports, there was sufficient labour to bring in the harvest, but shortages of horses and tractors remained.[58] Initially the local population blamed the Soviets for this wanton destruction. The subsequent impact of German requisitions, however, which further impoverished the country, was influential in turning much of the population against the new occupying forces.

The Germans began to encounter stiffer opposition on the Central Front as they approached the pre-1939 Soviet frontier. For example, motorized forces pushing forward north of Nesvizh ran into fierce resistance from scattered enemy columns attempting to escape between the advancing pincers. Large numbers of Soviet prisoners were taken, as battle-weariness and lack of supplies took its toll amongst the demoralized Russians. Nevertheless, some enemy formations succeeded in slipping through the gaps between the advancing German columns.[59]

By the first week in July the bold operations of the Germans began to lose some of their punch in the vast expanses of the Russian interior. On his visit to XXXXVII *Panzer* Corps, the *Panzer* Group Leader, Heinz Guderian, noted that a further attack across the Dnepr appeared almost impossible. Strong forces of the Corps were still being held to the west for the completion of mopping-up operations. Meanwhile the lead forces had become weakened by non-stop attacks and losses. From the start of the campaign up to 2 July the Corps had suffered some 6 per cent losses (killed and wounded) in personnel. On 4 July the Corps reported that only some 30 per cent of combat vehicles (tanks) were still operational.[60]

It was in this context that the German treatment of Soviet PoWs began to have an impact on the course of the struggle. As Red Army resistance stiffened, instances are known of Russian prisoners being shot whilst surrendering in the heat of battle.[61] Official records from the Central Front reveal a similar story:

> the enemy starts to dissolve and voluntarily surrender. In order to encourage this further, the Commanding General issues an order which again clearly sets out the provisions of the partly misunderstood *Führer* Decree. Through misinterpretation of this Decree, prisoners have sometimes been shot dead; these shootings dampen the actually existing willingness to desert and give rise to skirmishes, since every Russian is consequently intent upon selling his life as dearly as possible, and thereby ultimately work to the detriment of our own troops.[62]

As can be seen, some enlightened German commanders recognized the practical disadvantages of mistreating enemy prisoners;[63] nevertheless the sufferings of Soviet PoWs were apparent to the local population from an early stage. Once captured, they ran the gauntlet of being selected for execution by the Security Police as Jews, Commissars or 'Asiatics' in the transit camps.[64] In general the *Wehrmacht* co-operated with these measures without much protest.

The improvised PoW camps, staffed mostly by 'Home Guard' (*Landesschützen*) units, had inadequate supplies for the vast numbers of men captured during the first months of the invasion. A report on the situation in Minsk, where about 100 000 PoWs were crowded together within a small space, noted that some had received no food for 6–8 days.[65] Some more fortunate interness had bread thrown to them by their relatives or sympathetic local inhabitants from outside, but these people were in turn punished by the Germans if caught.[66]

Instructions received on 25 July from the Army High Command gave a clear indication of the small value placed on the lives of PoWs: 'Where it is necessary to assert oneself against resistance, disobedience &c., the weapon should be used immediately. In particular, fleeing prisoners of war are to be shot at immediately, without calling out "Stop" first.'[67] During transports and even within the camps themselves, the few guards sometimes made use of their rifles at the slightest provocation. The suspicion that former Red Army personnel might provide the nucleus for a renewed partisan offensive in the German rear contributed to a further radicalizing of the policy.

Given the wooded and marshy terrain in much of the northern and central areas of the theatre, it was not uncommon for encircled troops to disperse into the forests or assume civilian clothing in order to avoid capture. Many of these men then returned home, assuming that the war would soon be over. A typical example is the story of one man encircled during the first days of the invasion:

> In June 1941 our unit was surrounded by some German troops in one of the forests near the town of Belaya Tserkov. The political instructor (*Politruk*) mustered the remaining troops and ordered us to leave the encirclement in groups. I and two other soldiers from our unit...changed into civilian clothes and decided to go home to where we used to live. We took this decision because according to rumour, the German troops moving up towards us had advanced far away in the east.[68]

Others took jobs with local people, especially on farms where there was now a shortage of male manpower.[69] Most had no intention of heeding Stalin's call for continued resistance at this time. Some hid their weapons, lest they should they be required later. A few genuine partisan groups existed, like those described in an *Einsatzgruppen* report from early August:

> In addition, there is the problem of the activities of the partisans, groups of stragglers detached from the encircled Russian Army, who hide in the forests and rob the inhabitants of nearby collective farms, commit arson and carry out attacks...The partisan groups are obliged to extract provisions from the rural population by force.[70]

These initially sporadic acts of resistance caused the Germans to become highly suspicious of the numerous stray men living behind the front. A date was set by the Commander of Rear Area Army Group Centre for former Red Army soldiers to surrender themselves: 'all straggling Russian soldiers who are caught west of the Berezina [river] from 1 September 1941 are to be treated as guerrillas'.[71] In consequence former soldiers found working on farms or who surrendered too late faced the risk of being shot. In the long term these harsh German measures ultimately only worsened the very problem they were trying to solve.

The choice of 1 September for this deadline was in line with Hitler's plans to hand much of the army area over to a civil administration by this date. At a secret conference on 16 July 1941 Hitler told his closest advisers that it was his intention for the German conquest to be permanent. His aim was:

> to break the giant cake into manageable pieces so that we can firstly govern, secondly administer and thirdly exploit it. The Russians have

now given the order for a partisan war behind our front line. This partisan war again also has its advantage: it gives us the opportunity to exterminate anyone who looks askance at us.[72]

At this conference *Reichsmarschall* Hermann Göring stressed the need to obtain food from the occupied areas. This reflected the pre-war German calculation that the war could only be continued for a further year if the entire *Wehrmacht* was fed from Russia. This would cause the deaths of several million people in the east by starvation, due to the amount of resources extracted.[73] Alfred Rosenberg, Reich Minister for the occupied eastern territories, was more inclined to make some concessions to local nationalist aspirations, especially in Ukraine. Hitler, however, saw no place for client states within his new order. He declared that no persons other than Germans were to bear arms.[74] The next day Hitler confirmed the appointments of Erich Koch and Hinrich Lohse as the Reich Commissars for the new civil administrations in *Ostland* and Ukraine.[75]

Reichsführer SS (*RFSS*) Heinrich Himmler was not present at the conference, but the role of his police forces was discussed. It was decided that he would hold the same police responsibilities as he enjoyed within the *Reich*.[76] Nevertheless he did not accept Hitler's opposition to arming the local population. While denying them any direct participation in the struggle against the Red Army at the Front, Himmler issued orders at the end of July 1941 for the establishment of indigenous police formations, or *Schutzmannschaften*, subordinated directly to his own police structure.[77] Consisting of both mobile auxiliary police battalions and smaller units serving at local posts (*Einzeldienst*), these collaborators would be vital for the execution of all Himmler's police tasks in the areas under civil administration.

One reason for Hitler's rapid hand-over from military to civil administration was his concern for his own party henchmen to take over responsibility for the radical measures he envisaged in the east.[78] As recorded in his 'tabletalk', he recognized the practical difficulties which administering such vast territories would entail: 'we are forced to govern districts of an extent from 300 to 500 kilometres with just a handful of people. Naturally the police there will have to hold their pistols loose in the holster. The men of the Party will do it right.'[79]

Paradoxically the plans of Hitler, the *SS* and the army contrasted minute preparations for the deployment of their terror apparatus in the occupied territories with a blithe confidence in military success. The blueprint for 'Barbarossa' actually contained only vague notions of driving the Soviet forces into the east and awaiting the collapse of a system seen as rotten to the core. Nevertheless, in mid-July 1941 this confidence appeared well-placed. Advance German spearheads were already in the vicinity of Smolensk, well over half-way to Moscow. Over 600 000 Soviet prisoners had been reported captured during the first month of the campaign.[80] Hitler and the German military leadership expected that Soviet resistance would soon be broken.

Christopher Browning has identified this period in the second half of July as being decisive in the build-up of the necessary manpower for the implementation of the 'Final Solution' in the east. Confident of victory, not only were three brigades of the *SS* and at least eleven Order Police battalions made available, but authorization was given for the recruitment of local police collaborators to operate under Himmler's authority. These forces were to complete the task which the small units of the *Einsatzgruppen* had hardly begun in the vast expanses of occupied Soviet territory.[81]

So far *Einsatzgruppen* operations had targeted mainly specific groups of 'potential opponents', including Jewish leaders, as well as some 'reprisal' actions against Jews. As one early *Einsatzgruppen* report indicated, 'cleansing' operations were to be concentrated initially against the Bolsheviks and Jews. Except in urgent cases, measures against the Polish intelligentsia were to be deferred until later.[82] The mobile task forces (*Einsatzkommandos*) conducted small-scale selections in the outlying towns. In Gorodeya, just north of Nesvizh, fifteen 'Soviet workers' were arrested in July, three of whom were shot on the spot.[83]

In nearby Mir, a typical 'intelligentsia' action was carried out on Sunday, 20 July 1941. All male Jews aged between 16 and 60 were ordered to parade in the main square. Approximately 190 men showed up and a selection was conducted by the Germans, assisted by local Belorussian collaborators. Most chosen were wealthy Jews and heads of families, including at least one teacher. In addition to nineteen Jews, three Gentiles were also selected. The group was told they were being sent away to work. Other people received instructions to go home and fetch shovels for them. The selected group was then taken out of town by truck and killed in a nearby forest.[84] Confirmation of their fate is provided by a local Belorussian:

> Next day I was travelling to my father's field which was not far from Mir and close to the village of Simakovo. That is when I passed by their grave. It was poorly covered because arms and legs were sticking out of it. The grave was in the forest.[85]

In the larger Belorussian towns these actions were on a correspondingly greater scale. The first action in Slonim took place on 17 July 1941, as recalled by a local survivor:

> On that day *Einsatzgruppen* members came from outside Slonim with 12 big trucks from the Krupp German company. They rounded up about 2000 men in and around the area of the Community Centre, near the market and loaded 100 men on each truck, altogether 1200 men, who were led to

execution on the sands of Petralovichi. The rest of the gathered men were released, among them the father of my future wife.[86]

The veracity of this witness is confirmed by the corresponding *Einsatzgruppen* report, which noted that some 2000 persons [mainly Jews] had been detained with the assistance of the civil police: 'of these, 1075 were "liquidated" the same day'.[87] Local collaborators were also employed to assist, such as a man in nearby Derevna, who went about the town with the Germans, pointing out to them the communists and other persons who had been active in the Soviet administration.[88]

The Jewish 'intelligentsia', however, bore the brunt of the initial onslaught, which spread terror amongst the entire Jewish population. According to the *Einsatzgruppen* reports, Belorussians were only 'neutralized' (murdered) where they were 'identified' (denounced) as Bolshevik functionaries or agents.[89] The impact on the Jewish community can be estimated from the recollections of a Baranovichi survivor:

> During this time we heard that there were punitive detachments going around which went to small villages and killed Jews. 'We don't believe that they could go around killing everyone. Surely it's impossible to kill everyone to a man. They're trying to frighten us.' That is what people were saying. Then we heard that all the Jews in the town of Gantsevichi had been killed, to a man.[90]

During 'cleansing' operations in Baranovichi in July, German forces secured large sums in cash. The operation was conducted by *Einsatzkommando 8* assisted by the *GFP*, Counter-espionage (*Abwehr*) and Military Police of the *Wehrmacht*.[91] This reflected the close co-operation between the *Einsatzgruppen* and the rear area *Wehrmacht* units. For instance, the 252nd Infantry Division issued orders for any communists captured to be handed over to the Security Police.[92]

Responsibility for securing the rear areas behind the advancing German forces fell mainly to a number of Security Divisions specially designed for these tasks. Each Division contained a section VII, which was responsible for running the military administration through the *FK*s and *OK*s under their control. Behind Army Group South, Security Divisions 444, 213 and 454 operated.[93] On the central and northern sectors, the main Security Divisions were 221, 252 and 403. Some regular Infantry Divisions, such as 707 and 339, also performed similar security tasks.

For the area around Vinnitsa, which was captured by units of the 17th Army by 21 July 1941,[94] the details of the military administration are well documented in the reports of Field Command 675 for August 1941. A provisional town administration was appointed on 22 July 1941; its first task was to repair vital utilities, such as the electricity plant. Over the following weeks *rayon* heads (*Rayonchefs*) were appointed in the surrounding area, with a labour office (*Arbeitsamt*), housing office (*Wohnungsamt*) and food supply office (*Ernährungsamt*) all being established in the city.[95]

A local police force known as the *Miliz* (militia) or *Ordnungsdienst*, abbreviated *OD* (Order Service), was also established by and made answerable to the local mayors and the military administration. Initially this local police force remained unpaid. In the absence of available uniforms, the militia generally wore arm-bands.[96] In both Belorussia and Ukraine recruitment to the local police forces was to be voluntary. If insufficient recruits were found, however, it was also permitted to recruit Ukrainians from the PoW camps to be released for service in the larger towns.[97]

The recruits were to be screened first by the Security Police.[98] In Vinnitsa, however, German officers complained that some policemen had been appointed by Ukrainian nationalist activists who had helped to set up the local administration. The military authorities were not always satisfied with the loyalty of nationalist appointees and some were subsequently dismissed on these grounds. The policy with regard to arming of the militia depended essentially on how much they could be trusted. According to official instructions, at first weapons were to be distributed to the militia only in an emergency.[99]

The initial tasks of the Ukrainian militia included guarding factories and warehouses, street patrols, special duties and some economic functions in regulating markets and prices. They also guarded the Jewish population, ensuring that they performed their work duties. The Jews repaired war damage in the streets and worked as forced labour at the disposal of the German authorities. In Vinnitsa the Jews had to wear armbands bearing the Star of David, but there was no immediate ghettoization.[100]

The shooting of Jews began shortly after the occupation of Vinnitsa. Field Command 675 noted that the Jewish Council had been decimated during the first days of its existence by *SD* men working for the *Einsatzgruppe*. According to *Einsatzgruppe C*, the rabbis had been requested to gather together the Jewish 'intelligentsia' within 24 hours for the purpose of registering the Jewish population. When not all those requested appeared, those who did were sent out to collect the others. In this way nearly the entire Jewish 'intelligentsia' was gathered and 'liquidated'.[101] The direction of German policy can be seen from an order issued in August, which said that in cases of sabotage, if the culprits could not be found, reprisals were to be exacted against the Jews and Russians, rather than the Ukrainians.[102]

In the view of the German military administration, the OUN's economic plans posed a threat, as they made a direct appeal to the interests of the Ukrainian population. With regard to the issue of land reform there were widespread expectations that the collectivization policies of the communists would now be reversed. The military administration, however, did not permit any immediate changes in property ownership.[103]

Ukrainian nationalist sentiment was not as strong in the areas around Vinnitsa and Zhitomir as in Galicia and Volhynia. Following the arrival of nationalist organizers from western Ukraine in the wake of the German advance, strong support did develop, however, especially in the city of Zhitomir.[104] The western Ukrainians were well organized and soon occupied a number of significant positions as local mayors and police chiefs. The Nazi administration was suspicious of their ultimate aim of independence, but tolerated them, at least during the establishment of a functioning local administration.[105]

In Volhynia, further north, the Germans feared that the Ukrainian militia was being used by the nationalist organizations as the basis for a subsequent Ukrainian Army. Ukrainian nationalists sought to arm and train as many young people as possible. In order to retain it as a useful tool for their own purposes, the German officers were determined to keep a close eye on its leadership. As in Zhitomir, the militia units soon had to be purged of disloyal elements by the Germans.[106]

Reports about the presence of partisans, especially in the wooded areas north of Vinnitsa, were received from foresters and peasants, as well as the local outposts of the *FK*. These partisans were not seen as a danger at this stage, but as a possible seedbed for a partisan movement which might eventually materialize.[107]

The military administration in Vinnitsa was only of short duration. It aimed at maintaining order and establishing a working local administration that would serve German interests. In the summer of 1941 the Germans enjoyed a brief 'honeymoon period', as the Ukrainian population initially viewed them as liberators.[108] Nevertheless, the activities of *Einsatzgruppe C*, selecting particular groups for 'execution' as elements 'hostile to the *Reich*', provided a brutal foretaste of the repression and exploitation to come.

There was a greater reluctance to serve the Germans in those parts of Belorussia which belonged to the Soviet Union before 1939. This was due primarily to a fear of the consequences should the Soviets return.[109] Thus some 20 or 30 Belorussian émigrés, who arrived with *Einsatzgruppe B*, were installed in leading posts in the local administration.[110] German agricultural administrators ('Special Leaders') also arrived with the *Wehrmacht*. They were soon put in charge of the collective and state farms and were subsequently absorbed within the civil administration.[111]

As noted above, the effects of German occupation soon had an impact on the lives of every member of the Jewish population. Since the Germans encountered difficulties in identifying the Jews, one of the first measures introduced by the military administration was the wearing of a distinguishing patch.[112] Some confusion arose, however, regarding design as

successive German commandants passed through. A survivor from Baranovichi recalls:

> We had a Field Commandant's office there, that is, a military authority.
> When the advanced units left we had a Local Commandant's office and
> there was some sort of higher rear authority. And each Commandant's
> office gave different orders as to how these patches were to be worn.[113]

The implications of being branded in this way soon became apparent. For
instance, in one Belorussian town in August 1941 a Jewish boy was caught
without a yellow patch. As a result his whole family was hanged. 'The
Germans read out the verdict, but those who carried out the hanging were
[local] policemen from the *Hilfspolizei* (auxiliary police).'[114]

In due course the Jews were soon bombarded with an array of further
restrictions: 'They were forbidden (*verboten*) to walk on the pavement; *verboten* to go out beyond the city limits; *verboten* to go into a Christian home;
verboten to carry on a conversation with a Christian in the street; *verboten* to
buy necessities from farmers.'[115] In order to enforce their policies the Germans appointed a Jewish council (*Judenrat*) in each community.[116] As *Einsatzgruppe B* reported, their responsibilities included organizing the Jews for
forced labour:

> In every city a chairman of a Jewish Council has been appointed, with the
> task of forming a Jewish Council numbering between three and ten people.
> The Jewish Council is collectively responsible for the conduct of the Jewish
> population. It is also charged with the immediate commencement of
> registration of Jews living in the area. In addition, it is required to form
> work groups comprising all Jewish males between the ages of 15 and 55
> years to undertake clearance work and other works for the German
> authorities and military forces. A number of work groups composed of
> women between the same ages are also to be formed.[117]

A survivor from Baranovichi notes that he was caught and taken to work in
lorries every day at eight o'clock in the morning. On occasions even non-Jews
who looked Jewish would also be taken, despite their protestations.[118] The
Germans might receive payment from local inhabitants for work conducted
by the Jews. The most the Jews could hope for was a crust of bread in return.
Nevertheless the hope remained that if they carried out useful work the
Germans would not kill them.

A valuable case study in German occupation policies at the start of the
Barbarossa campaign is provided by the operations of the 2nd *SS* Cavalry
Regiment commanded by *SS-Sturmbannführer*, Franz Magill. The rich source
material available in the form of contemporary German orders and reports is
supplemented by post-war German investigative records and Jewish survivor
testimonies.

The area of the Pripyet marshes was a cause of particular concern to the German military High Command and the Nazi Party leadership in the summer of 1941. The main German spearheads had elected to by-pass the region as it was only likely to slow down their rapid eastward advance. It was feared, however, that the impenetrable swamps and forests might be used as a basis for Soviet raids against German supply lines, if not for a major counter-attack. A raid conducted by a Soviet cavalry unit from the area south of Slutsk towards German communications at Minsk during July 1941 alerted the German command to the dangers of leaving its flanks exposed.[119]

In view of such threats, it was decided to employ part of Himmler's personal reserve, the *SS* Cavalry Brigade, as a suitable mobile unit to sweep through the Pripyet marshes and pacify it, without at this stage setting up permanent German garrisons. As the two *SS* cavalry regiments had not previously been in combat, the operation would provide them with useful experience before being sent to the front line.[120] On 19 July 1941 Himmler ordered that the *SS* Cavalry Brigade would be placed at the disposal of the Higher *SS* and Police Leader (*HSSPF*), Erich von dem Bach-Zelewski, in Baranovichi for a systematic combing of the Pripyet marshes.[121]

The Cavalry Brigade was directly subordinated to the Staff (*Kommandostab*) of the *RFSS*, Himmler, who kept a close eye on its activities. Himmler laid down detailed guidelines for the forthcoming operation in an order issued on 28 July 1941. Careful co-ordination with the Security Police and Order Police during the 'cleansing actions' was to be maintained where possible. Himmler only sought to create local strongpoints where the population was friendly to the Germans:

> If the population, from a national standpoint, is hostile and racially and physically inferior, or as often in marshy areas, is made up of criminals who have settled there, then everyone suspected of supporting the partisans is to be shot; women and children are to be deported, cattle and food to be confiscated and secured. The villages are to be razed to the ground ... No opponent is to obtain support and provisions in this area.[122]

These orders document the development of German genocidal policies in response to both real and imagined partisan threats. At this time resistance to the Germans was restricted to a few dispersed Red Army units and communist activists, or to the so-called 'destruction battalions' left behind by the retreating Soviet authorities. Nevertheless, the references to 'criminals' and 'racially inferior populations' had a clear meaning in the context of Nazi anti-Semitic beliefs. Himmler chose to exploit the opportunities offered by Stalin's appeal for partisan resistance to intensify the murderous actions against the Jews.

During the operations of the *SS* Cavalry Brigade up to 12 August 1941, some 13 788 'looters' were reported as having been shot. The Brigade's own losses in the same period were only 2 dead and 15 wounded. Obviously these so-called 'looters' did not pose much of a threat to the members of the Brigade who shot them. Nevertheless, Brigade Commander Fegelein called for increased rewards for his men (in the form of battle decorations) in view of 'the most difficult tasks' they had to carry out.[123]

The precise nature of these tasks is indicated by the detailed account of *SS-Sturmbannführer* Magill, who commanded the 2nd *SS* Cavalry Regiment: 'Jewish looters were shot. Only a few craftsmen who were employed in the repair workshops of the *Wehrmacht* were left behind.'[124] At his trial the court concluded that Magill had received explicit orders for the subsequent shootings from Cavalry Brigade Headquarters in the first days of August.[125]

It was at about this time that the *Einsatzgruppen* and other mobile killing units began to extend their operations from actions against male Jews of military service age,[126] mostly intelligentsia and Commissar killings, to the rest of the Jewish population, including women, children and the elderly: for instance, the detailed record of killings in Lithuania – kept by Karl Jäger in charge of *Einsatzkommando 3* – indicates that the killing of women and children greatly intensified from around the middle of August.[127] Ralf Ogorreck, in his study of the post-war statements by former *Einsatzgruppen* members, concludes that by August 1941 all the *Einsatzgruppen* had received orders from Himmler to extend the killings to the entire Jewish population. It is interesting to note that several *Einsatzgruppen* commanders effectively resigned their posts shortly after this date.[128]

The operations in the Pripyet marshes provide a macabre demonstration of how Himmler's orders were put into practice. Whereas the initial order of 28 July indicated only that women and children were to be evacuated from 'criminal' strongpoints which were to be cleared, a subsequent telex, issued explicitly on Himmler's authority on 1 August, stated bluntly: 'all male Jews are to be shot. Jewish women to be driven into the swamps.'[129] In his concluding report, Magill remarked that:

> driving the women and children into the swamps did not have the intended success, as the swamps were not deep enough to permit a successful sinking in. At a depth of 1 metre there was in most cases firm ground, so that it was not possible to effect a sinking.[130]

Clearly Himmler's euphemistic language was interpreted literally by Magill, at least for the purposes of his report. Nevertheless, more explicit orders did get through at this time. During the mass shooting of Jews in Pinsk and the surrounding area from 5 August 1941, women, children and the elderly numbered among the victims.[131] Two squadrons of the 2nd *SS* Cavalry Regiment participated in the Pinsk actions. According to a Security Police report some 4500 Jews were killed in Pinsk at this time.[132]

The cavalry squadrons conducted smaller actions against the Jewish population in many of the villages through which they passed. For instance, about 250 male Jews were murdered in the cemetery of the village of Serniki in August 1941, having been collected together in the synagogue.[133] In David-grodek the male Jews were shot with the active collaboration of the Christian population, while the women and children were driven out of town and their property plundered. After about three weeks of wandering in the forests, most of the women and children returned. They were then permitted to reside in a ghetto with the few specialist workers who had been preserved.[134]

Of some significance is the organization of these actions, given that the German administration scarcely existed in these remote parts. The action in Pinsk was co-ordinated by the small Security Police unit of 18 men, detached from the Commander of the Security Police in Lublin.[135] No District Commissar had arrived in Pinsk, which was still under military administration. Nevertheless, mayors and a local police force had been appointed, either by the military administration or the cavalry squadrons themselves as they passed through the area. Local assistance was required in preparing the graves and filling them in afterwards. Some skilled workers were preserved from the shootings, partly at the insistence of the *Wehrmacht*.[136]

Participation by the newly established local police in these early actions is of particular interest. Magill comments:

> It was noticeable that the population in general was well-disposed towards the Jewish section of the population. However, they actively helped in collecting the Jews together. The local police employed, made up partly of Polish police and former Polish soldiers, makes a good impression. They perform their duties actively and also participated in the struggle against looters. In many cases they suffered losses in battle. However, their armament is very inadequate. In some places absolutely no weapons are available. Captured weapons were scarcely to be found in these areas, so that none could be distributed from these sources.[137]

Other witnesses also refer to the active role of the local police in identifying the Jews and helping to drive them out of their houses for collection.[138] The shooting was carried out mainly by members of the squadron, although thereafter local inhabitants participated in killing male Jews who were uncovered.[139]

The activities of the Cavalry Brigade in the Pripyet marshes are well known to Holocaust experts.[140] The deployment of units directly under Himmler's control is seen as a clear indication of the high priority and extra manpower devoted to this special task. Nevertheless, the cavalry squadrons also carried out other tasks during their progress from west to east.

The report of Commander Rear Army Area Centre on 10 August noted that 'by the appointment of mayors, the creation of an auxiliary police and the suppression of the Jews the region can be viewed as pacified'.[141] A few suspected communist activists (non-Jews) denounced by the local population were also shot. The cavalry squadrons even provisionally returned some cattle to the peasants from the collective farms.[142]

Magill's report includes a rough sketch of the countryside and population in the area. He notes that the population was primarily Ukrainian, with Belorussians in second place, some Poles and a handful of Russians. The Jews lived mainly in the larger settlements, where they made up a large proportion of the population: sometimes 50 to 80 per cent, but in other places only about 25 per cent. There were also many Jewish emigrants from the west. The Ukrainians and Belorussians were at this time reported as being well-disposed towards the Germans, even voluntarily bringing food to the arriving troops. The Russians and Poles were more reserved, although Magill received the impression that they were pleased that the Bolsheviks had left.[143]

In the Pripyet marshes almost no contact was made with organized enemy formations. The 2nd *SS* Cavalry Regiment managed to capture only ten prisoners, against 6526 persons shot. Amongst those shot only 76 were classified as Red Army personnel or communists, the remainder being 'looters' (Jews).[144] Nevertheless, as the separate squadrons approached the enemy front line to the east, they began to encounter stiffer resistance. In the town of Turov on 16 August the 3rd Squadron was repulsed with heavy losses after an initial attack. Therefore the Regiment halted and assembled its complete strength, in preparation for a combined assault on 21 August which was to prove more successful.[145]

It is most revealing to compare the detailed contemporary orders and reports with the post-war testimony of the cavalrymen and Jewish survivors. None of these sources is entirely reliable. The contemporary documents contain euphemisms and propaganda distortions related to the specific Nazi world view, demonizing the Jews as 'looters' and 'criminals' to justify the actions in their own eyes. The post-war evidence of members of Magill's Regiment is concerned primarily with diminishing their own personal responsibility, although several describe the killings in some detail. Jewish testimonies, however, can only provide the perspective of those who survived, usually by managing to escape or hide. The vast majority of Jews were not so fortunate and have left no testimony.

What does this operation tell us about the initial measures of the German occupation in this area? Many of the key elements of Hitler's 'war of destruction' in the east can be found in this pacification of remote areas, which were of little economic interest to the Germans. The written orders appear to be ambiguous, reflecting some of the difficulties encountered in extending the shootings beyond men of fighting age to women and children as well. If only with hindsight, the reluctance of men to admit their participation in the killing of women and children demonstrates an acknowledgement of the criminal nature of these actions.[146]

Units of Himmler's *SS* and police forces carried out similar 'cleansing' operations at other points behind the front. Police Regiment South was deployed in the area of Shepetovka-Rovno at the end of July 1941. Under the leadership of the *HSSPF*, Friedrich Jeckeln, the Regiment received orders that captured Commissars were to be held for interrogation by the *SD*, while female agents and Jews who assisted the Soviets were to be treated 'appropriately'. According to the concluding report some 370 Russians and 1643 Jews were shot as 'provocateurs and perpetrators' during this operation.[147] The shootings carried out by Police Battalion 322 of Police Regiment Centre, recorded in the unit's War Diary, leave no doubt about its activity as a killing unit.[148]

In the summer of 1941, it was the task of units of the Order Police and the *SS* to carry out pacification operations behind the front. These actions included, among their main tasks, the shooting of Jews as 'hostile elements'. Nevertheless, not all Jews living in these areas were killed in one fell swoop. Like the *Einsatzgruppen*, these mobile units had little time to prepare their actions or comb an area thoroughly during their rapid sweep through the area. Many Jews went into hiding or did not report when requested. Others were preserved as valuable skilled workers. The example of the village of Serniki, deep in the Pripyet marshes, demonstrates that many hundreds of Jews survived these initial actions, which were only a first strike against Hitler's chosen racial enemies. Magill concluded that a further sweep through the area would be necessary later on.[149]

In the ethnically mixed regions of the east, the Germans adopted traditional policies of divide and rule. Around Vilnius, for instance, both the Lithuanians and Poles looked to the Germans for patronage in their struggle for political and cultural power against each other.[150] Throughout western Belorussia, the Germans exploited rivalries between Poles and Belorussians in a similar fashion to establish their authority through the selection of personnel. Generally the superior education of the Poles gave them a great advantage as they sought to secure key positions.

The Belorussians by contrast were less well organized, lacking a strong sense of national identity. The Germans encountered difficulties in finding suitable Belorussians to fill key administrative positions.[151] By replacing some of the less reliable Poles, however, they were able to assert their own authority. There was also somewhat less anti-Semitism amongst the Belorussian population than was demonstrated in Lithuania. One report from *Einsatzgruppe B* noted that: 'the population undoubtedly harbours general feelings of hatred and anger against the Jews and approves of German measures... but is incapable of taking the initiative itself'.[152] This apathy was in part the lesson to be drawn from recent events. Having seen Soviet officials taken away to be shot by the Germans, it might be unwise to be identified too closely with the new regime lest the Soviets should one day return.

Nevertheless, as with almost every occupying force, using money and favours the Germans were able to find sufficient local collaborators prepared to assist with their 'dirty work'. The local police forces were initially only small, but volunteers came forward generally from the rougher sections of the population or those with a particular grudge against the communists. In Lithuania the (anti-communist) partisans played an active role in measures against the communists and Jews from the first days of the invasion. Pogroms in Ukraine also saw local participation from an early stage. In Belorussia the first actions were against communist officials and the Jewish 'intelligentsia', ostensibly to remove the threat posed by the 'Judaeo-Bolshevik' leadership cadres. Such actions required considerable local knowledge to help identify the relevant persons. This assistance was duly forthcoming in both Belorussia and Ukraine, even if the shootings were mainly carried out by the German units in charge of the operations.

Given the rapid German advance, the Jewish population, especially in the western areas, had little opportunity to flee. At the instigation of the *Wehrmacht*, they were placed under a series of restrictions which were much harsher than in Germany itself. Nazi propaganda sought to depict all Jews as identical with communists and inimical to German interests. Indeed, the social structure of the Jewish community was quite different from that of the population as a whole. However, the majority were craftsmen and traders who, especially in the former Polish areas, had no great affinity with communism:

> In fact only a small proportion of the Jews belong to the leading strata, if that proportion is quite extraordinarily high by comparison with the host population. The majority of the Jews live very poorly and are engaged in small-scale commerce and home-based trades, primarily retailing and small-scale agency businesses. There are, however, among the poor Jews, comparatively few labourers and even fewer peasants.[153]

Nevertheless, as Hitler's confidence in military success appeared to be confirmed by the successes of the summer, his campaign against the Jews was intensified towards genocide. The deployment of eleven police battalions and other *SS* units on 'cleansing operations' behind the front from mid-July greatly increased the manpower available for such 'special tasks'. At the same time Himmler extended the category of victims to include Jewish women and children. This obviously exceeded the measures necessary for political repression.

The anti-Jewish operations did not remain hidden from the *Wehrmacht*, which worked closely with the *Einsatzgruppen* on matters of rear area security. Front line troops were rarely involved directly, but rear area units, such as the *GFP*, Security Divisions and the PoW transit camp staff were required to support these operations. Acceptance of the initial pre-war 'illegal' orders had already implicated the *Wehrmacht* leadership. In view of this, it was difficult for individual officers to refuse requests by the Security Police, apparently required on security grounds. Others no doubt participated willingly.

The treatment of PoWs was another issue which was radicalized during the summer. The problem of dealing with vast numbers of prisoners was not solved effectively as there was widespread indifference to their fate. In addition, the existence of many former soldiers behind German lines became confused with the partisan danger. The adoption of a radical solution to this limited rear area threat undoubtedly turned many potential supporters into desperate opponents. Subsequently the high death rates in PoW camps and the hunting down of former Red Army personnel were significant factors in the emergence of armed resistance from among former Red Army soldiers who had evaded the German net.

Part of the problem no doubt lay in German overconfidence. This was fuelled by the stunning initial advances. In the retrospective view of Heinz Guderian, this was pure folly:

> The *OKW* and *OKH* [German Armed Forces and German Army High Commands] were so serenely confident of victory before winter set in that winter clothing had only been prepared for every fifth man in the army. It was not until 30 August 1941 that the *OKH* became seriously concerned with the problem of supplying major portions of the army with winter clothing.[154]

These initial advances, however, were achieved in areas essentially hostile to the recently imposed Soviet regime, against an army disorganized and demoralized. As they penetrated further into pre-1939 Soviet territory German supply problems and losses mounted, just as the Soviet *Stavka* was able to bring up second-echelon troops to block a further advance on Moscow. The outcome of the mobile battles around Smolensk in July 1941 was to convince Hitler of the need to divert forces away from the central axis. Against the advice of his generals, Hitler aimed to deprive Stalin of his 'vital areas', particularly Leningrad and the industrial base of the Donets basin, rather than pushing on immediately towards Moscow. In switching from an annihilation to an attrition strategy, however, the realization began to grow that the campaign might not be concluded before the Russian winter.[155]

Military overconfidence was matched by a failure of political planning. Nazi occupation policies reflected their extreme war aims. Assuming the campaign would be another *Blitzkrieg*, the Nazis paid almost no heed to the political ambitions of the subjugated peoples of the Soviet Union.[156] German economic policy failed to meet local expectations for a reversal of Soviet collectivization. Instead, Hitler sought the utmost exploitation and ruthless control of the territories conquered. The Soviet Union was viewed in Nazi plans as a vast territory, which first had to be depopulated in order for the Nazis to develop their own colonial empire.

Under the initial military administration, the *Wehrmacht* sought primarily to establish order and secure its rear areas. Himmler's *Einsatzgruppen* were deployed to carry out 'special political tasks' within the area of military jurisdiction, and by August they had initiated the genocide of Soviet Jews, including women and children amongst the victims. Hitler did not, however, trust the *Wehrmacht* to implement his radical programme fully. He was therefore keen to transfer authority in the occupied territories rapidly to a civil administration under Party control, and to lay the basis for his imperial 'New Order'.

3 Mass Killings in the Autumn of 1941

Once vast areas of the Soviet Union had been occupied, by the autumn of 1941, intensified efforts were made to shoot large numbers of Jews. The detailed reports of the *Einsatzgruppen* and post-war investigations reveal a definite shift from 'intelligentsia' killings to large-scale actions, including women and children amongst the victims, from the end of July.[1] In September and October 1941 this pattern was extended as *Einsatzgruppen* units in certain regions began the destruction of entire Jewish communities.[2]

Some historians have interpreted this intensification as Hitler taking revenge on the Jews, once his plans for the swift conquest of the Soviet Union had been thwarted. The real crisis for the *Wehrmacht*, however, did not come until December 1941. With regard to the Soviet Jews, it appears that the 'euphoria of victory' rather than frustration was the motivation for taking the final step towards genocide.[3]

Despite the stiffer resistance encountered by the *Wehrmacht* from mid-July, the capture of more than 450 000 additional prisoners around Kiev and preparations for the final assault on Moscow by the end of September served to bolster Hitler's confidence in victory. In mid-November the Army High Command still believed in the capture of Moscow and possibly even Stalingrad before the end of 1941.[4] The slaughter of the Jews was in line with Hitler's original conception of creating *Lebensraum* for the Germans in the east. It was solely due to practical considerations, such as the continuing need for Jews as specialist workers and the physical difficulties encountered, that this autumn wave remained only a 'partial solution'.

In accordance with Hitler's plans, authority was transfered from the military to a civil administration in *Weißruthenien* (western Belorussia) on 1 September 1941. *Gauleiter* Wilhelm Kube was named General Commissar. The transfer was celebrated with an official ceremony in Minsk on 31 August 1941 (see Photograph 2). In practice the real transfer of power was not immediate. The civil administration required more time to set up a government from scratch, whilst awaiting the arrival of personnel from Germany. In the meantime the 707th Infantry Division remained in the area to secure the army's lines of communication. Units of the Division continued to exercise authority as the *OK* in many of the main towns. The military authorities conceded that due to the weakness of the occupying forces, considerable reliance would have to be placed on the improvised local police.[5]

An impression of the difficulties encountered in establishing the civil administration can be gained from contemporary German reports. The District Commissar (*Gebietskommissar*) for Slonim, Gerhard Erren, complained of a shortage of all necessities from office materials to vehicles. A particular problem was the slow arrival of his small basic staff, some of whom did not arrive from Germany until January 1942. During these initial weeks the civil administration was preoccupied with sorting out offices and accommodation, and selecting local auxiliary staff.[6]

In western Belorussia the problem of personnel selection was compounded by the national conflicts between Poles, Belorussians and Lithuanians. During the period of Polish rule nearly all administrative posts had been held by Poles. The Belorussians in particular lacked men with sufficient education and experience to assume leading positions. Added to this was the greater energy and ambition of the Poles, who sought to secure influential positions under the Germans in order to protect their own interests.[7]

German military operations on the Central Front were diverted southwards in August to complete the encirclement of a large concentration of Soviet forces around Kiev. Following the successful conclusion of this operation, the *Wehrmacht* was then able to press on into eastern Ukraine. It was at this time that the first mass killings were carried out in the south. Some 23 600 Jews were murdered in Kamenets-Podolsk on 28–31 August by Police Battalion 320 under the command of *HSSPF* South, Friedrich Jeckeln. Further large-scale actions followed in mid-September in Berdichev and Vinnitsa, where in each case available sources indicate that more than 10 000 Jews were killed.[8] In Zhitomir 3145 Jews were murdered on 19 September. In this operation the Jewish quarter was sealed off by 60 men of the Ukrainian militia and twelve lorries were supplied by the *FK* and the local administration.[9]

Shortly after the capture of Kiev in mid-September a large fire broke out in the city. It was the result of Soviet sabotage against the headquarters of the 6th Army in the Continental Hotel. On 26 September the Jews of Kiev were requested by the *SD* to report for registration. Over 30 000 people reported, including women and children. They were shot in the ravine at Babi Yar just outside Kiev on 29 and 30 September.[10] German sources reported this as a reprisal action. However, Soviet sabotage served only as a pretext for anti-Jewish massacres that had already been initiated in this region.

A further large-scale action took place in Rovno on 6–7 November 1941, when over 15 000 Jews were killed by the Security Police, assisted by members of Police Battalion 320 and local Ukrainian police.[11] On 15 November the *HSSPF* South, Friedrich Jeckeln, was transfered to become *HSSPF* North in Riga, where he organized a large ghetto 'clearance' action in December which claimed a further 30 000 Jewish lives.[12]

Mass shootings of Jews were also carried out in central Ukraine. The participation of the local Ukrainian auxiliary police is mentioned in a German report from October 1941 concerning the police operation against the remaining Jews of Krivoy Rog. Here the whole of the Ukrainian auxiliary police (*Hilfspolizei*) was involved in an action designed to clear the city of Jews.[13] In Dnepropetrovsk it was reported that about 70 000 of the 100 000 Jews originally living there had fled before the arrival of the Germans. Of the remainder, some 10 000 were shot by units subordinate to the *HSSPF* on 13 October 1941.[14] In many places skilled Jewish workers were exempted from the killings to avoid further damage to the local economy.[15]

By the end of September preparations had begun for the final assault on Moscow. Behind the advancing troops, *Einsatzgruppe B* made efforts to increase its rate of killing. Whilst the *Sonderkommandos* were scheduled to follow in the path of Army Group Centre, the main *Einsatzkommandos* remained stationary to conduct a more thorough 'cleansing' of eastern Belorussia. Large-scale Jewish shootings were conducted in the main towns of Mogilev, Polotsk and Vitebsk during October, and in Bobruisk, Orsha and Gomel in November.[16] In Vitebsk the German authorities withheld food from the Jews in the ghetto and whilst many died of starvation, the remainder were shot because of the danger of their 'spreading disease'.[17] Only a few Jews were kept alive in Mogilev to work as skilled craftsmen in a forced labour camp after the ghetto was cleared.[18]

Numerous Jewish 'actions' were conducted in the towns and villages of eastern Belorussia and Russia under military administration through the winter of 1941–2.[19] For example, in the area around Mogilev small units of *Einsatzkommando 8* led by *SD* commanders scoured the surrounding villages for Jews. Some Jewish families were arrested and taken to the prison in Mogilev, where they were later shot. Others were killed on the spot where they were found.[20] The local police (*OD*) were often involved in rounding up and guarding the Jews, as in the actions in Mglin and Starodub in the autumn of 1941.[21] At Krupka in October the *Wehrmacht* played an active role in the mass shooting of Jews.[22]

By mid-November *Einsatzgruppe B*, commanded by Arthur Nebe, claimed to have 'liquidated' 45 467 people since the start of the campaign. Nevertheless, these figures lagged behind those for his colleagues and rivals in the other *Einsatzgruppen*.[23] He noted the tendency for the Jews to flee before the advancing Germans as they penetrated further east. Many undoubtedly left as part of the extensive Soviet evacuations, which had now become better organized.[24]

With the renewal of the advance on the Central Front, *Einsatzkommando 1b* was sent from Riga to take over Security Police duties in Minsk and western Belorussia (*Weißruthenien*). A Lithuanian *Schutzmannschaft* Battalion (later known as the 12th) was also detailed to Minsk from Kaunas in

October 1941, operating under the control of German Reserve Police Battalion 11.[25] This German Order Police unit was in turn subordinated to the Military Commandant for *Weißruthenien*, Gustav von Bechtolsheim, commander of the 707th Infantry Division. The arrival of the Lithuanian *Schutzmannschaft* Battalion coincided with a murderous wave of killings in the Minsk area in October 1941. Officially described as anti-partisan actions, the victims were mainly Jews, communists and other elements deemed by the Germans to be 'suspicious', such as Gypsies, who were also to be shot on the spot according to the military orders issued at this time.[26]

The commander of Reserve Police Battalion 11 arrived in Slutsk on 27 October with two German police companies and two companies of Lithuanian auxiliary police. He explained to the District Commissar, Carl, that he had orders to 'liquidate' all the Jews of the town within two days. The District Commissar attempted to save the Jewish craftsmen, whom he deemed indispensable to the maintenance of the economy:

> During the operation the town itself presented a terrifying picture. With indescribable brutality, both German police officers, and especially Lithuanian partisans, herded the Jews, and also Belorussians, out of their homes. Shots could be heard all over the town and in some streets the bodies of executed Jews were piled high.[27]

The majority of the Jews were taken out of the town and shot in pits. The Lithuanian forces were divided into three sections for the 'action': one group guarding, one shooting and one preparing to shoot. After a while the groups relieved each other in turn.[28] It appears that some victims were buried alive and subsequently dug their way out of the graves. District Commissar Carl expressed concern about the impact of the action on the Belorussian inhabitants, who were reportedly stunned by the events which had destroyed most of the confidence built up previously by the German administration. The operation was also accompanied by rampant looting by the indisciplined forces involved.[29]

Two days later, on 30 October, there were further Jewish killings in the nearby towns of Nesvizh and Kletsk. Post-war Soviet and German investigations conclude that members of the Lithuanian 12th Battalion were involved in both these actions, having moved on from Slutsk. According to a German military report, some 5900 Jews were shot dead in the Slutsk–Kletsk area at this time.[30] Detailed descriptions of the action in Nesvizh are available from a number of sources, including several Jewish survivors. The operation was preceded by demands for a ransom by the Germans in mid-October. On this occasion the adult male Jews were assembled in the market place and 200 hostages taken. When the initial German demands were met, the next day they were increased to half a million roubles and 2.5 kg of gold.[31]

On 29 October 1941 an order was issued by the Local Commandant for the entire Jewish population to gather in the square to have their papers examined.[32] The next day people turned up dressed in their best clothes and uncertain what to expect. In the light of recent events the Jews were anxious and suspicious. Shalom Cholawski recalls: 'we were full of dread. We imagined all sorts of reasons for the order.'[33] Yet, as he admits, they were reluctant to fear the worst. Another survivor echoes his sentiment: 'we could not believe that they would simply kill all the Jews'.[34] Most expected only that their houses would be looted while they were on parade.

A selection was conducted of the skilled workers on the basis of a list. Doctors, engineers, glaziers, blacksmiths, textile workers, saddlers, shoemakers and tailors were amongst the groups which were sent to one side and permitted to take their families with them. During the selection process some trucks suddenly appeared on the road which led to Slutsk. Uniformed men surrounded the entire market-place.[35] They were Lithuanians, recognizable to a Jewish witness by the language which they spoke.[36] Gradually those not yet selected began to sense the danger of their position and when 'it was announced finally that 20 carpenters were also to leave the lines, people who had never been carpenters started to run'.[37]

The skilled workers, about 560 people,[38] were then escorted to the school where they were guarded by the local Belorussian police. German soldiers and Lithuanian auxiliaries took the remainder, approximately 4000 Jews, to be shot at two separate sites. In the grounds of the Radziwill castle, Poles working under German supervision had prepared two pits in advance. The other site was on the road to Snov just outside the town. The old and infirm were transported to the killing site in lorries. The Germans took valuables from the victims and made them undress before killing them. After the war German soldiers from 8th Company, 727th Regiment, who were based in Nesvizh, claimed that the Lithuanians did most of the shooting.[39]

The German authorities collected the victims' clothes and sold them to the population. The most valuable property was sent on to Baranovichi.[40] There was also some looting of the houses by the local population.[41] After the action the skilled workers were released and given only a short time to move into the ghetto which was surrounded by barbed wire.[42] Over the following days members of the local police searched the ghetto and any persons found hiding who were not on the list of skilled workers were shot. The graves which had been filled in were reported to be moving. For the Pole, Josef Marchwinski, this was a sign: 'as if those killed wanted to shout out and protest saying "Look you, the living, this is Fascism, this is the new German culture!"' He realized then that: 'today they were killing Jews and tomorrow they would start killing Belorussians and Poles'.[43]

In early November the 11th Reserve Police Battalion was sent back to Kaunas and the Lithuanian Companies returned to guard duties in Minsk.[44]

Nevertheless the local commandant in Stolpce, Ludwig Göbel, in charge of 8th Company, 727th Infantry Regiment, continued the wave of killings, operating with the assistance of the local Belorussian police. Mass killings in Turets and Yeremichi on 4 November 1941 were followed by a large-scale operation against the Jews of Mir on Sunday 9 November 1941.[45] Recent court proceedings in England permit a detailed reconstruction of the events in Mir based on the testimony of a number of eye-witnesses.

Ze'ev Schreiber, a Jewish resident, awoke at first light and looked out of the window. He saw a group of armed policemen, including the *rayon* police chief, walking down Vilnius Street in a close group. As they passed his house two of the policemen fired automatic weapons at Abraham Resnik, a Jewish resident who was standing on the corner. He fell to the ground immediately, shot dead; the body was seen shortly afterwards lying in a pool of blood. This was the opening shot of the massacre which took place on the streets of the town.[46]

Nearby another Jew, Lev Abramovsky, was woken by the sound of shooting in the streets. His mother said: 'Children, get up quickly, we must run away from here. Now they will be killing everyone!' His whole family and many of his neighbours ran out on to the streets. They were trying to escape in all directions. It was total panic. Lev Abramovsky and his family headed towards the Jewish cemetery. As they ran many of them were hit by gun-fire from the local police. Near the Jewish cemetery Abramovsky ran into a barn. He climbed up into a hay loft, from where he had a good view of the surrounding area.[47]

As Ze'ev Schreiber went to his assigned work, decorating the house of a local policeman, he saw many Jews trying to escape by running towards the fields. They were being chased by Belorussian policemen who were shooting at the fleeing Jews. Many Jews were hit, as the policemen sprayed them with bullets using their automatic weapons. At the same time German soldiers were present on the streets. They were watching events, but did not join in the chase.[48]

The local police had been formed within a couple of weeks of the German arrival on the basis of voluntary service. It was composed of about 30 local men aged between 25 and 35. They were mainly of Belorussian nationality, with a few Poles and Tartars. These men did not enjoy a good reputation amongst the local population. Some had had relatives deported to Siberia during the brief Soviet occupation and a few were known as aggressive anti-Semites.

Amongst the more notorious policemen was a man named Litvin. Ivan Yatsevich, a Belorussian resident of Mir, spent the day at home. He watched out of the window as two Jewish girls were walking along the road. They were being followed by two local policemen. 'One of them was Litvin and the other was the Tartar. They shot them in the back of the head with pistols from about one and a half to two metres. The girls dropped dead, their heads were blown to pieces.'[49]

German soldiers and the local police drove many Jews out of their houses and escorted them to the market square. Thirteen-year-old Jacob Lipszyc arrived at the square with his family quite early. He saw shooting in the square and his mother told him to run. There were two machine guns manned by policemen situated in the corners of the square, which opened fire. His mother, brother and sister were all killed by this salvo. His father was put on to the back of a truck with other Jews.

Jacob Lipszyc managed to take refuge under the steps of the old pharmacy, which had been burned down. From here he observed the scene in the square. It was packed with hundreds of people, men, women and children. He saw a truck reversing into the square. The canvas cover was pulled back to reveal another machine gun. A policeman then fired the machine gun into the crowd of Jews.[50]

Another Jewish survivor, Shmuel Cesler, was brought to the square a little later, having initially managed to hide for a while. When he arrived some 1000 Jews had been gathered there. A German requested that any carpenters should come forward. Although he was without a trade, Cesler joined them voluntarily and was taken with 85 others to the courtyard of the Catholic church. Here they remained in safety until the end of the slaughter at about 3 o'clock.[51]

Apart from the square, there were two other main killing sites in Mir on this day. Columns of Jews were escorted away from the square by the local police and Germans using Alsatian dogs. One site was at the slaughter house, on a side street off to the left from Vilnius Street as it heads north-west towards Novogrudok from the main square. Menachem Shalev, from a house on Vilnius Street, observed a large column of several hundred Jews being taken here at about ten o'clock.[52]

The same column was also seen by Regina Bedynska, the daughter of the Polish schoolmaster. She spent the morning in the attic of the school building where she lived, which had a clear view from the windows. Earlier in the morning she had observed German soldiers arriving in trucks from Stolpce. At the slaughterhouse she also saw Jewish men, women and children being pushed into a hole and shot by Germans and the Belorussian police. She soon turned away as she could not watch it any more.[53]

The other killing site was at the sand-pit, not far from Count Mirsky's castle. From his hiding place in the hay loft Lev Abramovsky could observe events over a wide area. He could see the sand-pit site and the castle, as well as events in the Jewish and Tartar cemeteries. He watched as his mother and father and two brothers were murdered. Two sisters managed to survive, but his other sister, Zlata, was captured with her family. Her husband was shot and then the police picked up the children by the legs and hit them against the tombstones to kill them. Lev did not see what happened to Zlata, but he never saw her again.

Lev Abramovsky also watched as the police and Germans escorted a large number of Jews in a column to the sand-pit near the road to Stolpce. The column stretched from the Catholic church to the pre-prepared grave. There were four or five people in each row of the column: 'The Jews were being herded to the pit by the police.'[54] The same group was probably seen by Ze'ev Schreiber, who also witnessed a large crowd of Jews (including his own family) being escorted down Tartarski Street in the direction of Stolpce.[55] The scene at the killing site was watched by Boris Grushevsky, a local Belorussian inhabitant who had cycled into Mir that day:

> The policemen were sitting on the top of this pit. They had sub-machine guns. There were also several Germans. It was the policemen who shot. The Jews were standing in columns in front of the pit. The police were guarding at the sides of the pit. The Jews were made to take off their clothes a few at a time and approach the pit and enter it. They laid down and were shot ... Some of the Jews were only wounded and tried to get out. Blood was gushing from their wounds.

A German officer was in charge, but there were more Belorussian policemen than German soldiers present. The police guarding the column were armed with rifles and bayonets. Grushevsky witnessed one of them go up to a woman, take a child from her arms on his bayonet and throw it into the pit. The policemen were from Mir and the nearby villages of Turets and Zhukovichi. According to Grushevsky, the policemen seemed to be relishing their murderous work. He recalls that the police at the pit seemed merry and 'behaved as if they were at a wedding party'. As Boris Grushevsky returned to Mir, he counted thirteen bodies of people who had not wanted to go to the pit and had been killed where they stood.[56]

Once the shooting at the slaughter house had died down, Regina Bedynska came down from the attic to get some water from the well opposite her house. As she approached the well she saw four Jewish adults and a child walking towards the fields along a side street. At the same time the local Belorussian police chief and three policemen were standing in the main street armed with rifles. One of the policemen alerted his boss by touching his elbow. The chief of police turned round, aimed and fired at the Jews who were trying to escape. The shot hit a Jewish woman who fell down on top of her child. The child crawled out from under the woman shouting 'Mother, get up, Mother, get up.' However, the woman did not move. The police then chased after the other escaping Jews. Regina quickly returned home.[57]

Some of the worst scenes took place at the hospital. Here three of the most notorious local policemen with two Germans rounded up and shot about 15 Jews within the clear view of one of the patients. This woman, a

Jewish doctor, Zoya Pozniak, had recently given birth to twins. She was well-known to the local policemen and only saved by the presence of mind of the Christian nurses. They offered some surgical spirit to the policemen in order to distract them.[58]

Two Jewish survivors had particularly narrow escapes. Menachem Shalev, who spent the day hiding in a house on Vilnius Street, was subsequently discovered in the afternoon by two Germans. He was found under the bed with his brother. They persuaded the Germans that they were not Jews, but were told to take some looted clothing to the German lorries waiting outside. In the street there was also a group of Belorussian policemen.

As the two boys left to go home they were recognized by two local policemen, who chased after them. His brother tripped and was shot dead in the street. Shalev escaped into a nearby courtyard, where he was confronted by the policeman, Litvin, who told him to run. He was then shot in the left hand as he fled. He was shot twice, but only grazed. Feigning death, he was left lying on the ground. After a while he got up and hid in a nearby attic.[59]

Policemen and Germans discovered Lev Abramovsky and his brother in their hiding place during the afternoon. The Goldin family was discovered at the same time. Mr Goldin pleaded for the lives of his family and they held on to each other, refusing to be moved. The policemen and the Germans beat them with their rifle butts and started to shoot at them. The Goldin family were all shot in turn on the spot.

Lev and his brother were then added to the column of Jews being taken to the sand-pit site. It took about two hours shuffling along obediently in small steps, as there were other Jews being shot ahead of them. They were being driven along like sheep or cattle. There was a loud sobbing from the people. It was impossible to break out due to the close guards all around. They were beaten severely by policemen on the way.

Light was fading as they approached the killing site. Lev Abramovsky saw policemen shooting the Jews with heavy machine guns as they approached the pit. The victims fell in as they were hit. Nearby stood several Jews with shovels. They were instructed to cover the bodies with a layer of dirt. One of the workers, Yeshil, was at the edge of the pit with a shovel in his hands. Suddenly he lunged with the shovel at a policeman. Yeshil was immediately killed and fell into the mass grave.

Eventually Lev Abramovsky's group reached the pit. He was herded to the edge and the machine guns opened fire. His brother was killed by the bullets. Lev Abramovsky, however, was toppled in by those falling behind him and was not hit. About five or six people fell on top of him and he lost consciousness.

When he came to, he was surrounded by bodies and warm blood. He managed to scramble up towards the air and climb out of the pit. It was already dark and light snow was falling. Exhausted, he washed himself with snow and wrapped his feet in rags made from a torn jacket he found nearby. He then set off towards the Tartar cemetery.[60]

In town the Germans now instructed the non-Jews to clear up the bodies lying in the streets. Menachem Shalev observed this from his new hiding place.[61] There was also some looting of Jewish property. The next day the pogrom was over and the surviving Jews returned to the ghetto, once they were told it was safe. They were stunned to find that so few of their relatives and friends remained alive. Estimates of the numbers slaughtered vary. Given that about 800 Jews survived to go into the second ghetto based in Mir Castle in 1942, probably some 1600 people were killed at the various sites on 9 November 1941.

A similar large-scale action took place a few days later in Slonim on 14 November 1941. One Jewish survivor was prevented from returning to his home, after visiting a friend the night before, as the German forces had already cordoned off the ghetto. He described what he was able to observe from the loft of his friend's house:

> I saw German soldiers chasing people and beating them and also children being thrown to the ground. These people were screaming. I later heard the sound of engines coming from the direction of the old market place. Shortly after that everything went quiet. It remained quiet for about two hours. Then things returned to normal – shops opened and people came back out onto the streets.[62]

He never saw his mother, his father, his brother and his own child again.

This action was a joint operation between the District Commissar, Gerhard Erren, and the Security Police, assisted by the *Wehrmacht*, Latvian and Lithuanian police auxiliaries and the local Belorussian police:

> They entered the houses in the ghetto and told people that they would have to leave their homes to go and live somewhere else. The old people, the children and the women were driven on trucks to Chepilova to pits prepared in advance by other Jews who were the first victims to be shot and to fall into the pits they had dug themselves.[63]

Again a selection took place on the market square and those with a yellow employment card were spared.[64] In his report dated January 1942, District Commissar Erren boasted of having rid Slonim of 8000 'unnecessary hungry mouths'; he callously concluded that 'the approximately 7000 Jews in the town of Slonim are now all employed in the work process, they work willingly owing to their constant fear of death and in the spring they will be most carefully vetted and selected for a further reduction'.[65]

As in Mir, one Jew survived being taken to the pits. He fainted instead of being shot and subsequently managed to crawl out when he came to. The following description is based on his recollections.

At the square the Jews were told they were being relocated and initially they departed in an orderly fashion. Panic set in at the railway station, once it became clear that they were not leaving by rail, but being marched off into the forest in the direction of Baranovichi. From here the guard on them was tightened and those who fell out of the column were shot. It was too far across open fields to the forests for a successful escape. In the distance they could hear the sound of machine guns. After being marched for about an hour they were made to sit on the ground. The men were then separated from the women and forced to undress as their turn came, the guards often employing their rifle butts and whips.

Groups of 20 people, all naked, were then led by a path up to a hill. As he climbed over the hill he saw two pits, one completely full with bodies and the other half full. He was then ordered to run by the side of the half-full pit and was ordered to stop. From there he does not know what happened, but feels that half a second before the shooting started he fainted and slipped into the pit. He did not see any of the shooters.

On regaining consciousness he did not understand where he was and he gradually started to move and got one elbow free. He felt damp and hot. He then realized where he was, but did not know in which direction to go to get out of the pit. He moved like a snake and then felt a cold stream of air and made his way in the direction of the air. He then put his head out of the pit and saw the stars. It was cold outside on his head but the pit inside was warm. He managed to crawl out from amongst the pile of bodies and sneak away back to the ghetto.[66]

Several witnesses observed the participation of the local Belorussian police during this action. The police had been organized by the *Wehrmacht* as an *OD* and were at this time only dressed in civilian clothing: 'It was formed of young men from Slonim, from the villages and Poles.'[67] One survivor saw Belorussian policemen going into the houses and taking people out.[68] Others describe them being used as escorts and cordon guards during the shootings.[69] Following the 'action', the policemen held a party to celebrate.[70]

In Borisov further to the east a major action was carried out on 20 October 1941, when some 6500 out of 8000 Jews were shot. This was in spite of the reportedly exemplary conduct of the Jews in performing work and paying 300 000 roubles, as well as silver and gold, in contributions. The action was co-ordinated by *Einsatzgruppe B* (Security Police), but carried out primarily by their local 'Russian' auxiliaries under the command of an ethnic German named David Ehof.[71] A vivid description of the brutal action of the local police was given by Ehof during the investigation conducted against him after the war:

The police broke into the Jewish houses, chased the people to the square in the centre of the ghetto, drove them into the vehicles by force and transported them to the place of execution. There was no mercy shown either to old people, children, pregnant women, or the sick. Anyone who offered resistance was shot on the spot on my orders – in the square, in the houses, on the trip to the place of execution – or they were beaten half to death.[72]

According to the *Wehrmacht* officer, Sönnecken, who was present in Borisov during the massacre, the initial attitude of the local population was hostile to the Jews: 'Let them die, they did us a lot of harm!' The round-up took place in full view of the civilian population and German military personnel; in the distance the sound of rifle shots could be heard all day. Having observed the action, the attitude of the local population changed:

> The eyes of these non-Jews reflected either complete apathy or horror, because gruesome scenes were taking place on the streets. If, on the previous evening, the non-Jews had believed that the Jews deserved their fate, the following day they asked: 'who ordered such a thing? How can 6500 Jews be killed in one go? It's the Jews now, when will our turn come? What have these poor Jews done? All they did was work! Those who are really guilty are safe!'

The policemen received plenty of *Schnaps* in order to enable them to carry out their difficult task. The extent of the massacre could be judged from the large piles of clothing which were brought back into the town for storage on lorries.[73]

Other large-scale actions followed in the Belorussian towns of Novogrudok on 8 December and Jody on 16 December 1941. In Novogrudok more than 5000 Jews lost their lives; Belorussian policemen who were present at the pits described later the heart-rending scenes to one of the few surviving relatives.[74] In Jody about half the Jews managed to escape, partly due to a timely warning from the local chief of police. Nevertheless some 250 Jews were killed. According to survivor testimony: 'there were very few Germans involved in the Jody massacre. They supervised the actions and the round-ups. The mass killings were all done by Belorussians, Russians and some Poles.'[75]

Despite this massive wave of killings, more than half of the pre-war Jewish population of eastern Poland survived into 1942. In General Commissariat Zhitomir thousands of Jews remained, mostly in the smaller rural ghettoes and labour camps. In the Kiev and Nikolayev General Commissariats, despite a heavier toll by the *Einsatzgruppen* in 1941, hundreds of Jews were not killed until the spring or summer of 1942. Many communities, especially in Volhynia, were spared a major action in the autumn. Even during those actions which took place, a number of skilled workers were preserved, while others managed to hide until the action was completed. The reports of

Einsatzgruppe C from September 1941 indicate that there was a considerable need for scarce Jewish labour:

> In the western and central Ukraine the Jews are almost identical with the municipal worker, craftsman and tradesman section of the population. *If the Jewish labour force is dispensed with completely, the economic reconstruction of Ukrainian industry, as well as the development of the municipal administrative centres, will be almost impossible.*
>
> There is only one possibility which it took the German administration in the General Government a long time to recognize: *The solution of the Jewish question by the extensive work deployment of the Jews.* This would result in a gradual liquidation of the Jews – a development which is in accordance with the economic circumstances of the country.[76]

This theme was also taken up in the report of the Wannsee conference in January 1942, which mentioned the employment of Jews on road construction in the east, as part of a gradual destruction of remaining Jews through work, alongside the systematic murders.[77] In Galicia (and to a lesser extent in Ostland and Ukraine) these plans were realized by employing Jewish labour on the *Durchgangsstraße* highway construction and other labour projects in specific camps.[78] The inmates of these work camps were amongst the last Jews to be 'liquidated' in late 1942 and 1943, although many were killed by the brutal work conditions and inadequate supplies. Thus from an early stage there was a dual strategy of outright murders combined with the prospect of life preservation for those providing useful work. This strategy proved most effective in dividing and deceiving the Jews as to the Nazis' ultimate intentions.

In the aftermath of these autumn massacres a new routine was gradually established within the ghettoes for those who had survived. Surprisingly, in Nesvizh, of the 560 survivors, only 180 were local Jews and the remainder were from among the refugees who had arrived from the west. Soon workshops were set up for the skilled workers and other jobs found for those without work. Jews working outside the ghetto were escorted daily to and from work by the local police. The Jewish Council was responsible for monitoring the performance of Jewish labour and issuing food rations accordingly. Each person received 300g of bread and a small piece of meat per day. At around 7.30am the ghetto gate was opened briefly for the inhabitants to fetch water as there were no wells within the ghetto. Inevitably, on some days no water was available due to queues or if the well was not working.[79]

Nesvizh Jews were occasionally ordered to dig pits for non-Jews who were shot. The victims were suspected communists and partisans, Red Army soldiers and other people deemed guilty under the stringent and harsh Nazi regime. Several witnesses refer to the participation of the local police and military Commandant in these measures: 'at first the Germans were clearly mistrustful, but then they allowed the Belorussians "to join in the fun", after they had proved themselves during the first action'.[80] The estimate of the Soviet Extraordinary Commission, which should be treated with some caution, is that about 3000 PoWs were shot in Nesvizh during the occupation.[81]

At the same time the treatment accorded to those PoWs held in camps was also appalling. Insufficient food and shelter were accompanied by brutal treatment from the guards. A description of conditions at the PoW camp at Berezvetch, near Glubokoye, is not untypical:

> When the Germans, on rare occasions, would bring into the camp some frozen, rotten potatoes, and the prisoners would fall upon them, grabbing and clutching, the Germans would shoot them for 'failing to keep order!' The hunger was so oppressive that life threatening acts were not a deterrent. Better death by a bullet, than slow death by hunger.[82]

In one of the makeshift camps there were reportedly only 2 toilets provided for some 11 000 PoWs.[83] The death rate amongst Soviet PoWs in the General Government (Poland) rose to over 1 per cent per day in October 1941.[84] In the occupied Soviet Union conditions were equally bad. At a camp in the town of Gnivan near Vinnitsa, based around a stone quarry, it was estimated by the Soviet authorities that over 6000 Soviet PoWs were buried, mostly between late 1941 and early 1942.[85] In Vinnitsa itself the Soviet authorities estimated that over 12 000 PoWs 'died of emaciation, cold and epidemics with no medical aid rendered. Those prisoners who worked on a special construction project [Hitler's "*Wehrwolf*" HQ] were killed one and all after the works had been completed.'[86] On account of the army's own supply difficulties, Generalleutnant Wagner, the Quartermaster General, pronounced that 'non-working PoWs in the camps were to starve'.[87]

The co-operation between the army and the *Einsatzgruppen* was not without some friction. A camp commandant at Vinnitsa who disapproved of the transfer of 362 Jewish PoWs to the Security Police initiated court-martial proceedings against his deputy.[88] Nevertheless, as Ronald Headland observes, relations between the two organizations were generally good, with objections more often being of a practical rather than a principled nature.[89]

More than 2 500 000 Soviet PoWs are estimated to have died in German captivity during the Second World War. It was above all the terrible conditions in the PoW camps which were responsible for most deaths. Many were also shot 'trying to escape' during PoW transports when they were unable to keep up with the march columns.[90] About 140 000, however, were selected and killed as politically and racially 'intolerable elements'. The death rate amongst Soviet PoWs fell off considerably after the spring of

1942, as German leaders recognized the serious labour shortage within the German economy. Nearly half a million Soviet PoWs were employed in the *Reich* by the autumn of 1943.[91]

As explained in the previous chapter, German policy towards Soviet PoWs evolved in line with fears about rear area security. A deadline was set for former Red Army personnel behind the lines to give themselves up.[92] Any persons found after this date were to be 'executed'. Units of the 707th Infantry Division were reminded of this policy again in mid-October 1941:

> With reference to the order of the Commandant in *Weißruthenien* dated 26.9.41, item 3, it is again pointed out that *captured* Russian soldiers (in uniform or civilian clothes) or escaped prisoners of war, even if they are not carrying any weapons, are not to be delivered to a PoW camp but are to be shot on the spot. If they can give any information about partisans &c. they are to be immediately taken by the fastest possible means to the Secret Field Police Group 1 in Minsk.[93]

Evidence that this policy was also enforced comes from a former German Lieutenant:

> In October 1941 the German *Wehrmacht* issued an order, whereby all the Russian soldiers behind the front had to report to be taken prisoner. The final date was 4 November 1941. Anyone found after that was shot or suspected of being a partisan and was therefore also doomed. At this time there were lots of Russian soldiers who had laid down their arms and found shelter on farms.[94]

The effect of this harsh treatment proved to be a self-fulfilling prophecy. From the autumn of 1941 onwards, many of the former soldiers working on farms fled to the forests for fear of their lives. As a former Polish partisan explained after the war, 'this illogical action by the Germans against prisoners of war working peacefully and completely satisfied with having at last got rid of their politicians, the *NKVD*, Stalin, hunger and lice, led to mass escapes to the forests and the organization of partisan squads'.[95]

It was also not uncommon for some PoWs to escape from captivity, as one man recounts:

> We were held in a prisoner of war camp in the town of Lida. The prisoners of war were held in a dilapidated barracks. The camp was enclosed with barbed wire. One day when the prisoners of war were unloading firewood at Lida station, I managed to escape and return home to my village near Brest-Litovsk by December 1941.[96]

Others took advantage of the weak German guards to escape in transit.[97] Most were too weak, however, to even contemplate escape. Many were shot by their guards on marches to camps located in the rear, as they were unable to go on.

Given the poor treatment of PoWs, those in hiding found some support among the local population:

> In 1941, in our village, there was a group of Soviet servicemen who were all wounded. They were staying in a shed ... The villagers fed them and the village elder knew they were there. However, none of the villagers told the Germans or informed on them and they later went to join the partisans.[98]

In Ukraine, and to a lesser extent in Belorussia, certain groups of PoWs were released and permitted to go home.[99] German officers often required someone to identify and vouch for the liberated men (usually a relative or person from his home locality). The men were then released to work on farms or in factories.[100] An example from Belorussia demonstrates how arbitrary the process of release might be. A soldier from Nesvizh:

> was captured by the Germans and marched to Molodechno. The march took about two weeks and he arrived there in late 1941. He spent two to three months in a prisoner of war camp here, during which time he was starved. He was subsequently freed in the winter of 1941–2 with the help of his mother. She was informed of his location by a friend who had escaped and she asked for his release.[101]

The inevitable confusion between soldiers returning home and genuine partisans is revealed by a report from the Krivoy Rog area. This example confirms that actual partisan activity was probably exaggerated in many German reports at this time:

> No real partisans have been seized here. Among the 28 alleged partisans handed over to the Secret Field Police during the period 5–10 October 1941 there were no partisans. Rather these were Russian soldiers who had fled from the Russian front and had come home here without weapons. They were taken to the transit camp. Another 12 arrested were former Russian soldiers, on three of whom weapons were still found. The latter incur the penalty threatened in the announcement.[102]

The Soviet Union was in fact poorly prepared for a widespread partisan struggle in 1941 and the main emphasis of Soviet partisan operations in the first months of the war was focused on assisting the Red Army in the vicinity of the front line.[103] Some of the resistance organizations, such as that within the Minsk ghetto, grew up spontaneously.[104] Many of the Red Army men and Border Guards who went into hiding had no contact with the official partisan organization.[105]

German reports in the autumn of 1941 place much emphasis on an unspecified partisan threat, but their own losses at this time were minute compared with later in the war. For instance, Battalions I and II of the 727th Infantry Regiment based in the Baranovichi–Novogrudok area suffered only a handful of casualties during the winter of 1941–42. These were due mainly to mines or personnel being run over by trains rather than direct combat with partisan units. The first losses inflicted on the Regiment in skirmishes with partisans date from the early summer of 1942, when the unit was engaged in active anti-partisan operations closer to the front line.[106] As Christian Streit has commented, in view of German draconian punishments, it was not surprising 'if a Soviet citizen decided, in the autumn of 1941, that offering resistance was a useless act of suicide'.[107]

Nevertheless, in the winter of 1941–42 there were already some signs of the partisan struggle to come. In areas not directly occupied by German forces, the partisans began to shoot mayors, officials and the local policemen appointed by Germans, together with their families, in order to intimidate the population. As a result, it became increasingly difficult to get people to work in the local administration.[108] The military success of the Soviets in blunting the German thrust towards Moscow and developing their own counter-attacks inevitably encouraged further resistance behind the lines.

In practice the failure to achieve a swift military victory left the administration of the east as an uncomfortable compromise between distant plans for colonization and the practical necessity of exploiting the native population for the German war effort. These conflicting priorities provided fertile ground for the inveterate jurisdictional conflicts that were the hallmark of the competing Nazi institutions of occupation. In practice, the Germans only made firm allies of those loyal collaborators who joined their service. The mass of the rural population initially remained uncommitted. They were relieved to see the Soviets leave, but soon came to expect nothing better from the Germans.

The orders and reports of Gustav von Bechtolsheim, military commandant in *Weißruthenien*, provide a detailed picture of the role of the *Wehrmacht* acting alongside the civil administration. In particular his orders include considerable anti-Semitic propaganda, which at every opportunity equates the Jews with partisans and enemies of the German *Reich*.[109] This served to justify the harsh measures against the Jews both to himself and his men. Undoubtedly many of them broadly accepted the ideological principles espoused by the Nazi government. A comparison of Bechtolsheim's orders with actual events on the ground, however, demonstrates that there is very little evidence to support his assumption that the Jews formed the main support for the partisan movement. The more objective reports of men like Sönnecken and Seraphim show some sympathy for the Jews in recognition of their eagerness to work. Eye-witness accounts leave no doubt that the vast majority of Jewish victims undertook no resistance to the Germans at this time.

The description of the behaviour of the Jews given by Seraphim for Ukraine also appears to reflect the general situation in Belorussia:

there is no proof that the Jews *en masse*, or even just a large number of them, were involved in, amongst other things, acts of sabotage. Of course there were some terrorists or saboteurs amongst them – just as there were amongst the Ukrainians. However, it cannot be said that the Jews as such represent any danger whatsoever to the *Wehrmacht*. The troops and German administration have been thoroughly satisfied with the productivity of the Jews who, of course, were driven by fear and fear alone.[110]

Moreover, the vast majority of Jews were town-dwellers with no military training and little experience of the countryside. As the subsequent service of Jews as partisans later in the war demonstrated, some were best employed using their craft skills as locksmiths, shoemakers and tailors in a support role.[111] In 1941 they were performing these tasks for the Germans.

Hans-Heinrich Wilhelm has concluded that the inhuman policies towards the local population resulted in a worsening of the fighting conditions for the numerically inferior German Army. This contributed to its defeat.[112] Christian Streit comments with reference to the initial development of partisan resistance that: 'The majority of the partisans of 1941–42 ... were prisoners of war who had escaped and Red Army stragglers who had taken to the woods because they knew that they would either be shot or starve in a German prison camp if they were captured.'[113]

If during the summer the first steps were taken towards the 'solution of the Jewish question' in the east, the wave of massacres which followed in the autumn was on a much greater scale. Apart from the activities of the *Einsatzgruppen*, which were intensified, it was units of the Order Police and even the *Wehrmacht* which provided the additional German manpower required. The mass killings took place openly, usually not far from the homes of the victims, such that the policy could not remain a secret for those present at the time. Increasingly the actions were carried out with the assistance of local collaborators, many of whom proved most willing helpers in the murder of their Jewish neighbours.

In the former Polish areas the winter of 1941–42 brought a reduction in genocidal operations. The German civil administration and police structure, however, soon became more firmly established. On Himmler's orders, preparations were then made for an intended 100 per cent solution in the east by the end of 1942.

Historical controversy has been raised by the work of Hannes Heer regarding the participation of *Wehrmacht* units in anti-Jewish measures, especially during the autumn of 1941. Assisted by a wide variety of sources, Heer has demonstrated not only the role of local military commandants in enforcing ghettoization and the wearing of the Jewish star, but also the participation of German soldiers in mass shootings, particularly in Belorussia. During the actions in Nesvizh, Kletsk, Slonim and Novogrudok active assistance was provided by units of the 707th Infantry Division. Some of the smaller villages around Slonim were cleared of Jews by small *Wehrmacht* squads operating alone.[114] A close examination of the considerable evidence gathered regarding the Mir massacre on 9 November 1941 leads to the conclusion that the local *Ortskommandant* and the Belorussian police acted together, apparently without other outside help.[115]

There can be no doubt that, in the rear areas, units of the *Wehrmacht* were implicated in many punitive actions against the civilian population, including some local participation in mass shootings of Jews. Nevertheless, the proportion of *Wehrmacht* members actively involved in the Holocaust of Soviet Jews was very low by comparison with that of the Security Police, Order Police or local collaborators.[116]

Shortly after the anarchic scenes in Mir, the following order was issued by Gustav von Bechtolsheim, the military commandant in *Weißruthenien*, clarifying demarcation between the army and the police:

> As instructed in the above orders, the Jews must disappear from the countryside and the Gypsies must also be eliminated. The carrying out of *major* actions against Jews is not the responsibility of units of the Division. They are to be carried out by the civil or police authorities, where necessary ordered by the military commandant in *Weißruthenien*, if particular units are available to him for this purpose, or for security reasons or in the case of collective measures. Where small or large groups of Jews are encountered in the countryside, they can either be dealt with by the units themselves or assembled in ghettoes in some large towns which are determined for this purpose, where they are then to be handed over to the civil administration or *SD*. In the case of major actions of this kind the civil administration is to be informed beforehand.[117]

Overall responsibility for Jewish policy in the occupied Soviet Union lay firmly in the hands of the German police forces, directly under Himmler's control.

Recent research has directed attention to the considerable participation of German Order Police battalions in these extermination actions. The history of the *Einsatzgruppen* operations is well documented from the detailed reports they left behind. Less well known is the part played by the Security Police in co-ordinating ghetto 'liquidations' in 1942. These actions were not widely reported in the documentation previously available in the West. This study will draw particular attention to the contribution of the *Gendarmerie* and local police (*Schutzmannschaft*) in these actions, as the main police manpower pool in the vast rural spaces of Belorussia and Ukraine which came under civil administration control.

4 Local Police Organization, 1941–44

Due to the shortage of German personnel, the Nazi police structure in the east relied heavily on local manpower to carry out its various tasks. For patrolling the countryside, the German *Gendarmerie* established a network of small posts in each of the *rayon* towns. The ratio of Gendarmes to local police (*Schutzmannschaft*), however, was initially at least one to five and worsened from the summer of 1942. Accordingly the local police played an important role in the functioning and image of the German occupation regime.[1]

The nerve centre of the police structure was the Security Police, which gathered information about various categories of 'enemies' and organized executive measures, including arrests, interrogations and shootings. Made up mainly from the *Einsatzgruppen* personnel, offices of the Security Police were established in the major cities during the autumn and winter of 1941–42. Co-ordination of joint police operations fell to the SS and Police Leaders (*SSPF*). In addition to the Order Police units on fixed post duty (*Gendarmerie* in the countryside and *Schutzpolizei* in the cities), battalions of the Order Police and the *Schutzmannschaft* were also available to assist with specific tasks. For large-scale operations, such as the clearing of the Jewish ghettoes in the summer and autumn of 1942, nearly all available manpower was called in. The Order Police and *Schutzmannschaft* played a significant role under the direction of the Security Police.

The strength of the *Schutzmannschaft* increased dramatically during the course of 1942 from 33 000 to some 300 000 men. Of these the *Schutz-mannschaft* on individual post duty (as opposed to batallions) formed more than two-thirds.[2] Up until now very little has been known about this con-siderable force of indigenous helpers. Who collaborated with the Germans and for what reasons? How were they recruited and what were their main duties?

The *Schutzmannschaft* was designed to take over much of the leg work from the predominantly middle-aged Gendarmes who supervised them. The local militias (*Ordnungsdienst*) established under the military administration were generally taken over by the *Gendarmerie* to form the core of the *Schutzmannschaft*. Various motives influenced the initial recruits to the local police. Most important was the promise of food and pay provided by the Germans, reinforced by the hope of gaining booty from police service.[3] Some were also motivated by a desire for personal revenge, due to relatives having been deported or property confiscated under the Soviets.[4] Since almost no experienced policemen were available, most having fled before the German advance, training was a particular problem.[5] Inevitably under conditions of enemy occupation, police service tended to attract unsavoury characters, ambitious individuals and even criminals.[6] In the words of one man who worked as an undercover agent within the police in Mir: 'at the beginning of the war nobody was enlisted into the police by force...The police was formed at that time by those who wanted power and easy gains.'[7]

The organization of the offices of the Security Police and *SD* was based on that developed within the central office (*RSHA*) in Berlin, divided into the following sections: I – Personnel; II – Administration; III – *SD*; IV – *Gestapo*; V – Criminal Police (*Kripo*). A good impression of the activities of the Security Police can be gained from the operations of the Commander of the Security Police (*KdS*) in Kiev.

Following the mass execution of Jews at Babi Yar at the end of September 1941, numerous surviving Jews were reported and handed over to the Security Police by local inhabitants, the *Wehrmacht*, the civil administration and especially the local police posts in and around Kiev. Clear orders had been received that all Jews, including women and children, were to be shot. Investigative sources indicate that at least 350 Jews were briefly imprisoned by *KdS* Kiev during 1942 and killed either by shooting or the use of a gas van.[8]

The Security Police were also responsible for active counter-measures against partisans and other political opponents. Once arrested, prisoners were interrogated and then either condemned to death or released by the *Gestapo* officers in charge. From about April 1942 a third option of transfer to a labour camp became available. Regular 'executions' of condemned prisoners were conducted at a nearby killing site once sufficient condemned people had been collected in the cells. In the outpost of *KdS* Kiev at Uman, for instance, these would occur at intervals of between two and four weeks.[9] The Security Police offices were often based in the former *NKVD* buildings, which had their own prison facilities conveniently on site.[10]

The *SD* was officially the intelligence service of the *SS*. Within each Security Police office section III carried out certain specific *SD* tasks. These included the collection and analysis of information, often gathered via paid informants known as *V-Männer* (*Vertrauensmänner*). This intelligence network produced much of the information required by the *Gestapo* for its activities against suspected partisans and Jews. A large proportion of all Security Police officials simultaneously held ranks within the *SD*. For the local population the fine distinctions between the *Gestapo* and the *SD* were not apparent, as they often performed the same functions.

The Security Police numbered only a few hundred officers throughout the occupied east. These were supported by some clerical staff (often female), interpreters, a transport section with drivers and maintenance workers, and guards provided from units of the *Waffen SS*, Order Police or auxiliaries recruited in the east. Nevertheless the Security Police relied heavily on assistance from other German offices.[11] For example, in the Zhitomir *Generalkommissariat*, which had a population of 2.9 million, there were only six Security Police posts: at Zhitomir, Vinnitsa, Ovruch, Mozyr, Berdichev and Gaissin.[12] In practice executive tasks were therefore often delegated to the *Gendarmerie* posts in the outlying districts.[13] For example, on 15 July 1942 the Commander of the Security Police in Zhitomir issued instructions via the *Gebietskommissar* for the *Gendarmerie* post in Marchlevsk to 'give special treatment to' (execute) three persons who had been arrested for partisan activity. The executions were to be carried out by a suitable local *Gendarmerie* official.[14]

As the war progressed the Security Police became increasingly pre-occupied with co-ordinating measures against the partisans. In the Brest area the Security Police was reinforced in August 1942.[15] This enabled small squads of Security Police to work alongside the *Gendarmerie* in many of the *rayon* towns as well as in the main cities. Nevertheless, the complaint remained that: 'Unfortunately the strength of the Security Police is so weak that an adequately effective observation of all suspicious elements is not possible and also the war against the bandits cannot be supported sufficiently.'[16]

To carry out large-scale operations against the partisans, the Security Police could draw upon support from a variety of mobile units, such as Order Police battalions and *SS* police cavalry detachments (*Reiterabteilungen*). A number of motorized *Gendarmerie* platoons were established in the main cities to act as a mobile fire-brigade against shifting partisan threats. In addition there were also *Schutzmannschaft* battalions, mainly from Ukraine and the Baltic states, which were distributed in various garrisons.[17]

The task of co-ordinating these diverse Order Police formations fell to the *HSSPFs*, who with regard to certain matters could also issue orders to the Security Police.[18] Their role became increasingly important in partisan warfare, where the effective orchestration of all available forces was essential. Nevertheless, instances are known of German units and their allies losing casualties to 'friendly fire', not least due to inadequate intelligence and the variegated and improvised uniforms worn by the indigenous units.[19]

Of the *Schutzmannschaft* battalions, the most notorious was the 12th Lithuanian Battalion from Kaunas. Men were recruited to this unit on a voluntary basis from the first days of the German occupation. Members of the unit took part in the mass execution of Jews in Kaunas at the Ninth Fort in the summer of 1941. According to Lithuanian Battalion orders, some members left during the first months of service on a variety of grounds.[20] The involvement of the unit in mass executions in the Minsk area in October 1941 has been documented above. Subsequently the 12th Battalion was deployed as guards and in fighting partisans in a number of places around Minsk, including Shatsk and Dukora.[21]

That the 12th Lithuanian Battalion was not the only mobile *Schutzmannschaft* unit to become involved in actions against the Jews can be seen from evidence regarding the 102nd Ukrainian Battalion in Kremenets. This unit participated in the mass execution of Jews in Kremenets in late summer 1942, before its transfer to anti-partisan operations in Belorussia.[22] In fact the Ukrainian closed units generally enjoyed a worse reputation than the *Schutzmannschaft* on local post duty. In the Zhitomir region unreliable local policemen were transferred to the battalions as a punishment, as it was thought they were less likely to desert to the partisans if based in barracks away from their home area.

The active role of Order Police battalions in anti-Jewish measures is well known to historians, not least due to the study of Reserve Police Battalion 101 conducted by Christopher Browning for south-eastern Poland. He documents the recruitment and background of these men and notes that police battalions were involved in similar operations in the former Soviet Union.[23] Further examples of police battalion activities can be found for units of Police Regiment 15 in the Brest area in the autumn of 1942. This unit was involved in brutal anti-partisan repressions as well as anti-Jewish actions, including the clearance of the Pinsk ghetto at the end of October 1942.[24]

In the autumn of 1941 detachments of the *Gendarmerie* and *Schutzpolizei* arrived from Germany to take over general security duties from the *Wehrmacht* in the towns and outlying villages. The Gendarmes deployed in the east consisted of a mixture of conscripted police reservists and full-time career policemen, most of whom were too old to serve in the army; according to a rough sample of more than 80 men serving with the *Gendarmerie* in the east, only some 10 per cent were under the age of 30.[25] More complete figures are available for 37 of the 38 Gendarmes who served in the I/3 platoon in the Rechitsa district, Zhitomir *Generalkommissariat*. Thirteen (35.1 per cent) were born before 1901, 21 between 1901 and 1910 (56.8 per cent) and only 3 were born after 1910 (8.1 per cent).[26]

Many of the reservists were called up in 1939 and had seen some service with the Order Police in Germany first. For some, however, only very basic training was received before deployment to the east:

I ran my own business until I was called up to join the *Gendarmerie* on 18 August 1941 . . . because of my previous training, after a short time I was sent to the stores. The training consisted of weapons and shooting and a short introduction to the laws, for example the hunting laws. It was intended to use us as Gendarmes in our own country. In October 1941, about 15 to 20 of us left Schneidemühl and went via Brest-Litovsk to Minsk.[27]

According to marching orders for the Gendarmes deployed to *Weißruthenien* in September 1941, the complement which left for Minsk in October was to consist of 168 reservists and 146 career policemen.[28] As regards the career policemen, it was more likely that they would be people who sympathised with the regime because under Himmler's direction the police service had been carefully assimilated. One man has described his own route into police service in the east:

> On 1 April 1932, I joined the *SA* [Storm Troopers] because they promised me work. A year later I joined the Nazi Party. In 1934 I was sent to an *SA* voluntary work camp in Breslau...In 1939 I applied to join the police [*Schutzpolizei*]...I finished my training at about the end of 1940 and then served as an ordinary policeman. In autumn of 1941, myself and some of my comrades were mobilized to go to the east.[29]

As with the civil administration, it still took some time for the new police posts to establish themselves. *Wehrmacht* orders noted on 10 October 1941 that *Gendarmerie* posts had been created at Minsk, Slutsk, Baranovichi and Slonim.[30] The first Gendarmes arrived in the town of Mir in mid-November 1941, shortly after the mass killing there: 'It was only on our arrival that the station in Mir was set up. For our office, we took over the building which the local police had previously occupied...After the post had been set up, members of the *Schutzmannschaft* went on patrol with the Germans.'[31]

A local *Miliz* or *OD* had been appointed at the start of the occupation on the authority of the military administration. In some areas members were issued with passes bearing the stamp of the relevant field post number.[32] Understandably the Germans were initially cautious about entrusting local collaborators with weapons. On formation the local militias were only to be armed insofar as it was required by the local situation.[33] For instance, in the area of Rogachev in Ukraine problems were encountered with the local militia (*OD*), such that most of them had to be disarmed. In the town of Rogachev itself, in the autumn of 1941 only those men were armed who were given the task of guarding the Jews.[34]

With the transfer of the German administration from military to civilian control and the arrival of *Gendarmerie* units responsible for policing in the country districts, the provisional militias were to be dissolved and replaced by a permanent *Schutzmannschaft* (police) force. A *Gendarmerie* Captain, Max Eibner, has described this process in his district of Baranovichi: 'The Belorussian *Schutzmannschaft* were subordinate to me. I took them over from the previous *Ortskommandantur* (local commandant's HQ). When I took them over they consisted of about 250 local volunteers spread over the whole area.'[35] In practice the personnel of the *Schutzmannschaft* remained much the same as that of the militia, although the reorganization provided the opportunity to remove some unreliable, especially active nationalist elements and reassert German control. According to instructions issued for the Brest area, a careful selection was to be made of the best people who were politically above criticism.[36]

In areas where the Poles played a prominent role the reorganization was used to weaken their control over the police:[37] for instance, in December 1941 interviews were conducted with the policemen in Nesvizh to establish their national identity. One man recalls: 'I replied that I was Polish and could not state that I was of a different nationality. Once the interviews were over a list was drawn up of all those who had stated that they were Belorussian ... I was then dismissed from the police.'[38] In nearby Novaya Mysh one Polish policeman records that he was advised by his colleagues to say he was Belorussian as Poles were being thrown out.[39]

Recruitment to the militias had initially taken place by the Germans asking for volunteers; one man recalls that soon after the German invasion notices were put up on walls asking for volunteers to join the police in Minsk.[40] Some men sent in letters of application.[41] Volunteers were selected following a vetting procedure. The majority of policemen were recruited from among the rural population in the villages: 'Within one or two weeks of the Germans occupying Mir, they established a police unit made up of local Belorussian men. All of the men in the police unit were volunteers. The type of men that volunteered for the police were peasants.'[42] Oswald Rufeisen has described the situation in Mir after he joined the police at the end of November 1941:

> These policemen were not conscripts, they were all volunteers ... They were aged between 25 and 35 years ... Generally the local policemen were not held in great esteem by the local population ... Some of them were inclined to alcoholism ... There were about 25 local men in the police at this time and 12 Gendarmes to cover an area of some 20 to 25 villages. The Germans relied on the local officers as they did not know the country or the language.[43]

The voluntary nature of service during this period is also demonstrated by the ability of men to leave the police if they wished.[44] According to an order dated February 1942 for the Zhitomir district, *Schutzmänner* could only request their release in 'especially urgent cases for personal or economic reasons'.[45] Nevertheless this was sometimes granted.[46] In practice later on this often meant bribing a doctor for a certificate proving unfitness for police duty.[47]

The main exceptions to voluntary recruitment during the initial months were the translators, who were much sought after as the police could scarcely function without them. Translators were ordered to report to the police and had little option in serving:

On 1 December 1941 I was called to the police station. I was told by the police chief: 'you will be the secretary here.' It was impossible to refuse and so I agreed. I think that if I had refused then I would be shot, because the policemen shot everyone who did not obey their orders. And that was an order. I think that I was chosen as a secretary because...[it was known] that I was literate and spoke German, and also that I could translate into German and from German.[48]

Frequently ethnic Germans were employed as translators where available, as they were seen as likely to be more reliable in this key position. The status of ethnic Germans within the police was slightly different from that of other locals. Many started off serving with the *Schutzmannschaft*, but were sent on training courses in 1942 or 1943 and returned wearing the dark green uniforms of the *Gendarmerie*.[49] In the Zhitomir region in 1942 they were given the special status of *Volksdeutsche Hilfspolizei*, clearly above the *Schutzmannschaft*, but not enjoying the full civil service status of the German *Gendarmerie* officials.[50] In areas where ethnic Germans made up a large proportion of the population, for instance north of Odessa, they organized their own self-defence forces (*Selbstschutz*).

From about the summer of 1942, a greater degree of compulsion was used in order to obtain further recruits for the *Schutzmannschaft*, as one former policeman from the Baranovichi area explains: 'At the beginning of the occupation the local Belorussians went to work at the police units voluntarily, for example there were four such Belorussians from our village. Later on in 1942 the partisan movement began and we were forced to work for the police.'[51]

The main expansion of the *Schutzmannschaft* occurred from the summer of 1942 as a result of forcible recruitment for local post duty (*Einzeldienst*). Hitler's War Directive No. 46 dated 18 August 1942 expressly approved an expansion of the indigenous forces with regard to partisan warfare.[52] In the Mir *rayon* the beginning of September 1942 was a crucial date. Numerous witnesses indicate that from this time local young men were forcibly recruited. According to recommendations for promotion found in the Moscow archives, a great many new recruits were taken in on 1 September 1942, with another large group commencing service in November.[53] Almost half of all the men who served in Mir during the occupation were recuited during the autumn of 1942 (see Table 4.1). One conscript recalls the situation at that time:

Towards the end of the summer of 1942 over a period of time the Germans tried to get me to join the local police, but I avoided this. They eventually arrested me and took me to the police station and told me I had to join the police. They were losing men to join the partisans and others who were shot by the partisans, I had no choice.[54]

Table 4.1   Date of joining for the local police in the Mir *rayon*

Date of joining	Other ranks	NCOs	Total	% (where known)
1.7.41–31.12.41	22	6	28	13.4
1.1.42–30.6.42	8	1	9	4.3
1.7.42–31.12.42	94	5	99	47.3
1.1.43–30.6.43	35	–	35	16.7
1.7.43–31.12.43	18	–	18	8.6
After 1.1.44	20	–	20	9.6
No information	131	1	132	–
Total	328	13	341	100.0

Source: WCU 93/1 Appendix II/1–11.

The process of recruitment is described by another policeman, who subsequently made it to the west:

> The mayor sent letters to various men in our village ordering them to attend the police station, here they were forced to join the police and sent on to various villages...We were examined by a doctor and then sent to some barracks, where we were issued with a rifle and shown a bed.[55]

In post-war investigations a number of different means of compulsion are suggested as having been used to encourage men to serve. Some 'were locked up and held until they expressed their agreement to join'.[56] Another claimed he and his family were threatened by the police chief with a pistol in 1943.[57] Some men were even recruited from among those who had been rounded up for work in the *Reich*.[58] Certainly exemption from deportation to Germany for policemen and their families acted as a welcome incentive:

> At the end of 1942 or the beginning of 1943 the Germans began to send former prisoners of war and young people to work in Germany. I wanted to stay at home and to make this possible I decided to go to work for the Germans in the police and so avoid transportation to Germany. At this time I voluntarily joined the police.[59]

For others it was the guarantee of good food rations and pay which persuaded them to serve the Germans.[60] As one former policeman reportedly explained: 'I haven't got a lump of bread, I have joined the police service to feed my children.'[61] However, this did not always solve all family problems. In another case a man's wife left him, as she did not want him to join.[62]

Not all were reluctant; the promise of land offered by the Germans encouraged recruitment, while others joined for nationalistic reasons.[63] Some men were still bitter about close relatives who had been taken away by the Russians and wanted to fight against the Soviet partisans.[64] By the autumn of 1942 it had also become very difficult to leave the police voluntarily. One man who was conscripted in the late summer of 1942 explains:

> Like other policemen that were conscripted, I had no choice but to remain with the police, because if I returned to my home village there was every likelihood that I would be shot by the partisans and if the Germans or other policemen caught me I'd be shot for desertion.[65]

The *Schutzmannschaft* initially wore distinctive arm-bands bearing the word *Schutzmann* with a service number and place of service to identify them.[66] Subsequently they were to receive uniform clothing, when such became available. For instance, instructions were issued for any Red Army PoWs who had been released to return home to surrender great coats in their possession, so that they could be used by the *Schutzmannschaft*.[67] One member of the *Schutzmannschaft* search platoon (*Jagdzug*) in Baranovichi has provided a description: 'Our uniform was black, we had soldiers' coats they were black, the sleeves had grey cuffs, the buttons were made of white metal in two rows, the epaulettes were black, the belt was also black with a white metal buckle.'[68] Nevertheless the problems encountered in finding sufficient uniforms for the *Schutzmannschaft* continued even into the autumn of 1942.[69] In terms of weapons, ordinary policemen were armed with captured Russian rifles and NCOs often carried a pistol as well. Machine guns of some description were in particular demand for anti-partisan actions.[70] Subsequently even some heavy weapons and mortars were used, although the *Gendarmerie* and *Schutzmannschaft* did not receive such weapons until the latter stages of the war.[71]

On local post duty there were no officers in the *Schutzmannschaft*, the highest rank being that of *Feldwebel* (equivalent to sergeant-major), followed by corporal and vice-corporal. In Belorussia and Ukraine there was in any case a severe shortage of officers with military experience, as both the Polish and Soviet regimes had been reluctant to give commissions to men of these nationalities. In former Polish areas, NCOs were chosen initially from those older men aged between 25 and 35 who had served before in the inter-war Polish Army. As the *Schutzmannschaft* expanded from 1942 many of the younger volunteers were also promoted to NCO ranks.

Members of the *Schutzmannschaft* took an oath, swearing 'to be true, brave and obedient and to carry out their duties conscientiously in the struggle against murderous Bolshevism'. They were to be prepared to lay down their lives for this oath taken in God's name. The oaths were sworn in the autumn of 1942, with new recruits subsequently taking oaths after four weeks' service. Written records of the oaths were kept in the men's personnel files by the *Gendarmerie*; these were signed by the *Schutzmänner* personally.[72]

The personnel files also contained details relating to the education, religion, nationality, military experience, postings, police training, decorations, promotions and medical records of the *Schutzmänner*. Each *Schutzmann* was assigned a personal number similar to those of the infamous 'Travniki men' who staffed the death camps and labour camps in Poland.[73] As with the 'Travnikis', generally the higher the number, the later the date of recruitment, although it appears that some numbers may have been reissued for those who were killed or dismissed. A number of these personnel files have survived for the Baranovichi district, providing valuable raw data on the membership of the *Schutzmannschaft*.[74]

Initially members of the *Schutzmannschaft* in Ukraine undertook to serve up until 31 December 1942. At the end of 1942, however, the German authorities introduced *Schutzmannschaft* service for an indefinite period, in accordance with the introduction of compulsory labour service in the occupied territories. Payment for the *Schutzmannschaft* was in *Reichsmark* (*RM*), the amount depending on their rank and family status, with those from the Baltic states receiving more for political reasons. Members of the police also received free food from the police kitchen in addition to their salary. Pensions were paid to the families of those who were killed in combat with the partisans.[75]

German regulations stated that the *Schutzmannschaft* formed an integral part of the *Gendarmerie* post. The commander of the post was responsible for overseeing all the activities of the *Schutzmannschaft*. Members of the *Schutzmannschaft* had no authority to arrest a German citizen or to conduct a search or confiscation order against him. Such actions could only be conducted by officials of the German police. *Schutzmänner* could be given rewards of up to *RM* 100 for exceptional achievements on behalf of German interests and especially in relation to the war against the partisans.[76]

One of the tasks carried out by the *Schutzmannschaft* from the start was the guarding of public buildings, especially at night, against sabotage or attack.[77] In many places the local police were also entrusted with guarding the ghetto perimeter to prevent smuggling and with escorting the Jews to places of work outside the ghetto.[78] At the beginning of the occupation the *Schutzmannschaft* also dealt with everyday crime, such as theft and burglary. At this time a *rayon* police unit generally had only about 30 members and was not much stronger than had been the case under the Poles or the Soviets. Regular police work largely ground to a halt, however, once the partisan war intensified by the autumn of 1942.[79] In addition, selected policemen were sometimes assigned to assist the *Gendarmerie* with what Oswald Rufeisen has described as 'special actions':

> A 'special action' was orders to kill specific groups of people. The first group of people falling into the category for 'special actions' were ex-communist 'activists' who remained. The second group were Jews who remained in the small villages outside Mir. The third group were

ex-prisoners of war who happened to be Soviets. The fourth group were the Polish intelligentsia.[80]

It was the treatment of former Red Army soldiers which probably made the greatest impact on the local population. During the winter of 1941–42 orders were issued by the local Commandant's office in Brest for Soviet PoWs to be brought in from the outlying villages, where they had been working on the farms.[81] Evidence from the area south of Brest indicates that many former Red Army men were shot at this time as suspected partisans.[82] In Nesvizh, near Baranovichi, the local police were observed by schoolchildren escorting Soviet PoWs to the killing site near the school. Shortly afterwards shots were heard.[83] According to post-war interrogations, about 20 former Soviet soldiers living at the homes of individual farmers in the villages around Polonka, near Baranovichi, were arrested, escorted back to Polonka and shot by the local police and *Gendarmerie*.[84] The Germans sought to prevent these men from escaping to the forest to join the partisans.[85] Inevitably the result was to cause many men to do just that and take up arms against their oppressors.

As the war progressed, the nature of the tasks carried out by the *Schutzmannschaft* also diversified. One recruit at the post of Gnivan, near Vinnitsa, has given a brief résumé of some of the jobs he carried out during his police service. These included guard duty at the police building and at the nearby camp, which held persons who had escaped from deportation to work in Germany or had committed other crimes. He also went to carry out the arrest of young persons from neighbouring villages for transportation to Germany. In the summer of 1943 he was detached to nearby villages to force the peasants to bring in the harvest. Other tasks included accompanying other forced labourers (usually prisoners held at the labour camp) working on the roads, and searching for partisans in the forests.[86] To this list can be added the collection of taxes in the form of food and livestock from the local peasants and the arrest and execution of suspected partisans and their helpers.

Given the limited degree of supervision by the Gendarmes, the local police held considerable arbitrary power within these rural communities, which they often abused. In the view of one former *Schutzmann* from the Mir *rayon*: 'All members of the Belorussian police had enough power to arrest and shoot people, nobody could forbid them from doing so, nor could they be punished for it. The police commandants had even greater power.'[87] Prisoners were very often beaten by the policemen during interrogation in order to extract information.[88] There are also widespread allegations that members of the Belorussian police in Mir raped Jewish girls.[89] Instances of unauthorized shooting were numerous, with policemen exploiting their position to settle old scores, rob their neighbours, or merely to show off and demonstrate their arbitrary power. Indeed policemen were subject to many common human vices, as one man recalls: 'I got to know A. when he began his service in the police. I know that he often over-indulged in alcohol and was very fond of the company of [prostitutes]. In Nesvizh it was generally said that he was a lady's man and enjoyed a drink.'[90] Members of the local police were also renowned for their desire for personal enrichment.[91] For instance, in the spring of 1942, five *Schutzmänner* from Brailov, in Ukraine, were arrested for plundering during the Jewish action there.[92] In the Kiev district there were many complaints that the *Schutzmannschaft* conducted its work with a view to personal interests; policemen were said to be enriching themselves through corruption and blackmail: 'there are also frequently attacks on the population under alcoholic influence, which strengthens even further the popular dislike of the *Schutzmannschaft*'. The report goes on to comment that there were insufficient Gendarmes to prevent these problems arising.[93] Inevitably the local population came to distrust and fear the local police.[94]

As one Jewish survivor put it succinctly: 'the volunteers were, in my opinion, bandits and murderers'.[95] Others described them as opportunists, or as ordinary people who became corrupted by the position of power they held: 'the police volunteers were absolutely normal people and nobody could imagine that they could change like that. They became real beasts.'[96] One of the Gendarmes in Mir noted after the war that he received the impression 'that the local volunteers took pleasure in shooting Jews'.[97]

Certainly it is fair to make a distinction between the early volunteers who had thrown in their lot with the Germans from the start, and the later conscripts who were generally less enthusiastic, especially once they began to doubt the certainty of German victory. The volunteer leaders of the *Schutzmannschaft* committed themselves to the Germans from a combination of anti-communism and personal ambition. Many of these men took an active part in the murderous actions against the Jews and partisan families.[98] The majority of the conscripted policemen, however, only took their oaths in the autumn of 1942 (that is, following the main actions against the Jews).

By this time they could be in little doubt about the nature of the organization they were joining; but for most able-bodied men of military age the choice was one between paid service in the police, deportation to Germany or joining the partisans in the forests. Dangers were involved in all of these options. But for those who had no love for the communists, police service may have seemed the more attractive of the available alternatives. Most of these men obeyed German orders but, given the exploitive nature of the German regime, their loyalty was in many cases half-hearted, their main aim being survival. Many collaborators, including some volunteers, revealed the limits of their loyalty to the Germans once sent to the west, where they took the first opportunity to desert and abandon their German paymasters.

The distinction between the early volunteers (who eagerly supported the Germans and generally went on to become NCOs) and the more reluctant conscripts can also be seen in the differing treatment they received within the police, as depicted by a man who was questioned by the partisans:

> Every day 200–300 grammes of bread was given to each of those mobilized, the rest of the food was very poor, if we had not gone to Turets, it would have been very difficult with food supplies. The volunteers were fed separately. They ate very well. If a police official got drunk, he would be flogged. However, the police chiefs themselves were drunk every day.[99]

The expansion of the police was partly in response to the partisan threat, to prevent young men from joining the partisans. In some areas of Ukraine it appears that the heaviest recruitment took place in 1943: for instance, the *Gendarmerie Zug* (platoon) in Kazatin, Zhitomir region, had a strength of 170 *Schutzmänner* in January 1943 which had almost doubled to 330 men by August of the same year.[100] The overall figures for the Zhitomir district rose from 5682 *Schutzmänner* in November 1942 to some 9400 later in 1943. It was noted, however, in 1943 that these forces remained insufficient, especially as the *Schutzmannschaft* was no longer proving reliable.[101] As the partisan war intensified, some districts found it increasingly difficult to find suitable recruits.

The story in Belorussia is a similar one. According to the numbers of the identity cards issued, there were only about 300 *Schutzmänner* in the Baranovichi district in the period up to the summer of 1942. By November 1942 the strength of the rural police force in this area was 71 Gendarmes and 816 *Schutzmänner*; by June 1944 this number had more than doubled again to some 2263. Many of the later recruits were sent to mobile formations of more than a hundred men based in Baranovichi (*Jagdzug* I and II), from which desertion was more difficult.[102]

The *Gendarmerie* and *Schutzpolizei* (Order Police) were also thinly spread over the vast territory to be covered. In some areas there were only three or four Gendarmes available for each main *rayon* post.[103] Many smaller *Schutzmannschaft* outposts were left with only one German in charge, or even no German supervision. Specific instructions were given to appoint the most energetic Gendarmes as post commanders.[104] The intention was for them to lead from the front and keep a close eye on their indigenous subordinates. In practice they were often tied down with administrative paperwork, leaving considerable initiative in the hands of the local police commanders. In Brest the civil administration complained that of 44 *Schutzpolizei* officers stationed in the city, exactly half of them were concerned only with administrative matters. There were hardly any German policemen available for actual police duties.[105]

Built into the almost autonomous German police structure, which was subordinated to Himmler as Head of the German Police, were inevitable conflicts over competence and jurisdicton with the civil administration. The offices of the civil administration were formally subordinated to Rosenberg's Ministry for the occupied eastern territories; in practice the often self-willed Commissars, Erich Koch and Hinrich Lohse, were effectively in charge. As was Hitler's wont, there was no clear subordination of one rival institution to the other.

The guidelines issued in November 1941 indicated that the District Commissars could give technical instructions to the *SS* and Police District Leaders.[106] In practice, however, this was largely ignored by the German police officers on the ground.[107] Volumes of correspondence in the German files relate to such questions of mutual rivalry over competence and jurisdiction between separate offices. The effect of this dualism was to undermine the coherence of German policies as they were implemented in practice. In some places, as in Slonim, the District Commissar even employed his own local guard formation alongside the *Schutzmannschaft*.[108]

Some basic training in drill and weapons was given to the *Schutzmänner* on joining. However, due to the shortage of qualified NCOs, training courses for selected members of the *Schutzmannschaft* were held at special schools organized in each district:[109] for example, there were schools at Maloryta in the Brest district, Vileyka in *Weißruthenien* and Pogrebichi in the Zhitomir area. These courses lasted for up to eight weeks.[110] *Schutzmänner* were rated on their performance and suitable candidates were selected to act as training personnel for the others.[111]

Training for the *Schutzmannschaft* included courses of political education.[112] Amongst the matters to be covered in these courses were overtly anti-Semitic headings such as: 'The common enemy of the European Peoples – The Jew'. Detailed points under the headings included: 'Jews in leading positions in the Soviet Union. Jews are Commissars. The Jew must be destroyed'; 'Adolf Hitler speaks to his people and shows them the Jewish danger'; and 'A people will be strong and happy once the Jew has been driven out.'[113] It should be noted, however, that this anti-Semitic indoctrination was generally not received until the autumn of 1942, by which time in many areas the final ghetto liquidations had already taken place. The effectiveness of such propaganda, conducted through an interpreter with a partly illiterate audience, must also be open to some doubt.

The average age of the *Schutzmänner* was considerably less than that of the Gendarmes. According to rough figures collected for the Mir *rayon*, in 1944 about 50 per cent of the *Schutzmänner* were under 25 years of age, 43 per cent were aged between 25 and 35 and only some 6 per cent were over 35 years old (see Table 4.2). The local self-defence organization established in many of the villages of Belorussia by 1943, the *Samookhova*, was comprised mainly of men over 35 years old, who acted as guards against partisan attack, but usually did not go out on raids and patrols.[114]

Table 4.2   Age structure of the Mir *rayon* police unit, 1944

Born	Other ranks	NCOs (from Corporal)	Total	% (where known)
Pre-1910:	13	–	13	6.2
1910–14	35	4	39	18.7
1915–19	45	5	50	23.9
1920–24	94	3	97	46.4
Post-1925	10	–	10	4.8
Unknown	131	1	132	–
Total	328	13	341	100.0

Source: WCU 93/1 Appendix II/1–11.

With regard to occupation, nationality and education, the *Schutz-mannschaft* roughly corresponded to the overall population in the area (with the natural exception of the Jews). Above all it should be stressed that the conscripts recruited from the summer of 1942 were mostly quite young, aged between 17 and 21, as the older age groups had been conscripted previously into the Red Army under the Soviets. The members of the local police in the Baranovichi area were primarily ethnic Belorussians (about 75 per cent), who were of the Orthodox religion. The Roman Catholic Poles made up some 20 per cent, apart from those who had been purged in the winter of 1941–42. A few Russians and Tartars made up the rest. For historical reasons there was quite a large community of Muslim Tartars in the area around Baranovichi. Several Tartars served in the police units in Nesvizh and Slonim.[115]

In the Brest district (now in Belarus), ethnic Ukrainians were the largest group, making up around 70 per cent of the local police. The Poles here formed some 20 per cent, with the remainder made up of Russians and Belorussians. Many Polish *Schutzmänner* were also secretly members of the Polish underground organization. Later some of these men deserted to join the Polish partisans. A few were shot by the Germans when they uncovered their secret activities.[116]

According to the available sources approximately 75 per cent of the police-men in the Baranovichi district were farmers or peasants, as was only to be expected in a rural area. About 20 per cent had worked previously as crafts-men or tradesmen (for instance, as a blacksmith, chimney sweep, miller, car mechanic, butcher or carpenter). Less than 5 per cent had more than a very basic education, two having been employed as teachers and another as an organist (see Table 4.3). The NCOs were mostly recruited from amongst those with a trade or above average education, such as the sons of priests. Owing to the youth of many recruits, they often had not worked previously and only the profession of the father is given in their papers. Others men-tioned their work on the family farm. The previous occupation and education

Table 4.3 Occupations of 100 local policemen in the Baranovichi district

Agriculture	74
Trades	(20)
Blacksmith	2
Chimney sweep	1
Carpenter	4
Decorator	1
Fitter	1
Locksmith	1
Tanner	2
Car mechanic	1
Butcher	1
Miller	3
Tailor	3
Professions	(4)
Organ player	1
Road engineer	1
Teacher	2
No trade	2
Total	100

Sources: WCU 93/1 Appendix II/1–11 and 91/143 Appendix II/1.

also influenced the rank held within the *Schutzmannschaft*. Naturally the Poles had certain advantages, thanks to their superior social standing and education under the pre-1939 Polish regime.

The age group from 1914 to 1920 is shown to be slightly underrepresented, partly due to Red Army conscription and partly due to the lower birth rate during the war and revolution period. Only a few Red Army deserters and released PoWs were among those recruited to the *Schutzmannschaft* due to obvious German suspicions of such men. Even persons deserting from the partisans were more likely to be shot as spies than accepted into the local police, unless an existing member could vouch for them. Nevertheless, a few *Schutzmänner* did act as partisan agents, secretly passing on information through contacts amongst the local population. Eventually most of these men fled to the partisans. Some committed acts of sabotage as a parting gesture.[117] Others lost their lives playing this dangerous double role.

How important was anti-Semitism as a motive for the participation of the *Gendarmerie* and *Schutzmannschaft* in actions against the Jews? Answering this difficult question is necessarily constrained by the inadequate nature of the available sources and has to be done with some care. Ultimately we will never know exactly what was going on in the minds of the killers and which among several possible motives predominated. The generalized characterization of the Order Police as consisting of 'willing executioners' motivated primarily by anti-Semitism does not in my view suffice to explain the full range of behaviour patterns to be found in the evidence.[118] Christopher Browning's discerning analysis is more convincing. He expresses shock at the ability of 'ordinary men' to adapt to the killing process; yet he also identifies differing behaviour and a variety of motives operating within the group as a whole.[119]

The evidence of the Jewish spy who later took holy orders as a Catholic priest, Oswald Rufeisen, is of some interest in this respect. He notes that he got on very well with the *Gendarmerie Meister*, Reinhold Hein, in charge of the Mir police post. Indeed he was perturbed by the apparently honest character of Hein despite his responsibility for implementing orders to murder the Jews and other groups.[120] Hein's deputy, Schultz, was clearly a brutal type, but Hein's long service as a policeman in Germany before the Nazi period, when order was kept, meant that he at least attempted to ameliorate the worst effects of the orders he received, whilst still obediently carrying them out.[121] Amongst the twelve men who served at the *Gendarmerie* post in Mir, there were two or three who never took part in killings.[122] Rufeisen also noted that, apart from one occasion, he did not hear any anti-Semitic expressions during his frequent meals with the Gendarmes.[123] This clearly independent, if limited, evidence from one *Gendarmerie* post appears to bear out Browning's similar conclusions regarding Reserve Police Battalion 101.[124]

Careful differentiation should also be applied to the local policemen serving at the Mir post, on the basis of the extensive testimony of local inhabitants. A few of the early volunteers were known as anti-Semites before the German occupation and these were amongst the most active participants in the murders both of the Jews and subsequently of partisan families. In Mir and other villages, however, both Jews and Gentiles agree that relations between the two communities were generally 'normal' prior to the German invasion, if some anti-Semitism did exist. Under German occupation, surprisingly, several witnesses report that the local police behaved worse than the Germans with regard to the Jews and other local inhabitants.[125] Anti-Semitic insults and beatings by the local police became regular occurrences, once the overall policy of anti-Jewish discrimination had become clear. Nevertheless, only a few names of individuals crop up repeatedly in connection with the beatings and killings. Other policemen appear to have been less active and employed only as perimeter guards; they appear to have kept themselves out of trouble where possible. At *Gendarmerie* posts, such as that in Mir, prisoners were periodically taken out to be shot, usually by a small group of willing volunteers from among the local policemen.[126] A description of how this group operated has been given by a former police secretary, who secretly worked for the partisans:

1. Jewish work column in Mogilev, summer 1941.

2. Ceremonial handover of authority by General Walter Braemer of the Wehrmacht (*right*) to Generalkommissar Wilhelm Kube (*left*) of the newly formed civil administration in Minsk, 31 August 1941.

3. Members of the Gendarmerie post in uniform, Mir, 1942.

Rayonposten Sarig
Районний пост Заріг
Ukr. Schutzmannschaft
Укр. Шуцманства

4. Gendarmes and local police at the *Schutzmannschaftsposten* Sarig, Kiev district, December 1942.

5. Jewish women and children guarded by local police (wearing armbands) prior to the mass shooting of Jews from the 'liquidation' of the Mizoch ghetto, Sdolbunov district, 14 October 1942.

6. The shooting of women and children near Mizoch, Sdolbunov district, 14 October 1942.

7. German deportation of local inhabitants to Germany for work, 1942–43.

8. Results of an anti-partisan action in the Minsk area, 1943.

The policemen could kill or beat anyone without any reason... It was enough to say that the future victim was a partisan or a communist to justify themselves in the eyes of the *Gendarmerie*. They killed people to prove their loyalty to the German authorities. That group was very enthusiastic about the murders... There were very many people killed in Mir. Most of them were killed on suspicion of their connections with the partisans. I had not seen the shootings for myself but I know where they were carried out.[127]

There were, however, also instances of local policemen assisting Jews, or at least turning a blind eye.[128] Rufeisen has characterized one of the Belorussian police chiefs as being not especially anti-Semitic; his obedience resulted from a belief that the Germans would remain victorious and an expectation of corresponding promotion and rewards.[129] Other motives which played a part were those of greed or revenge for Soviet injustices.

Nevertheless inherent local anti-Semitism was clearly exacerbated by the anarchic conditions of the war, as had happened previously during the Russian Revolution and Civil War. Recollections of Jews from Davidgrodek stress the anti-Semitism of the 'local Christians', which was conditioned in part by the Jewish welcome for the Red Army in 1939.[130] German propaganda was successful in equating the Jews with a Bolshevik conspiracy, despite the visible evidence that the majority of Jews were ordinary citizens engaged only in handicrafts and trade. The fact that some partisan groups also hunted down and killed the Jews confirms that existing local anti-Semitism coincided with German approval and thoroughness to produce terrifying results.

The *Gendarmerie* and *Schutzmannschaft* comprised the sharp end of German police administration, which enforced the harsh German occupation regime. The local policemen were perceived as instruments of local terror on behalf of the Germans, implementing German policies of genocide and terroristic revenge.[131] Information regarding the history and composition of these organizations is vital to an understanding of the men and their motives. When orders came in the summer of 1942 to liquidate the remaining ghettoes, the *Schutzmannschaft* and *Gendarmerie* were employed in rounding up the Jews and acting as cordon guards at the shootings. Some Gendarmes and local policemen also took part in the shooting of surviving Jews found hiding in the ghettoes and forests. There is no doubt that many local policemen carried out these orders with ruthless enthusiasm, but it should be recognized that the motives and degree of participation varied according to specific circumstances. To explain the precise nature of local collaboration in the Holocaust, it is necessary to conduct a detailed examination of events during the ghetto liquidations which took place during the summer and autumn of 1942.

5 The Ghetto 'Liquidations' of 1942–43

In contrast to the mass killings reported in detail by the *Einsatzgruppen* in 1941, much less is known about the ghetto 'liquidations' in 1942. In the areas under civil administration in *Weißruthenien* and western parts of *Reichskommissariat* Ukraine, however, the majority of Jews were killed during the 'Second Wave' in 1942 and 1943.[1] Moreover these were total 'liquidations'. Only a few Jews were exempted from these so-called 'actions', usually to be killed themselves within a couple of months. A large proportion of the victims were women, children and the elderly. By the end of 1942 only a handful of 'work ghettoes' remained in these areas.

The actions of the 'Second Wave' were generally co-ordinated by officers of the Security Police sent from *KdS* offices and their outposts in the main cities. Investigative sources make reference to the Security Police (often described as '*SS*' or '*SD*-men') carrying out the shooting at the pits.[2] Nevertheless it is clear that a great deal of manpower was required to shoot several hundred people, escort the victims and act as cordon guards. Nearly all persons involved with the Nazi German administration were likely to have been aware of what was taking place and might have been asked to provide assistance. This applied to the civil administration (*Gebietskommissariat*) and units such as the *Organization Todt* (labour service), as well as the *Gendarmerie* and other police or military units in the vicinity.[3] Some Hungarian and Slovakian units, as well as Lithuanian guards deployed in the Zhitomir region on security duties, became involved in this manner.[4] Yet the most numerous force available was the local police (*Schutzmannschaft-Einzeldienst*), which duly played its part.

During the 'Second Wave' the element of surprise was no longer available to the Germans. The Jews began to make elaborate preparations to conceal themselves and to escape to the forest. In some places the ghetto clearance forces encountered armed resistance and attempts at mass escape. The local police played a key support role in these actions. They were frequently used to seal off the ghetto on the eve of the action. They were actively involved in ghetto clearance and had explicit orders to shoot anyone resisting or attempting to escape.[5] Small squads of Security Police generally organized and conducted the mass shooting at the pits. However, on occasion members of the the local police also took part in the shooting.[6] In particular, the *Schutzmannschaft* proved especially active in searching the empty ghettoes in the days following the main action and in the shooting of any Jews found in hiding or brought in from the forest.

In the winter of 1941–42 the main Jewish killings in the East were conducted by the *Einsatzgruppen* and supporting units in the military-occupied areas of Belorussia, Russia and Ukraine. In the areas under civil administration there were only a few murder actions against the Jews before the onset of spring. Several reasons can be identified for this partial respite. The cold weather reportedly made it difficult to dig pits due to frost, dynamite being used in some places to prepare the required graves.[7] Due to the critical situation at the Front in December 1941, some police battalions and *SS* units previously involved in anti-Jewish operations in the rear were sent forward to help stabilize the German position.[8] At the same time the civil administration complained in a few districts about the excesses involved in the anti-Jewish operations and the loss of valuable labour.[9] The *SS* leadership was reluctant to permit economic considerations to interfere with their racial goals; nevertheless 'selections' of skilled workers continued in practice even during the actions in 1942.

The inhabitants of the ghettoes were still in shock after the slaughter resulting from the large-scale actions in the autumn of 1941. During the winter the Germans finished clearing the countryside (*das flache Land*) of those Jews living in small scattered settlements. In the Slonim area, as has been shown, units of the *Wehrmacht* shot the Jews in some of the smaller villages.[10] At the end of 1941 the civil administration issued orders for all Jewish communities of under 1000 persons to be concentrated in the main ghettoes. The District Commissar in Slonim requested that the local military commandant, Glück, continue with his assistance in this process. Glück, however, replied that this was currently impossible due to the absence of the necessary transport.[11]

In the Mir area, a small squad of *Schutzmänner* commanded by the Gendarme, Willy Schultz, carried out the clearing of the smaller villages around the *rayon* town. The role of the local police in these actions was crucial as only they knew the identity of the Jews.[12] These operations have been described in some detail by Nechama Tec, based on Oswald Rufeisen's numerous testimonies.[13] Corroboration has been obtained recently on the basis of witness statements from local inhabitants.

The first action took place on about 16 January 1942 in the village of Krynichno, 16km to the north of Mir. A police squad of about 10 men went out to the village on sledges, picking up one or two Jewish families at the village of Berezhno on the way. One of the local inhabitants, who subsequently joined the partisans, saw them arrive:

> At about mid-day I was looking through a window in my house and saw two horse-drawn sledges arriving in Berezhno on the road leading from Mir. The first sledge had 4 people on it, there was a policeman driving the sledge and behind him sat a German in a green uniform... In the second

horse-drawn sledge there were a number of policemen in dark overcoats armed with rifles.[14]

He then fled and hid in the forest. About an hour later he heard separate shots. When he returned home he was told that the Jews had been killed. Oswald Rufeisen recalls what happened:

> When we reached Krynichno the families from Berezhno and all the Jews from Krynichno were gathered in one room of a Jewish house. Schultz registered every Jew he was responsible for or killed himself. He had a notebook. Twenty-one Jews were gathered in that room...Schultz counted those under 16 years out loud and then wrote in his notebook '*acht Stück bis sechzehn Jahre* (eight items up to the age of sixteen)'.[15]

The Jews were then taken outside behind a nearby barn. In Rufeisen's words, they were led 'like sheep to the slaughter'. He managed to absent himself to avoid witnessing the killing, but when he arrived at the site after hearing some shots, the Jews were lying on the snow. The policemen lifted the legs of the bodies and let them fall, to check whether any were still alive.[16] One survivor from Krynichno, Ester Gorodejska, had gone to Mir that day to clarify a coded warning received from the *Judenrat*. On her return she discovered that only her brother had survived. He was fortunate to have been away from home when the police turned up.[17]

A similar operation was conducted against the Jews of Dolmatovshchina and its neighbouring villages to the west of Mir about two weeks later on 2 February 1942. On this occasion the Gendarmes and local police arrived in two separate groups to cover all the scattered Jewish communities. At the village of Luki, Schultz shot seven Jews personally, after Oswald Rufeisen had refused to carry out a request that he shoot them. Then a further 41 Jews who had been collected together on the journey were shot in Dolmatovshchina, where local inhabitants were requested to dig and fill in the graves. Only a few Jews managed to escape by hiding, including one young girl who slipped away whilst saying good-bye to a friend. Another Jew was found hiding behind a snow-drift and was taken away to be shot with the others.[18] The grave-sites for the small Jewish communities of Krynichno and Dolmatovshina can still be found just inside the forest with the assistance of local inhabitants.[19]

In most areas the civil administration did not implement the clearing of the flat lands by shooting the Jews living in the villages. More frequently the civil administration ordered the Jews to be transferred to the nearest large ghetto. For example, this was the case for the villages around Kamen-Kashirsk and Brest in *Reichskommissariat* Ukraine,[20] and also for those living near Novogrudok, just to the north of Mir. In a circular to the mayors and village elders of the region, the District Commissar of Novogrudok, Traub, issued instructions in March 1942 for any Jews still found in the villages to be brought to Novogrudok by members of the *Schutzmannschaft*.[21]

The policy of ghetto formation in western Belorussia and Ukraine was not uniform throughout these areas. Some military commandants ordered the creation of some form of separate living quarters or ghetto for the Jews at the same time as they imposed other initial restrictions in the first weeks of the occupation. In many cases, however, clearly defined ghetto areas, cordoned off with fences and barbed wire, were not established in cities such as Brest until December 1941.[22] In some smaller towns the ghetto remained more or less open until well into 1942;[23] the General Commissar for Volhynia-Podolia issued orders in March 1942 for the ghettoes to be more tightly sealed.[24] The German authorities in Mir did not transfer the remaining 800 Jews to the closer confinement of the castle building until May 1942.[25]

In Nesvizh the ghetto was established immediately after the first action. According to Shalom Cholawsky it was about 150 metres wide by 250 metres long. It contained a handful of frame houses and five brick synagogues encircled by a fence.[26] For those remaining cramped within this enclosure, life settled back into its harsh routine; Cholawsky recalls only two further deaths in the initial months after the first action.[27] Few Jews starved in the rural ghettoes, as it was usually possible to trade with the local population or smuggle food in from outside.[28] Nevertheless small incidents could easily lead to the death of a Jew. Oswald Rufeisen in Mir witnessed the shooting of four Jews who had been condemned to death for specific offences such as possessing a piece of leather or a chicken.[29] In particular, being found outside the ghetto other than on work duty could be punishable by death: for instance, some Jewish women and children who had escaped from the ghetto in Baranovichi were shot by members of the local police in Polonka at this time.[30]

By March and April of 1942, mass slaughters had been recommended against the Jews in some areas under civil administration. In Baranovichi there was a further large-scale action in early March 1942. Under the direction of the Head of the Security Police outpost, Waldemar Amelung, more than 2000 Jews were selected and driven away to a railway cutting just outside the town, where they were shot.[31] According to evidence from post-war investigations, the Germans killed several thousand Jews in the city of Vinnitsa in a mass shooting on 16 April 1942.[32] In Ukraine, especially in Volhynia, many of the remaining Jews had survived the autumn wave of killings. The armaments inspectorate of the *Wehrmacht* still employed large numbers of Jews as specialist workers in Volhynia in 1942.[33]

From the beginning of 1942 there was a concerted effort by the Nazi German authorities to 'liquidate' the remaining Jewish population in the *Generalkommissariat* Zhitomir. The aim was probably to 'cleanse' the district of Jews by the summer of 1942, when Hitler was due to move into his newly constructed secret field headquarters at Vinnitsa, the '*Wehrwolf*' camp.[34] Documents of the Reich Security Service (*RSD*), which served as Hitler's personal bodyguards, reveal the shooting of Jews in the vicinity of the planned *Führer* bunker near Vinnitsa in January 1942 in co-operation with the local Security Police commander.[35]

The smaller rural communities of the Zhitomir region also experienced a murderous 'wave' of killings against their Jewish population in the first half of 1942. Detailed evidence of these actions can be found in post-war investigation records. In the town of Gnivan, near Vinnitsa, about 100 Jews were killed early in the summer of 1942, including women and children. The Jews were driven out of their houses at dawn and collected together by German and Lithuanian guards from the PoW camp, together with men from the *Gendarmerie* and the Ukrainian *Schutzmannschaft*. Once all the Jews had been assembled, they were marched into the woods in a large column under escort. A pit had been prepared at a construction site only a few hundred metres from the village. Here the Jews were shot by members of the *SD* from Vinnitsa. One Jewish survivor who hid during the round-up was able to show Australian investigators the scene of the crime in 1991.[36]

The Security Police conducted similar actions throughout the towns and villages of the Zhitomir *Generalkommissariat*, including, for example, Ruzhin, Illinzi, Lipovets, Brailov and Khmelnik.[37] The monthly situation report of the Zhitomir *Generalkommissar*, dated 3 June 1942, includes the following entry: 'The Jewish question has for the most part been settled in my region. That valuable labour was often eliminated is well-known. 434 Jews were resettled in the district of Illinzi, 606 Jews in Ruzhin.'[38] After the war the Soviet authorities recorded the following confession from the former police chief in Samgorodok:

> In June 1942 I participated together with the Germans in the shooting of the Jews. In total about 500 people were shot including children, women and the elderly. My participation in the destruction of the Jewish inhabitants of Samgorodok consisted in the fact that I and the policemen under my command collected the Jews from their houses and drove them into the school building. I selected the specialist workers, who were to be employed on various tasks by the Germans, and under my direction the Samgorodok police kept the Jews under strict guard during the shooting.[39]

Such confessions have to be treated with considerable caution as historical evidence. None the less, in the context of the other available sources, there can be little doubt that the local police were active during these ghetto 'liquidations'. According to contemporary German documents, Ukrainian *Schutzmann* W. P. in Samgorodok was recommended for a decoration in 1943, as he had 'especially distinguished himself during the resettlement of the Jews in June 1942 and in the subsequent apprehension of individual Jews who variously concealed themselves'.[40]

Further orders and correspondence from units of the Zhitomir *Gendarmerie* at this time corroborate the overall pattern. The Vinnitsa *Gendarmerie* Captain issued an order in June 1942 that Jews were no longer to be employed by the *Gendarmerie*. On 14 June the *Gendarmerie* District Leader in Ruzhin replied that there were no Jews left working at the posts in his district. He confirmed that his post leaders had received express instructions to comply with this directive.[41] Strict orders were also issued against photographs being taken during 'executions'.[42] Most of the remaining specialist workers did not survive the summer sweep for long. At the beginning of August 1942 members of the Security Police outpost in Berdichev shot more than 300 Jewish workers with Ukrainian 'militia' acting as guards to cordon off the killing site.[43] In Ruzhin 44 Jews were shot by members of the *SD* on 1 October 1942.[44]

A letter written by one of the *Gendarmerie* post commanders in the Kamenets-Podolsk region west of Vinnitsa, also from June 1942, reveals the nature of the tasks carried out:

> Every week 3–4 actions, sometimes Gypsies, on other occasions Jews, partisans and other rabble. It is very nice that we have here now an *SD* unit [*SD Außenkommando*] with which I work excellently. Only 8 days ago a Ukrainian policeman was murdered in the most bestial manner. The reason: he drove Jews to work in a minefield. The Jews united with the partisans and murdered the policeman.[45]

In southern Ukraine the remaining Jews were also 'liquidated' by the summer of 1942. In Kamenka, Cherkassy district, the local police participated in the shooting of more than one hundred Jews in March.[46] On 29 May 1942 in Stalindorf, Kherson district, the remaining elderly Jews and Jewesses were rounded up and shot, after their menfolk had been sent to work on the Dneprpetrovsk–Zaporozhe highway in April.[47] In the *rayon* town of Ustinovka the *Gebietskommissar* issued orders in June 1942 for about 30 Jews from the surrounding villages to be arrested and brought in to the local police station by the *Gendarmerie* and local *Schutzmannschaft*. Another 30 or so Jews were brought in from the nearby town of Bobrinets.

In the village of Izraylovka, not far from Ustinovka, there lived about 60 Jews. A small squad of police from Ustinovka was sent there and briefed by the Head of the *Gendarmerie* post at 2 o'clock in the morning to 'immediately take all necessary steps to round up each and every Jew and deliver them to the school building in Izraylovka in a short space of time, not more than 3 or 4 hours'.[48] A grave had been prepared in advance a few kilometres outside Izraylovka on the road to Ustinovka near Kovalevka.

In the morning the Jews of all ages collected in Ustinovka and Izraylovka were escorted to the grave site. Here they were made to undress and shot by members of the Security Police, *Gendarmerie* and *Schutzmannschaft*, with other colleagues acting as perimeter guards. The German *Gebietskommissar* and the agricultural administrator were also present at the killing site.[49]

Having taken away the 'racially pure' Jews in the morning, some policemen were sent back to Izraylovka in the afternoon to collect about 20 half-Jewish children from mixed marriages. In June 1991 a team of forensic experts employed by the Australian Special Investigations Unit carried out an exhumation of the mass Jewish grave near Ustinovka. The skeletal remains of 19 children aged under 11 years were uncovered lying at the top of the grave. Under these bodies a layer of soil was found and then further adult human remains. It was estimated that about 100 more bodies were buried in the grave.[50]

In Belorussia the summer of 1942 also saw the 'liquidation' of most remaining ghettoes. The report by a squad of the *Waffen SS* attached to the Security Police outpost in Vileyka records several operations in northern *Weißruthenien*. Jewish actions were conducted at Kryvichi on 28 April 1942 and at Dolginov on 29 and 30 April, in which only some of the Jews were killed. 'The action in Dolginov was remarkable in that the Jews had prepared proper bunkers as hiding places. For two days we had to search and clear out [the ghetto] partly with the aid of hand-grenades.' On 10 May a further action was conducted in Volozhin followed by a final action against the Jews in Dolginov on 21 May. The *Waffen SS* section reported that 'the Jewish question in this town was finally solved'.[51]

The wave of killings continued in the Glubokoye district. On 29 May the ghetto in Dokshitsy, holding 2653 Jews, was 'liquidated'. The Jews were so well concealed within the ghetto that it took a whole week to find the last ones. The District Commissar went on to report: 'On 1 June 1942 the ghettoes of Luzhki, holding 528 Jews, and Plissa, holding 419 Jews, were liquidated, and one day later the ghetto of Miory, holding 779 Jews. Here the Jews made an attempt at a large-scale break-out. 70 to 80 persons may have escaped.'[52]

An impression of the desperate Jewish resistance at the grave-site in Miory can be gained from one author's account of these events:

There were shouts and gunfire all around. Young Jews broke out of the lines near the mass grave, scattering. Some threw themselves at the Germans and beat them with their bare fists. Michael saw Germans lying on the ground, unconscious. He rushed another German standing off to one side. Then he felt something hit him in the back. He fell, rose, ran and fell again. Bullets were whizzing past him. He lost the German, but he kept on running, farther and farther into the woods, as though he was driven by some mysterious force: rather live among the wild animals of the woods than among the 'civilized' men who had turned into beasts.[53]

The brutal wave of killings continued two days later on 3 June, when 2000 Jews were 'liquidated' in Braslav. Further actions followed a few days later in Disna (2181 Jews) and Druya (1318 Jews). These were conducted by the Security Police supported by forces of the *Gendarmerie* Vileyka. The latter two ghettoes caught fire soon after the action commenced and were burned to the ground. Other actions were conducted in Glubokoye and Sharkovsh-china; in Glubokoye the skilled manual workers and specialists working for the *Wehrmacht* were preserved.[54]

The division of labour amongst the forces involved in these actions has been described in the Glubokoye Memorial Book. The Security Police would arrive to carry out the slaughter in a few hours and then leave:

> The local police would then complete the unfinished work. The local White-Russians and Poles, in their black 'police-crow' uniforms, would diligently search for the hidden Jews over a period of days and weeks and then murder them. They searched for the unfortunate hidden Jews in the houses, in the attics, ditches, the surrounding woods, and other such places. Those who distinguished themselves in catching Jews, the Germans rewarded handsomely with gifts.[55]

A surprising setback was encountered in the German campaign against the ghettoes on 9 June 1942. A Security Police command from Baranovichi was ambushed by partisans and virtually wiped out on its way back from a Jewish action in the town of Naliboki. Among the losses were ten Germans and eleven Lithuanians attached to the Security Police.[56] Up until this time the partisans had generally avoided contact with other than small patrols. Henceforth greater caution was shown in conducting such actions.

Closer to Baranovichi, an action was carried out in the town of Novaya Mysh during the summer of 1942. A former policeman relates:

> Germans came from Baranovichi and brought an 'execution squad' of Lithuanians. The police took the Jews to the assembly point. The action was led by [the Head of the police], he declared himself a Belorussian. The representative of the *SD* was Lieutenant Amelung. Novaya Mysh was surrounded by a cordon so that the Jews could not escape. In the town there was a market place with a fire station, and the assembly point was in the fire station. Policemen were drawn from the surrounding sta-tions...The Jews were taken from the fire station beyond a copse and shot there. Several hundred people were executed – perhaps 600.[57]

According to eye-witness evidence, several Jews were shot during the round-up and on the following day by members of the local police.[58] The killing site was guarded by a dense cordon of men from the German 'special unit'. On this occasion the Germans also surrounded the killing site with machine guns nests, in order to prevent any intervention by the partisans.[59]

The co-operation between the various German offices involved in the ghetto clearances can be seen from the example of Slonim. Following the recent losses from Baranovichi, a squad of *Waffen SS* and Security Police from *KdS* Minsk travelled to Slonim to take part in a large-scale action there at the end of June 1942.[60] They were assisted by local policemen, members of the *Wehrmacht*, Lithuanians and men from the District Commissar's office.[61] Here it appears that the German forces deliberately set fire to the houses in order to drive out those still in hiding. One Jewish survivor concealed himself with his brother in a store-room close to the house in which the rest of his family was hiding. From here he observed a group of Germans and Lithuanians approaching:

> The Germans were giving orders and shouting with their weapons pointed '*Juden raus*' [Jews come out], but nobody came out. Then an order was given to throw phosphorous grenades into the house and it caught on fire. We saw all of this through the gaps in the wooden planks of our hiding place. Since there was no room for the whole family to hide under the kitchen, some of my family members hid in the attic. I saw that my cousin jumped down and he was shot by a Lithuanian whilst he was still in the air. The District Commissar, Erren, clapped his hands and shouted '*Bravo Litauer*' [Bravo Lithuanian]. At some stage when the house was on fire my grandmother came out of the house wearing all of her clothes and some fur coats, she was on fire. Some of the Germans shouted 'here comes the burning witch'. Erren took out his pistol and shot her three times until she fell to the ground. A Lithuanian asked Erren for permission to set the wood store on fire but Erren did not allow it and said in German 'leave it alone, there is no one there'. They continued from house to house.[62]

A similar version of events is given by one of the firemen, who was called out to deal with the burning ghetto:

> I was off duty when I heard the siren going indicating that there was a fire. I went to the fire station and went with the fire engine to a bridge that crossed the river to where the Jewish ghetto was. I saw that the houses which were wooden in the ghetto were on fire. I saw German soldiers in the ghetto area, I think White Russian Police and maybe Ukrainians. The ghetto was situated next to the river and I put the pump in the river to draw water to put out the fires. I started to pump water on to some of the houses and I then heard people shouting and coming out of the cellars. I aimed the hose on the area that the people were in but a German told me not to do this and shot the people in the cellars. I remained at the ghetto for a couple of hours putting fires out.[63]

On the day of the main action it appears that members of the District Commissar's office, including Erren himself, played a leading role, whilst, according to their own testimony, many Gendarmes were absent on an anti-partisan operation outside Slonim. Nevertheless over the following days members of the *Gendarmerie* and about 50 *Schutzmänner* were responsible for combing the ghetto once more for any survivors. Any who tried to escape were shot on the spot, while the rest were escorted to the prison. From here they were taken in batches to be shot by the *Gendarmerie* shortly afterwards.[64]

Approximately 8000 Jews were killed in Slonim at this time.[65] Apart from the action in Slonim, other ghetto 'liquidations' were also carried out in the surrounding towns (for example, in Byten on 25 July).[66] In September District Commissar Erren boasted that of the 25 000 Jews originally living in his district, only some 500 remained. These had been preserved due to important considerations regarding the war economy.[67]

The Jews of Nesvizh had drawn their own conclusions from the first action there on 30 October 1941. A group within the Jewish community began to speak openly of resistance, not wanting to go meekly to their deaths.[68] Others prepared hiding places before the expected action.[69] The 'liquidation' of the ghetto in the nearby town of Gorodeya was carried out on 16 July 1942. Two local bystander witnesses observed how the Jews were taken towards the pits, some in lorries and the rest on foot under the guard of known local policemen. As they were escorted to their deaths, those who fell and were not able to continue were shot on the spot. In the distance the sound of machine gun fire could be heard for four or five hours. In total about 1500 people were shot.[70]

News of events in Gorodeya rapidly dispelled any delusions among the Nesvizh Jews that they might be spared.[71] The chairman of the Jewish Council considered contacting the partisans, but was opposed to people escaping from the ghetto as this might only precipitate the action.[72] During a memorial service in the Nesvizh synagogue, Shalom Cholawsky urged his co-religionists to fight for their lives: 'A plan of attack was agreed. It was decided to set fires and resist with weapons in order to gain the opportunity, for those Jews who could, to flee to the forest.'[73]

In the meantime the German police began their own preparations. In May the Commander of the Security Police for *Weißruthenien* had issued urgent orders for the *Gendarmerie* to conduct a census of the remaining Jewish population.[74] Under the organization of the Security Police a combined force of German police and Lithuanian auxiliaries arrived in Nesvizh from Baranovichi on trucks the day before the action. In addition the local Belorussian policemen from all the police stations in the district were mobilized and brought to Nesvizh.[75] It was customary for all available forces to be mobilized for such large-scale anti-Jewish operations; usually only one or two policemen were left behind to man the police station.[76] In the evening all the policemen were assembled and the police chief explained to them that the

Jews were to be shot on the following day. Instructions were given for a cordon to be thrown around the ghetto to prevent any Jews from escaping. Clear orders were issued to the policemen that they were to shoot any Jews attempting to escape.[77]

At dusk on 20 July 1942 the Nesvizh ghetto was surrounded by the Belorussian police. During the night there was some sporadic shooting before the action began.[78] The events of the following day are difficult to reconstruct from the available descriptions. According to Shalom Cholawsky's account, a few Germans and police appeared at the ghetto gate early in the morning and informed the Head of the Jewish Council, Magalif, that there would be a 'selection'.[79] It appears that some Jews were transported away in an orderly fashion, but soon it became clear that on this occasion the Jews would not co-operate. When the police then opened fire, the Jewish fighting unit in the synagogue replied with a surprise volley from a machine gun operated by a former Polish officer and a battle ensued. In the meantime fires were lit within the ghetto to assist Jews trying to escape in the smoke and confusion.[80]

One of the former policemen has given his view of these confused events:

> The noise of vehicle engines being run could be heard from the opposite side of the ghetto where the gate was. It was clear to me that the policemen had begun to load the ghetto residents on to the trucks to transport them to the place of execution. Between an hour and a half and two hours after the loading of the Jews on to the trucks had commenced, fire broke out in various parts of the ghetto area. Soon the flames had engulfed all the buildings. Sub-machine gun and rifle fire began in the ghetto in quick succession. Due to the smoke from the fires it was difficult to recognize what was happening in the ghetto. At that moment I could only guess that the policemen were finishing off the condemned people on the spot. Soon the shooting in the ghetto stopped. Some of the policemen who had been part of the cordon were hurriedly moved straight to the place of execution.[81]

According to the various accounts, several Germans and local policemen were killed and others wounded during the brief battle.[82] One Belorussian policeman serving on the outer cordon has described to the Soviet authorities how about 20 Jews tried to break out on his sector. He and the other police nearby opened fire on them. He was wounded in the shoulder and another policeman was killed by the Jews. At this time he was drunk, as the Belorussian police had been drinking vodka before the shooting began.[83] Shalom Cholawsky has described these desperate attempts to flee from the standpoint of the victims:

> Small groups of Jews like ours burst forth from the ghetto. Once outside, some were beaten by zealous peasants. Others were killed in flight. Small

groups succeeded in reaching the forest. I saw Simcha R. carrying his small son wrapped in a pillow. As Simcha ran, he passed the bundle to a Christian woman standing near the gate and then continued running towards the woods.[84]

Meanwhile the fires within the ghetto had unfortunately trapped and killed some of the Jews still in hiding. One of the policemen entered the ghetto shortly after the shooting had died down:

I was faced with a terrible scene. There was only fire in the place where the wooden buildings had been standing. Walking through the former streets and side streets of the ghetto, I saw the skeletons of burnt people and charred corpses. In the cellar of a house that had been burned down I saw the corpses of two Jewish men which had been discovered by one of the policemen. They had been between 40 and 45 years old and they had probably been suffocated by the smoke from the fire. I didn't notice any visible injuries that would have been inflicted by firearms.[85]

Some of the local inhabitants living outside the ghetto were also witnesses to the murderous events of the day. One woman saw Belorussian policemen chasing and shooting at Jews after the synagogue had been set on fire. She and her family spontaneously hid one of the fleeing Jews.[86] Another Polish witness has described how:

during the clearance of the ghetto a Jewish woman with a young child in her arms appeared on Ogrodova street. She was stopped by a Belorussian policeman. He took her child, who was perhaps one year old, from her, struck it against a wall and hurled it towards a burning house. He shot the Jewish woman dead with a handgun. I also heard rumours that even after the clearance of the ghetto, any Jews who were captured – men, women and children – were shot on the spot for several days afterwards. That was done by the Belorussian police.[87]

In the meantime those Jews who had been escorted out of the ghetto by the police were now being taken to be shot. According to one of the policemen the Jews were loaded on to trucks and taken to a pit outside the town. Here they were shot by the Lithuanian and German policemen who had arrived from Baranovichi, although five local *Schutzmänner* were also reported to have been involved in the loading and shooting of the Jews.[88] A policeman who claimed only to have acted as a perimeter guard describes his view of the killing site:

I was standing about a hundred metres away from the pit where the shooting of the Soviet citizens of Jewish nationality was carried out . . . The policemen led the condemned people, including women, children and old men, to the edge of the pit in groups consisting of six to eight individuals each. The butchers . . . were shooting their victims in the back of the head, and the latter were falling into the pit.

The witness confirmed that local Belorussian policemen were also amongst those actually carrying out the shooting.[89] These few men were probably volunteers. A former Nesvizh policeman maintained in post-war testimony that: 'For shooting Jews only those who had voluntarily expressed their wish were taken from among the police, they were not simply assigned, so that if anyone did not have such a desire, he did not take part in the executions.'[90]

During the rest of the day the police continued to comb the remains of the ghetto looking for further survivors. They concentrated on basements and attics in those buildings still standing. A local policeman recalls his experiences during this process:

Coming up to a clothes closet standing in one of the rooms, [one of the policemen] pricked up his ears and began listening to something. I then saw him draw a revolver from his holster and fire one or two shots at the closet door. He shot from approximately the level of, or slightly lower than his breast. While shooting at the closet, he ordered the remaining members of the punitive force to open fire on the same closet . . . After the shooting was over, the door of the closet opened slowly and the dead body of a young Jewish woman fell out: she showed no signs of life.[91]

For those still in hiding this was a particularly nerve-wracking time. One survivor recalls:

At around 12 noon we heard my flat being searched. During the search a Belorussian shouted to his comrades that he had found some *Schnaps*. They certainly took with them anything which they found to be of value. At around 8 o'clock some Germans came into the flat. They tapped on the floor, looking for a hollow space . . . They did not find our hiding place.

This group waited until 3 o'clock the following morning before creeping out through a hollow under the ghetto fence which had been used previously by Christians to smuggle food into the ghetto. The witness became separated from some of his colleagues during the escape. Despite hearing shots and some Germans or policemen on patrol, Mr Lachowicki succeeded in making his way through the high corn fields out to the forest where he met up with other survivors the next day.[92]

The Jews from Mir were more fortunate in being able to organize their escape without a battle. In particular they enjoyed the vital assistance of a Jewish spy within the local police, Oswald Rufeisen. He overheard part of a telephone conversation between his boss, *Meister* Reinhold Hein and the *Gendarmerie* Captain Max Eibner in Baranovichi, which revealed the date of the planned ghetto 'liquidation' in Mir.[93] Acting on this information, he not only succeeded in smuggling a number of weapons into the ghetto, but also managed to send nearly all of the Gendarmes and local police on a wild-goose chase after non-existent partisans just before the 'liquidation' was due to take place.[94]

Nevertheless, many within the ghetto were reluctant to follow his advice to flee, as one survivor recalled:

> Rufeisen advised us to risk escaping. We were not inclined to do so. The unnerving experiences with many gentile fellow-citizens, who willingly – in order to get a share of the loot – joined in the massacre of our fellow-creatures, had shaken our trust in our once good neighbours.[95]

The situation was hotly debated within the ghetto. As in Nesvizh, some feared that escape would only hasten the end for those who could not leave. One woman recalls the tense arguments within families:

> Elderly parents implored their – reluctant – children to escape, for perhaps by a miracle their children would succeed in escaping death... Fathers could not decide to leave their wives and children – for dying seemed more bearable together with their families. On 10 August 1942 we broke out – trotted through a ripe cornfield into the nearest wood – the miracle became reality.[96]

In total about 250 of the younger Jews decided to try their luck in the forests. Meanwhile Oswald Rufeisen also managed to escape, probably thanks to his good relations with the Gendarmes. Shortly before the 'liquidation' he was betrayed by one of the Jews and confessed to *Gendarmerie Meister* Hein:

> I am neither an enemy of the Germans nor a Pole, I will tell you the truth because so far I have always worked with you openly and honestly, but nevertheless I consider the planned anti-Jewish operation to be very wrong for I myself am a Jew. And this was the only motive for my action.[97]

Despite this confession, the guard on him remained lax and he was able to slip away without great difficulty. One Gendarme recalls his version of events:

> The local volunteers wanted Rufeisen to be handed over and shot. When Rufeisen escaped, I had just come off duty. I was probably the first to see it. However, because we had such a good relationship with Rufeisen, I only reported what I had seen when Rufeisen was far enough away.[98]

The shooting of the remaining Jews followed shortly afterwards on 13 August as planned. A grave was prepared in advance in the nearby Yablonovshchina wood on instructions from the chief of the local police.[99] On the evening before the 'liquidation' a reinforced guard of local police with machine guns was set up around the castle. The next morning a number of police auxiliaries from Baranovichi appeared in Mir.[100] The remaining 560 Jews, consisting mainly of the elderly and women with children, were loaded on to lorries and taken to the killing site.[101] Members of the *Gendarmerie* guarded the route and were ordered to ensure that no Jews escaped. According to one account the Jews were made to lie on top of each other in the pit before being shot.[102]

Gendarmerie Captain Max Eibner duly reported on 26 August the completion of his task:

> From the District Commissar in Baranovichi I have instructions in general terms, as far as my manpower permits, to rid the region, especially the countryside, of Jews. The major actions carried out in recent months have resulted in Jews fleeing on a very large scale and going over to the bandit groups. In order to prevent further escapes I have eliminated the Jews still present in Polonka and Mir. A total of 719 Jews have been shot. Meanwhile 320 Jews who had fled during the major actions have already been recaptured and summarily shot by the *Gendarmerie* posts.[103]

The process of searching for those in hiding continued for some time after the actions. According to Hein some 65 of the Mir Jews had been captured by 20 August 1942.[104] Investigative records reveal that four Jews were found in the cellar of Mir Castle about three weeks after the ghetto 'liquidation'. They were dragged out by local policemen from Mir who shot them nearby.[105]

The *Gendarmerie* in nearby Stolpce ordered the concentration of all local Belorussian policemen in the *rayon* alongside a Latvian police battalion for an operation there on 23 September 1942. Some 750 Jews were shot, while another 850 managed to conceal themselves, mostly within the ghetto. The *Gendarmerie* post commander, Willy Schultz, has described how over the following days up to 2 October another 488 Jews, mostly women and children, were brought in and shot under his personal supervision. Another 350 Jews were killed on 11 October, including many more who attempted to hide amongst the work Jews in the reconstituted ghetto. He concluded that after this there were no children or persons unfit for work remaining.[106]

In Minsk a series of large-scale actions were carried out by the Security Police, assisted by the *Waffen SS* and Latvian auxiliaries, over the summer. According to one contemporary German report 6000 local Jews were killed on 28 July, followed by 3000 German Jews the following day.[107] At this time Himmler wrote openly about the difficult task given to him by Hitler: 'The occupied eastern lands are becoming free of Jews. The *Führer* has laid upon my shoulders the implementation of this very difficult order. In any case, nobody can relieve me of the responsibility.'[108] For the General Government territory to the west a deadline of 31 December 1942 had been set by Himmler to complete the 'resettlement' of the entire Jewish population.[109]

In the autumn of 1942 a concerted police operation was undertaken to clear the ghettoes of Volhynia-Podolia, which according to German sources still contained over 300 000 Jews at this time.[110] Transcripts of German Security Police documents, fortunately preserved in Polish archives, provide a rare insight into the German book-keeping for these 'Second Wave' actions.[111]

On 6 August 1942 the Security Police outpost in Kamenets Podolsk reported to the *KdS* Volhynia-Podolia, Dr Heinrich Pütz, that he had recently carried out two actions in the Dunayevtse *rayon* in co-operation with the *Gendarmerie*, shooting some 1204 Jews from three villages. In mid-August other Security Police posts reported, for example, the 'special treatment' of 6402 Jews in Kremenets, 3399 Jews in Kamen-Kashirsk, 1792 Jews in Shumsk and the killing of 420 Jews in Mikasevichi, Pinsk district. This last report was compiled by *Sturmscharführer* Wilhelm Rasp, who was in charge of the Pinsk post. In his post-war testimony, Rasp gives a detailed account of the wave of ghetto 'liquidations' in his district in the autumn of 1942.[112]

Over a three-month period from August to the beginning of November actions were organized in the towns of Ivanovo, Lakhva, Stolin, Davidgro-dek, Vysotsk, Luninets and Pinsk as well as their surrounding villages, sweeping away more than 20 000 Jewish lives. A combined force of Security Police, *Gendarmerie* and local police was employed for most actions, with members of the Security Police generally conducting the shooting at the pits. According to Rasp the orders for the 'liquidation' of the ghettoes came from Berlin and were passed on to him from his superiors, *KdS* Pütz and *Befehl-shaber der Sicherheitspolizei* (*BdS*) Thomas. He also notes the active role played by members of the Pinsk *Gebietskommissariat* in the measures against the Jews in his district.[113]

Internal correspondence within the civil administration in Volhynia-Podolia indicates that, against the wishes of the *Generalkommissar*, some large *rayon* town ghettoes were 'liquidated' before those in the surrounding villages. The result was that the village Jews were warned and some attempted to break out by setting fire to the ghetto.[114] The ghetto 'liquidations' were discussed at the meeting of District Commissars in Lutsk from 29 to 31 August 1942.[115] Here it was explained that the planned 100 per cent clearance was at the express wish of *Reichskommissar* Koch personally. A 'stay of execution' for two months was permitted only for small groups of vital workers, not to exceed 500 men. These small remnants were then also to disappear within this period. The General Commissar requested that in future the Security Police outposts discuss preparations for the actions not only with the *Gendarmerie*, but also with the District Commissars.[116]

Since the District Commissars retained overall responsibility for the Jews, they keenly defended their right to be consulted on these matters.[117] The practical role of the civil administration in the ghetto 'liquidations' consisted mainly in organizing for pits to be dug in advance, providing transport if required and disposing of Jewish property after the actions.[118] It was not uncommon for members of the *Gebietskommissariat* to be present personally during the shootings.[119]

A consistent pattern has been identified by Shmuel Spector with regard to the Volhynian 'liquidations'. In most cases the pits were dug only a short distance from the ghetto. The Jews were marched there on foot, with the aged and sick being taken on carts. Only rarely was motorized transport employed. Persons who attempted to hide within the ghetto during the round-ups were shot on the spot by members of the local police.[120]

The remote village of Serniki in the Pripyet marshes demonstrates the improved chances of escape for Jews living in rural communities. Approximately 1000 Jews lived in Serniki in 1942. They had been gathered together into a ghetto by April 1942. This ghetto was 'liquidated' by a German Security Police unit with the help of the local police in September 1942. The Jews were killed 3km outside Serniki in a pre-prepared grave. During the course of the action there was a break-out by the Jews. According to Spector's sources some 279 people succeeded in reaching the forests, mostly men aged between 13 and 40.[121] Of these escapees, some 102 died later in the woods: 10–12 in battle as partisans, the rest from the effects of hunger, cold, illness and pursuit. Nevertheless the proximity to, and familiarity with, the forests facilitated initial escape compared with the larger towns, where survival rates were generally much lower.

Particularly significant in the Jewish killings from the summer of 1942 onwards was the fact that many of the victims were women and children.[122] The German builder Hermann Graebe, who was a spectator at a mass shooting near Dubno, Ukraine, in October 1942, has described the scene at the killing site in some detail:

When I visited the site office on 5 October 1942 my foreman, Hubert Moennikes of Hamburg-Harburg, *Außenmühlenweg* 21, told me that Jews from Dubno had been shot near the site in three large ditches which were about thirty metres long and three metres deep. Approximately 1500 people a day had been killed. All of the approximately 5000 Jews who had been living in Dubno up to the action were going to be killed. Since the shootings had taken place in his presence he was still very upset.

Whereupon I accompanied Moennikes to the building site and near it saw large mounds of earth about thirty metres long and two metres high. A few lorries were parked in front of the mounds from which people were being driven by armed Ukrainian militia under the supervision of an *SS* man. The militia provided the guards on the lorries and drove them to and from the ditch. All these people wore the prescribed yellow patches on the front and back of their clothing so that they were identifiable as Jews.

Moennikes and I went straight to the ditches. We were not prevented from doing so. I could now hear a series of rifle shots from behind the mounds. The people who had got off the lorries – men, women, and children of all ages – had to undress on the orders of an *SS* man who was carrying a riding or dog whip in his hand. They had to place their clothing on separate piles for shoes, clothing and underwear. I saw a neat pile of shoes containing approximately 800–1000 pairs, and great heaps of underwear and clothing.

Without weeping or crying out these people undressed and stood together in family groups, embracing each other and saying good-bye while waiting for a sign from another *SS* man who stood on the edge of the ditch and also had a whip. During the quarter of an hour in which I stood near the ditch, I did not hear a single complaint or plea for mercy. I watched a family of about eight, a man and a woman, both about fifty-years old with their children of about, one, eight and ten, as well as two grown-up daughters of about twenty and twenty-four. An old woman with snow-white hair held a one year old child in her arms singing to it and tickling it. The child squeaked with delight. The married couple looked on with tears in their eyes. The father held the ten-year-old boy by the hand speaking softly to him. The boy was struggling to hold back his tears. The father pointed a finger to the sky and stroked his head and seemed to be explaining something to him. At this moment, the *SS* man near the ditch called out something to his comrade. The latter counted off some about twenty people and ordered them behind the mound. The family of which I have just spoken was among them. I can still remember how a girl, slender and dark, pointed at herself as she went past me saying 'twenty three'.[123]

The 'experience report' of Captain Saur, who commanded a Company from Police Regiment 15 of the Order Police, presents a stark account of the lessons learned during the large-scale action in Pinsk from 29 October to 1 November 1942. This can be compared with the post-war account of *Sturmscharführer* Wilhelm Rasp, who claims to have encountered Saur during the action. Several companies from Order Police battalions had arrived in Pinsk, as all available police forces from the area were concentrated there, including Security Police, *Gendarmerie*, *Schutzpolizei*, Ukrainian *Schutz-mannschaft*, German mounted police and police dog handlers. On the first day most Jews reported themselves voluntarily and about 10 000 persons were murdered at the grave-site 4km outside the town. Effective cordoning by police cavalrymen thwarted an attempted break-out by 150 Jews who were all recaptured.

The ghetto was combed carefully again over the following three days, so that altogether about 15 000 Jews were taken away to be shot. Sick Jews and individual children left behind in the houses were shot on the spot. In this way a further 1200 Jews were killed within the ghetto. Wilhelm Rasp says he carried six dead children to the grave. Captain Saur stressed the need for careful searches using axes and other tools to discover those concealed in cellars and attics. Young Jews were to be used to reveal those in hiding in exchange for (false) promises of their lives. According to Rasp, who collected the Jewish valuables during the action, his attempts to preserve a few hundred specialist workers were thwarted by his more enthusiastic colleagues from the *Gebietskommissariat*, who claimed 'all the Jews had to go'.[124]

At the same time the last remaining ghettoes were also being 'liquidated' in the countryside. The co-operation between German Order Police battalions and the local *Schutzmannschaft* is demonstrated by an action conducted in the village of Samary, near Dyvin, on 1 November 1942. Here 72 German Order policemen from Police Regiment 15 were supported by 39 *Schutzmänner*. They started surrounding the village at 2.45am and searched the houses once it was light. Twenty-seven Jews were shot trying to escape during the round-up. After a second search of the village the action was completed with 74 Jews captured and shot in total. One Ukrainian family, consisting of a man, two women and three children, was also shot for concealing a Jew.[125]

Despite these severe punishments, a few Christians still took great risks to assist their neighbours. During the 'liquidation' of the Brest ghetto in mid-October 1942,[126] a Jew and his family avoided the initial round-up by hiding in the cellar of their house. Just over a week later he and his family were discovered and taken to a central collection point. Here he managed to leave the group and escape to a Christian friend's house, who took him in. He stayed here for the remainder of the war. He was the only member of his family to survive.[127]

A report by the Polish Underground from this period confirms the active role of the local police, which also included many Poles in Brest:

Brest. The liquidation of the Jews has been continuing since 15 October. During the first 3 days about 12 000 people were shot. The place of execution is Bronna Góra. At present the rest of those in hiding are being liquidated. The liquidation was being organized by a mobile squad of *SD* and local police. At present the 'finishing off' is being done only by the local police, in which Poles represent a large percentage. They are often more zealous than the Germans. Some Jewish possessions go to furnish German homes and offices, some are sold at auction. Despite the fact that during the liquidation large quantities of weapons were found the Jews behaved passively.[128]

This report indicates also the widespread looting, which was a particular feature of these 'liquidation' actions. A local policeman from the Brest district reportedly gave this account to post-war Soviet investigators:

All of the Jews' property was looted by the Germans who took the best things like wardrobes, soft sofas, crockery, clothes and shoes for themselves, and sold the poorer quality things in shops for the general public. I also took part in the looting of the Jews' property. Namely, a week after the execution of the Jewish population, I went to the ghetto and unearthed a suitcase in a woodshed. In the suitcase were: two blouses, a jumper, three metres of material, and a pair of women's slippers. From behind a stove in one house I took a sailor's suit, yellow sailor's shoes and pyjamas. Other Jewish property taken by me included a wardrobe... a mattress, a wall mirror and a painting, which I got from the same Jews [previously] for some bread and three kg of groats and potatoes.[129]

Jewish property clearly served as an incentive for the perpetrators of these crimes.[130] Officially the *Gebietskommissar* was not permitted to retain any of the property collected from the Jews, which was to be handed over to the financial administration. A letter from the Kazatin *Gebietskommissar* in the Zhitomir region complained that the Ukrainian police had privately acquired considerable amounts of Jewish property. He maintained that an exception to the regulations could only be made for those locals who acted on German instructions and actively supported the German administration.[131] Some policemen moved into the former houses of Jews following the mass shootings, as happened for instance in Novaya Mysh, near Baranovichi.[132] The Germans also offered material rewards to those bringing in Jews from the forests.[133]

The campaign against the Jews was not completed with the ghetto 'liquidations'. The Germans recognized that many Jews had escaped and pursued an active policy of searching for hidden Jews within the empty ghettoes and in the surrounding forests. The Brest *Gendarmerie* report for November listed amongst its future tasks 'dealing with the fugitive Jews still at large in the district'.[134]

The Jews hiding in the forest continued to be hunted down by local police and other available forces loyal to the Germans, including local foresters in German pay. For example, shortly after the massacre in Serniki, a local forester was observed by a neighbour escorting a group of Jews at gunpoint:

There were 13 persons. I recognized the wife of a former resident of Serniki and his seven daughters, who were ten to twenty years old. All of them lived in Serniki. The forester herded his victims up two high hills. I heard sub-machine gun fire shortly after. I was terrified. He returned alone.[135]

An order issued by the town administration in Slonim in December 1942 warned that anyone found to be hiding Jews would be shot. Any Jews who were found were to be handed over to the *Gendarmerie* or *Schutzmannschaft*.[136]

These examples, taken with other evidence, indicate that standing orders were issued by the Security Police that any surviving Jews who were found in the countryside after the main actions were to be shot. This process of hunting for Jews using patrols in the forests has been described by Christopher Browning regarding southern Poland.[137] Numerous *Gendarmerie* reports from Belorussia and Ukraine record the capture and shooting of stray Jews uncovered after evading the ghetto 'liquidations'.

In the Zhitomir region a series of brief reports indicates the everyday nature of such incidents: in September 1942 two 'stray' Jewesses were 'shot escaping' near Ruzhin; on 2 October two Jews were shot 'while escaping' in the village of Ohievka; on 1 March 1943 a patrol from the *Gendarmerie* post in Samgorodok found two Jewesses hiding in a hay-rick who were then 'shot trying to escape'.[138] Clearly the attitude of a local policeman from Selets also applied here, that there was no point in handing the Jews over to the Security Police if they were only going to shoot them anyway.[139] As these Jews were not active partisans there was no need for interrogation; they were shot on the spot where they were found.

A *Gendarmerie* report from the Mir district in Belorussia is quoted here in full to illustrate clearly the nature of this policy:[140]

Gendarmerie Post 'Mir'   Mir, 15.11.1942
Gendarmerie District Baranovichi
General District *Weißruthenien*

To the *Gendarmerie* District Leader
in Baranovichi

Re: The arrest and summary execution of five Jews, and the destruction of a Jewish camp near the forest warden's lodge in Miranka, Mir District.

Ref: None

On 14 November 1942 at about 6pm, the forest keeper at the forester's lodge in Miranka, Mir District, informed me that he had discovered a bunker in which there was a gang of Jews in a wood about 6 km north of Mir. I immediately dispatched three *Gendarmerie* officers and 60 *Schutzmänner* to this place and they took the forest keeper with them. They established that what the forest keeper had said was true. They discovered a bunker which had been covered over with a wooden lid and well camouflaged. After the cover had been removed, the occupants of the bunker were told to come out without their weapons, otherwise a hand grenade would be thrown in. They complied with this request and three Jews, namely the Head of the Jewish Council from Mir and two Jewesses came out. After a short interrogation they were summarily shot and buried as ordered. Apart from a few tattered items of clothing they had no articles of value on them. The bunker was then searched. Around 100 kg of potatoes, some loaves and a few old cooking pots were found. No weapons or ammunition were found. The bunker was then destroyed by the police officers. The food and the tattered items of clothing were handed over to the *Schutzmannschaft* in Mir.

(Signature)
Hauptwachmeister of the
Schutzpolizei

Hunting down and shooting the last remaining Jews in their hiding places in the forest formed a routine element in the work of the *Schutzmannschaft* at this time. Although careful not to incriminate himself, a former policeman from Mir has recalled his participation in a similar search, which on this occasion proved fruitless:

> I remember soon after joining the police [in autumn 1942]...about twenty of us searched a forest near Mir looking for Jews who had escaped from the ghetto, there were no Germans, the local police NCOs were in charge of this operation on horseback...we followed them on foot, searched the forest but did not find anyone. I must say it was only after we returned from the search that we were actually told we were looking for Jews. This action lasted for half a day.[141]

Similar examples are also commonplace for the Brest district. In the village of Medno four Jews were shot by a member of the local police in full view of many local inhabitants.[142] In nearby Rogozno a Jewish woman who had escaped from the Brest ghetto was recaptured and shot by the 11th Company of Police Regiment 15 on 8 November 1942, just over three weeks after the action.[143] In a report for the month of January 1943 the *Gendarmerie* for the Brest district reported that a further 55 Jews had been given 'special treatment' (shot).[144]

What was the attitude of the local population to these public massacres? In the Brest region the initial reaction was one of fear. Rumours circulated that after the actions against the Jews, first the Russians, then the Poles and then the Ukrainians would be shot.[145] Confidence soon returned, however, as one month later it was reported that:

> The sympathy of the local population for the Jews during the actions in October 1942 was very great. During November, however, it was observed that the population now no longer feels afraid of being shot. The local population is now working with particular zeal to find the Jews still hidden in the woods. These people subsequently welcomed with particular gratitude the fact that they were able to acquire second-hand household goods cheaply from the ghetto in Brest-Litovsk.[146]

Some of the locals clearly had no sympathy for the Jews. Examples of voluntary denunciation are common, such as a woman from Lan, near Nesvizh, who ran straight to the nearest police station when two Jews appeared at her farmstead begging for bread.[147] In Kobryn local peasants are reported to have tied captured Jews to their carts and driven them into town.[148] Despite a degree of short-term enrichment, the loss of so many valuable craftsmen was, however, a further blow to the devastated local economy. Now there was almost nothing left for the peasants to buy in return for their produce. In economic terms, as Oswald Rufeisen has commented, 'the Jews needed the farmers and the farmers needed the Jews'.[149]

There was some truth in the widespread fear as to which group would be next to suffer. Even as the ghetto 'liquidations' commenced in the summer of 1942, measures were also being taken against the Polish intelligentsia and the Gypsies. As partisan resistance mounted, the Christian peasants themselves increasingly became victims of the brutal policies of the *Wehrmacht*, Himmler's police forces and their local collaborators.

In the Baranovichi area a number of prominent local Poles were rounded up simultaneously at the end of June 1942. The operation was prepared secretly by the Germans, as they feared local collaborators might tip off the intended victims. The schoolteacher in Mir was arrested on 27 June and sent to the Koldychevo detention camp near Baranovichi, where he subsequently died along with many other Poles.[150] In the Nesvizh *rayon* more than 80 persons were arrested on 28 June and 73 were subsequently shot by the *Gendarmerie* and *Schutzmannschaft* at the Hayka wood on the Malevo estate on 5 August. Amongst those killed were eleven women and several local priests. Only one man survived the shooting to recount what happened after the war.[151] In Slonim over 100 Poles were arrested on the night of 29 June 1942. Amongst those arrested were teachers, lawyers, priests and their families. Eleven men were transferred to Baranovichi and shot there in July. Of the remainder about 90 were taken to be shot at Petralevichi near Slonim on 19 December 1942.[152]

Gypsies and the mentally handicapped were two other groups which were treated in more or less the same manner as the Jews: for instance, in the town of Chernigov in Ukraine the Germans killed almost 500 mental patients between October 1941 and June 1942, initially by shooting and later using a mobile gas van.[153] In the Nesvizh *rayon* a group of Gypsies were shot by the Belorussian police on the Gorny Snov estate in February 1943. A local woman witnessed this incident:

> The Snov police came in several vehicles…bringing the Gypsies. The police started shooting them. They shot the old people immediately, on the spot, and the surviving children…in the well. I saw this clearly because at the time I was not far from the execution site…I don't know how many Gypsies were shot.[154]

Similar actions against Gypsies were conducted by members of the *Schutz-mannschaft* in the Khoiniki district, *Generalkommissariat* Zhitomir.[155] In these actions the local police acted as loyal helpers in killing women and children.

What were the main differences between the manner of implementation of the Holocaust in the occupied Soviet Union and the measures applied else-where in Europe? Shmuel Spector has highlighted the public nature of the mass shootings in the east, conducted in the open for all to see. This contrasted with the more secretive organization of the gas chambers in the Polish death camps.[156]

Certainly those Germans who served in the police or civil administration in the occupied east for any length of time 'must have known that the Jews were to be executed'.[157] Considerable participation by the local collabora-tionist police forces (including *Schutzmannschaft* units made up of local residents) and the distribution of some Jewish property established a degree of local complicity in their genocidal plans.

The significance of the Ukrainian and Belorussian police in the implemen-tation of the Holocaust can be seen from the fact that in these predominantly rural areas at the time of the massacres in the summer and autumn of 1942 they outnumbered the Gendarmes by between five and ten to one.[158] Other units were also brought in to conduct the ghetto 'liquidations', especially German Order Police battalions for the larger actions; and overall direction lay firmly in the hands of Himmler's Security Police, who usually provided the firing squads. Neverthless, the rounding up and escorting of large num-bers of Jews would have been difficult without the active support of the local police units. Individual local policemen appear to have distinguished them-selves particularly in the subsequent search for and shooting of Jews who went into hiding. As with the German Order Police, there was no shortage of volunteers for such 'Jew hunts' and firing squads.[159] The willingness to carry out such actions can be seen in the numerous descriptions from a wide variety of sources depicting local policemen acting on their own initiative in accordance with the general policy.

For the Jewish victims it was difficult to understand why their former neighbours should turn against them with such violent hatred:

> The Ukrainian police were animals. They were killers. They turned against fellow Ukrainians simply because they were Jews. There was anti-Semitism before Hitler, the pogroms and even in the First World War. We even had to bow to Polish policemen, they didn't beat us up or anything like that. The Ukrainians were murderers.[160]

In western Ukraine ardent nationalism was turned directly against the Jewish and Polish communities during the German occupation, as a form of what is now called 'ethnic cleansing' took place.[161] Anti-Semitic expressions were widespread in the local press and in the teachings of some Orthodox priests, who on occasions even took part in excesses against the Jews.[162] Ukrainian national aspirations, however, were frustrated by German rule and from the autumn of 1942 onwards Ukrainian policemen deserted in increasing numbers to form their own nationalist partisan units in the forests, where they continued to fight against all 'enemies' of a Ukrainian state:

> The Ukrainian police searched the woods for people who had run away. The Ukrainians wanted a country of their own. At first they fought with the Germans, then they turned against the Germans and fought against them and against the Russians and partisans. But in the beginning when they were working for the Germans they came into the forest searching for us every day.[163]

By contrast, local nationalism was much weaker in Belorussia, but the participation of the local police in actions against the Jews was not markedly dissimilar. Whilst anti-Semitism clearly formed a very important motive and was linked to some extent in people's minds with revenge for communist excesses, indoctrination and propaganda do not appear sufficient to explain the killing of former neighbours.

The other motives which spring to mind are those of personal enrichment and advancement, obedience to authority and group behaviour (peer pressure). Alcohol was readily available to the local police even during the actions, and in practice looting was widespread. Those who carried out German orders eagerly and efficiently could expect promotion and rewards. Direct disobedience of orders was rare, but was subject to punishment, mainly in the form of beating or arrest. No instances are known in which a local policemen was actually shot for refusing to shoot Jews.[164]

From analysing the behaviour of local policemen, it appears that the exertion of the power of life and death over others had a most corrupting effect. It is clear that the worst members of the police 'liked killing people'.[165] Thus not only the Jews, but also other Ukrainian inhabitants, were constantly at risk from self-willed acts of police violence:

> A notorious policeman appeared. He was drunk and had a pistol. He shouted: 'I will kill you, I will kill you.' He aimed at my head, but I was frightened and cowered. As a result he missed his target and shot me through the right forearm: the bullet passed right through. I am sure he wanted to kill me but missed because he was drunk and I still have a scar on my arm.[166]

The unprecedented genocidal campaign against the Jews was accompanied by similar measures against other target groups. For those who served most actively as Nazi henchmen it does not appear that their attitude towards former communists, Gypsies or the families of suspected partisans differed greatly from that towards their Jewish victims.

The perspective of the Jews had changed since 1941 as many people were now prepared for the worst. More strenuous and elaborate preparations were made for concealment or escape and, in some cases, for open resistance. Nevertheless many still went stoically to their deaths, sometimes putting family loyalty before the chances of individuals to flee. As one anguished survivor has described: 'The question was thrust on each of us and it defeated us all. The ties which held our families together could not be broken, desertion of our weaker kin was beyond our capacity, beyond our morality, beyond our strength.'[167] It is in this context of impossible moral choices that the arguments about passivity and resistance must be examined. The paralysing effects of constantly facing death cannot be imagined. Unfortunately, for the majority of Jews, there was no chance of escape. After months of deprivation and terror, it was religious faith and family loyalty which gave them strength to face their tormentors with dignity in death.

Shmuel Spector and Shalom Cholawsky have paid tribute to the heroic efforts of Jews who resisted, including those who defied the Germans by hiding. In some ghettoes, such as Nesvizh, the Jews put up an organized fight, in the hope that at least some might escape. In other places individuals used whatever weapons came to hand to gain some revenge; in Polonka, for instance, one *Schutzmann* was wounded during the action by a Jew armed with a knife.[168] Nevertheless most Jews had no military training and were ill-equipped to defend themselves. As one Jew in Hoshcha commented: 'The weakness of the Jews expressed itself perhaps in presenting gifts at the last moment. In any event, we don't have arms and even if we did, the Jews would have been afraid to use them.'[169] German reports such as those from the Brest district confirm that in many places the Jews were afraid, and anxious not to provoke an action by their own behaviour. There were only a few Jews serving with the partisans in the forest prior to the ghetto 'liquidations'. In October 1942 it was noted: 'As a result of the anti-Jew campaigns, which they always hear about very quickly, a great sense of restlessness has taken hold of these [the remaining] Jews. But they are only frightened, there should be no fear of any kind of resistance.'[170] German casualties remained negligible in these cowardly murders of defenceless and innocent civilians. A few losses were caused by their own men during escape attempts. In Antopol a German police cavalryman was killed accidentally: when a Jewish lady tried to escape, a policeman fired at her and a stray bullet went through a door to kill a squadron member.[171] Some men even committed suicide after participating in these gruesome killings.[172]

It is impossible to provide a precise figure for the number of Jews killed during 1942 in the occupied east. A reasonable estimate, however, would be in the order of half a million victims for the combined area of the *Reichskommissariate* Ostland and Ukraine alone. In a report from Himmler to Hitler in December 1942, the total of 363 211 Jews killed is given for southern Russia, Bialystok and Ukraine for the previous three months.[173] In areas under military administration there were also further killings in 1942 by the *Einsatzgruppen*, assisted by the *GFP* and collaborationist units, such as the *OD*. Mass killings were conducted in places such as Smolensk, Lokhvitsa and Kislovodsk.[174] In these areas, however, the 'First Wave' conducted by the *Einsatzgruppen* in the winter of 1941–42 had been more thorough and a greater proportion of Jews were able to flee before the German advance.

At the beginning of 1943, the tide of war finally began to turn following the German defeat at Stalingrad. By this time there were only a few thousand Jews under German control in the remaining 'work ghettoes' of occupied Belorussia and Ukraine. These ghettoes, such as those in Slutsk and Glubokoye, as well as the remnants of the Minsk Jews, were 'liquidated' in turn during the course of 1943.[175] For the thousands more who had succeeded in fleeing to the forests, the harsh battle for survival had only just begun.

6 Local Administration and Exploitation, 1941–44

For most of the local population the German occupation was experienced primarily in terms of economic exploitation. Hopes of land redistribution were frustrated and instead the peasants faced burdensome requisitions. Compulsory labour registration and mass deportations for work in Germany signified the direct control of labour resources. Economic conditions deteriorated further from the poor situation under Soviet rule; the urban population became impoverished as real wages fell and the peasantry reverted to producing only for their own needs. Not only was the German state squeezing the last drops from an economy already dislocated by war damage, Soviet evacuation and scorched earth, but within the economic administration itself German officials and their collaborators enriched themselves through corruption and the abuse of their power.

German economic exploitation began at the very start of the occupation. Shortly after the arrival of the Germans in the village of Velika Lipa near Nesvizh, the former village elder (*starosta*) and his deputy from the Polish period were reinstated in their posts. In July 1941 they organized the first requisition of cattle and foodstuffs, which were sent to Baranovichi for the German Army. These requisitions were implemented locally as a means of settling old political scores: the main burden was laid on the 'collective farmers', who had actively co-operated with the Soviets. The German authorities enforced further requisitions up to the summer of 1944, such that many farms had not a single cow or sheep remaining.[1]

The example of Velika Lipa demonstrates well the main tasks carried out by the village elders. They participated actively in the selection of young people for deportation to work in Germany. In the spring of 1942 two former *Komsomol* members were selected, to be followed a year later by five other young persons, mainly from the families of 'collective farmers'. The village elder and his deputy were both present at the medical commission in Gorodeya which made the final selection. Generous bribes enabled some of the more wealthy peasants to gain exemptions for their children.[2]

Another major task was the allocation of forced labour, which in Velika Lipa included unpaid work on a nearby German estate and the collection of wood from the forest. The village elder and his deputy selected individuals for this work and set the requisite quotas, again opening the door to corruption. Those who did not fulfil the work as requested were denounced to the German administration and either fined or beaten by the local police.[3]

Above the village elders the most senior local official was usually the *Rayonchef* based in the main market towns. His responsibilities included control of work permits through the Labour Office, the collection of taxes, registration of the population and the running of schools and other utilities. The *Rayonchef* was answerable to the District Commissar (*Gebietskommissar*) and his German representatives in the various departments, such as the Labour Office or the agricultural leaders. Local courts continued to function under the German administration, but increasingly punishments were applied directly by the police on the spot. It appears that the majority of the crimes dealt with were of an economic nature linked to the black market, such as illegal distilling or slaughtering.[4]

Frequently the personnel of the local administration would be fused with nationalist political organizations. In Belorussia, for example, the 'Belorussian Self-Help Organization' (BSO) under the control of Ivan Ermachenko was established, ostensibly as a charitable organization. It was intended to assist groups such as the elderly or orphans affected by the war: for instance, it ran soup kitchens in some towns and distributed pensions or clothes to the needy. However, it was manned by Belorussian nationalists who usually also held positions within the German administration. Its main strength was concentrated in a few towns and cities, where it also organized sports clubs and choirs for its supporters. Among the sources of income exploited by the *BSO* was 'ownerless property' from the resettlement of the Jews. In its collection and redistribution of goods the *BSO* was not immune from corrupt practices: Ermachenko himself was subsequently called to account by the German authorities for embezzlement and fraud.[5]

In Ukraine there was a similar overlap between the Ukrainian nationalist organizations and the leading personnel in the local administration and police. Despite purges carried out against Polish and Ukrainian officials, especially the Bandera faction of the OUN which was seen as unreliable during the first months of the occupation, Ukrainian nationalists frequently used such local positions to follow their own agenda.[6] It was in order to forestall any developments towards a Ukrainian national state that no Ukrainians were given positions of responsibility above *rayon* level.

The main departments within the German Ministry for the occupied eastern territories were for political, administrative and economic affairs respectively.[7] The offices of each *Reichskommissar, Hauptkommissar* and *Gebietskommissar* were structured in a similar manner, but with correspondingly fewer personnel on the lower levels. A District Commissar would have only a handful of German officials to deal with all matters such as administration, health, finance, law, culture, propaganda, industry, labour, prices, transport, agriculture and forestry. Considerable reliance had to be placed on local officials and translators in order for the administration to function at all; in *Reichskommissariat* Ukraine, for example, in January 1943 25 000

Reich Germans were responsible for almost 17 million inhabitants scattered in some 443 separate *rayons*.[8]

Only a limited selection of German personnel remained available to staff the offices of the civil administration. These were generally men of poor quality, as many *Reich* offices saw recruitment to the east as a welcome opportunity to rid themselves of personal enemies, obnoxious meddlers and incompetent chair-warmers.[9] According to the research of Bernhard Chiari, among the reasons given by German civilian officials for going east, expectations of material gain and improved career prospects were more prominent than ideological convictions. One man explained his decision as an opportunity to escape from a broken marriage and make a fresh start. Many of the 'golden pheasants' serving in the civil administration (so nicknamed for the elaborate plumage of their yellow-brown uniforms) gained a dubious reputation among their other German colleagues as 'good for nothings' who marched around with a revolver and a whip, enjoying the exercise of power.[10]

An interesting insight into the mentality of many German officials in occupied Ukraine is provided by the rescue efforts of Fritz Graebe. A civil engineer working for a private company contracted to the *Reich* railroad administration, he was often able to get his own way against the civil and police authorities by sheer bluster. In an oft-repeated theatrical scene, taken straight from the play, *Der Hauptmann von Köpernick*, he would skilfully turn the tables on lowly officials who dared to question the source of his instructions:

'I can only tell you, Berlin, no more. It is secret.' If pressed for additional information, he would shake his finger, cock his head to the side, and tell the inquisitor, 'Better for you that you do not know. Now that's all I will tell you. You do understand? My secret is that we want to win the war, isn't that right? So you don't want to interfere with me. It could be very serious for you.'

In this manner he managed to protect and help many Jews and Polish refugees in Ukraine. He provided them with work at the company's offices in Sdolbunov, Dubno, Ostrog, Poltava and other locations. Not all of his Jewish workers managed to survive the numerous mass shootings in the region, but his bold interventions were successful on many occasions. Petty officials generally chose to avoid an open confrontation with someone who appeared to have greater authority.[11]

Agricultural policy in the countryside was implemented by the local agricultural leaders (*Landwirtschaftsführer*) who arrived from Germany with the army and were soon transferred to the civil administration. The examination of available records for 201 German agricultural leaders has shown that three-quarters were aged between 37 and 43, and only 35 were Nazi Party members. The majority of the men came from small villages and possessed little relevant experience for managing large estates, which was to be their chief responsibility in the east.[12] The activity of the agricultural leaders consisted primarily of collecting farm produce from the local population and sending it on to the regional agricultural administration.[13] On visits to other farms they often received police protection in order to assist with enforcing requisitions. Alexander Dallin concluded that many *Landwirtschaftsführer* were unable to adjust to their alien environment and remained isolated from the local population.[14]

The main aims of the German administration were economic exploitation and the maintenance of a peaceful rear area behind the German Army.[15] However, there was clearly considerable conflict between these goals and the manner in which the indigenous population was treated. Instructions issued in the summer of 1941 to the agricultural leaders pronounced that the Russians had put up with hunger and poverty for centuries and should not be shown false sympathy.[16] The obvious failure to meet expectations for a reversal of Soviet collectivization added to the growing list of economic grievances which turned the inhabitants against the Germans.

Within the German leadership there were different views about the privatization of land in the east. The decision to maintain the collective farms in 1941 was supported by the Ministry for the Four Year Plan and the *SS*, which both saw it as a means for effectively exploiting the area in preparation for their own large-scale resettlement plans. Experts on the Soviet Union, such as Otto Bräutigam, however, favoured giving the local population more incentive to produce the urgently required agricultural surpluses. Attempts at land reform were made in 1942, especially in the areas under military control. In practice the collective system was largely retained: by the end of 1942 less than 8 per cent of collective farms in Ukraine had been converted into co-operatives. The limited reforms proposed by the civil administration soon became bogged down by intractable technical difficulties. In 1943 the German authorities proposed that grants of land be issued to local peasants, as a specific reward for active assistance in fighting the partisans. By then, such was the partisan threat that it all proved to be too little, too late.[17]

In the field of cultural policy a similar story of belated recognition of cardinal failures has to be recorded. In Ukraine the restriction of education to only four years of school provoked criticism from the local population.[18] In 1943 *Reichskommissar* Koch issued a press release noting that 'if in Germany universities are being closed, the Ukraine has no right to maintain its own higher educational institutions'.[19] A similar situation existed in Belorussia, where by 1942 less than a third of the schools which had existed under the Soviet regime were still in operation.[20] *Einsatzgruppe B* in the area of military administration reported in December 1942 that the fulfilment of local demands for the resumption of schooling had a positive effect in some areas,[21] but many school buildings had been requisitioned as police stations or by other German institutions. In general the school system continued to decay, due to shortages of equipment and personnel. At the same time children stayed away from the available schools in droves, in order to help out with work on the farms.[22]

The failure of practical reform efforts reflected the indolence and loss of direction of many officials in the east, once the expected rapid victory did not materialize. The German historian, Bernard Chiari, has observed that even in 1943 'many bureaucrats were unsure exactly what they were supposed to do with an ethnically divided and impenetrable swampland such as Belorussia'. One official requested fresh instructions regarding the political, national and cultural plans for Minsk and all of *Weißruthenien*, as otherwise he would be unable to organize cultural policy there. The German administration gradually lost the initiative and only reacted to crises as they occurred. This frequently resulted in the adoption of hasty and unrealistic administrative measures.[23] As mounting partisan activity increased the sense of isolation which haunted those serving in the east, growing numbers of 'ordinary Germans' fell into moods of uncertainty and depression.[24]

A symptom of this deterioration in morale was the mounting incidence of corruption, alcoholism and even fraternization with the local population. In the *rayon* town of Kossovo, south of Slonim, a series of irregularities by members of the local *Gendarmerie* post caused Himmler to call for a detailed investigation. The post, which consisted of ten Gendarmes and about 40 local policeman, was abandoned by its commander without authorization on 8 August 1942. The forces retreated to the nearby town of Ivatsevichi, in order to avoid an expected attack by strong partisan forces. The post commander, *Meister* Gustav Lange, committed suicide shortly afterwards.

According to the results of the *SS* investigation, Lange and other *Gendarmerie* officials had relationships with local women, who in turn were in contact with the partisans. It was alleged that when the partisans took control of the town from 8 August to 29 September, Lange's former mistress was seen to be living in the partisans' headquarters for the duration of their stay. Other members of the *Gendarmerie* were punished with sentences from ten days to two years for offences such as stealing Jewish valuables, taking a Russian mistress or concealing Jews from the *SD*.[25] This surprising story reveals some of the realities which rarely found their way into the official German reports.

A careful reading of available sources, however, reveals further evidence of everyday irregularities. Official orders warned sternly against trading on the black market and entering into contact with local women.[26] Such warnings are often a good indication of what was really going on. Postings to the rear areas in the east were notoriously dreary and increasingly dangerous. Home leave was a rare luxury of not more than a few weeks per year, and it was forbidden for spouses to come out to the east.[27] Despite strict Nazi racial laws, local sources reveal several further instances of German officials taking local women as mistresses, in some cases even Jewish women.[28] More widespread was the incidence of alcoholism: one Gendarme was reprimanded for casting a shadow on 'German honour' and endangering life when he went on a drunken rampage at an isolated outpost that was under constant threat of partisan attack.[29] The traditional image of German discipline and obedience does not always stand up to close examination. The temptations of the black market were a consequence of the catastrophic economic conditions in the east, which affected the cities worst of all.[30]

The aim of German economic policy was not to establish rival industries in the east, but to extract raw materials and supplies which were to be made into finished products in Germany.[31] Above all there were high expectations that the bread basket of Ukraine would ease the effects of the Allied blockade, which had contributed to increased death rates in Berlin during the First World War.[32] Priority was given to feeding the army in the east directly from the land, as well as meeting the army's needs for clothing, transport and other equipment. Civilian production, especially of consumer goods, which was already limited under the Soviets, virtually collapsed under German occupation.

A detailed analysis of the practical effects of German economic policies can be made on the basis of the regular reports available for the Brest district from the end of 1941. The short-sightedness of German exploitation soon worked to their disadvantage as the war developed into a more prolonged struggle. In February 1942 the new district agronomist in Brest complained that bread rations had been reduced by half for the 'Aryan' population and the Jews had received nothing for three months. The reason was that his predecessor had extracted everything possible from the peasants.[33]

The shortages were especially acute in the towns, where by the summer of 1942 the population was receiving very little apart from the meagre bread ration. City-dwellers made forays into the countryside to buy food at any price. The food shortage was such that people were leaving their jobs in the city to work on the land, simply in order to get enough to eat. This brought some of the urban population into contact with the partisans, who then exploited their dissatisfaction with the harsh economic conditions. The German report for August 1942 concluded that food supplies for the natives had to be improved if the partisan situation was to be mastered.[34]

A similar report prepared in late 1942 by *Einsatzgruppe B* for the area under military administration further east illustrates the main problems encountered in the cities. In spite of the introduction of rationing, the town-dwellers continued to suffer from food shortages: fat and meat were scarce and the set rations for staple goods were not always available. At the markets the peasants were keen to barter food for items such as soap, matches, vodka or clothing. The prices requested for cash products, however, were prohibitive for most city-dwellers, who now often had nothing left with which to barter. Most of the available clothing had migrated from the towns to the countryside due to the shortage of food in the towns. The lack of proper clothing and heating and the shortages of electricity made winter an especially grim time for the remaining city-dwellers.[35]

The 'liquidation' of the Brest ghetto in October 1942 brought an end to the smuggling of food for sale in the ghetto.[36] Black-market trading, however, at inflated prices continued otherwise as before. By the spring of 1943 it was clear that offering increased wages was not sufficient to encourage better work. Monetary wages were of little value on the black market, which was the only reliable source of supplementary food. German officials suggested that payment in kind would prove a more effective incentive for the native population.[37] Some state employees, including members of the *Schutz-mannschaft*, were paid benefits, such as vodka rations, directly in kind in order to boost their waning loyalty and morale.[38]

Part of the German economic problem lay in questions of distribution. In the late summer of 1942 the German administration in Minsk was unable to provide food supplies in accordance with the ration cards issued. Sufficient potatoes were in fact available, but these could not be brought in from Baranovichi and Novogrudok due to the shortage of petrol.[39] As the partisans came increasingly to dominate the countryside and attack German communications, more security forces (including the local police) had to be diverted to bringing in the harvest and escorting supply convoys.[40]

During the occupation the German authorities organized the collection of vast amounts of grain and livestock to be sent forward in support of the troops or to be delivered to the *Reich*.[41] They extracted such a large proportion of production that farmers were left with little incentive to work other than compulsion. The punitive level of requisitions in practice reduced the peasants to subsistence farmers. Typical are the instructions issued in the Nikolayev *Generalkommissariat* in August 1942, setting the level of requisitions:

> The amount to be delivered is calculated by deducting from the total harvest the seed corn required (also for spring), the requirements of the country population (12kg of corn monthly for each person capable of work over the age of 14, half this for children under 14) and the foodstuffs for the draught animals ... any amount remaining after this is to be handed over.[42]

Naturally these contributions became more onerous with time, as the monetary economy collapsed and remaining reserves became exhausted. An inhabitant of Yeremichi recalls: 'At first we paid our taxes to the Germans with money and as far as I remember there was someone who collected the money from us. Later the Germans came to our houses and took the cattle away from us.'[43]

Failure to deliver the grain and livestock requested by the German authorities resulted in punitive measures. As during Tsarist times, the local police acted not only as law enforcement officials, but also collected taxes and enforced other economic regulations: the police, together with the village elders, were often the only agents of the state with whom peasants came into contact.[44] The local police conducted searches looking for concealed grain. In the village of Studenitsa near Vinnitsa a woman was beaten and subsequently hanged by the police after concealed grain supplies were found in her house.[45] According to one former policeman, his unit from Novaya Mysh went to several villages in the district 'on the business of collecting grain from the peasant farms which had . . . not fulfilled the quotas appointed for the Germans'.[46]

An even greater imposition on the local population was the introduction of compulsory labour service from December 1941.[47] Jews had experienced forced labour from the start of the occupation. Under the new regulations, non-Jews who were unemployed had to register at the Labour Exchange and would be assigned to specific work. Work was to be paid according to fixed rates and the sanction of imprisonment was available to punish those refusing to comply. A subsequent ordinance forbade the poaching of workers by other employers and attempted to prevent wage competition.[48] These measures, however, only reflected the acute shortage of labour exacerbated by the vast deportations of workers to the *Reich* to work in agriculture, the arms industry or as domestic servants.

Forced labour was nothing new for the local peasants. They viewed it as a return to familiar systems of exploitation. A woman from the Nesvizh area recalls: 'my husband lived with me and he worked on his land, but once a week he was made to work in the fields'.[49] The increasing labour shortage was made worse in the summer and autumn of 1942 by the 'liquidation' of the ghettoes. One official in the civil administration in Brest reported: 'the loss of Jewish workers has created a shortage of labour in all offices. This gap can only be closed by taking workers from the countryside, which will have some impact there, but has to be coped with.'[50]

In the field of labour policy, the mass deportation of workers to Germany proved to be most damaging to German credibility with the local population. This policy, which commenced in January 1942, soon became unpopular and encountered widespread evasion and resistance. By June 1942, the German authorities had despatched over 100 000 workers from Ukraine. However, it was not expected that the civil administration in the western half would be able to fulfil its quota of over half a million workers. Resistance to the deportations had begun to develop, especially in the wooded areas in the north where partisan activity was most widespread.[51]

Any voluntary recruitment had dried up almost completely by 1943, such that large-scale round-ups were organized in the form of dawn raids by the *Gendarmerie* and *Schutzmannschaft*. For larger transports of workers, *Schutz-männer* from neighbouring outposts were employed to assist with rounding up and escorting the workers. However, the *Schutzmänner* were initially not to be told what sort of action was planned.[52]

In an order issued by the *SSPF* in Korosten on 31 May 1943, he describes the failure of large round-up actions in the area and recommends a more cautious course:

> The round-up of the year age-groups [born] 1923–25[53] in this area has remained almost completely without success. The female and male Ukrainians concerned remain hidden, have partly fled and then returned after the transport of those who have been taken. Another large action would only cause further trouble. Therefore, the male and female Ukrainians of the said years should be rounded up occasionally in their district and handed over to the collection point in Korosten. Those found with a white pass from the Labour Office in Korosten are not to be rounded up. These measures should be carried out as unobtrusively as possible.[54]

A further order issued by the Commander of the Order Police in Zhitomir dated 17 June 1943 stressed the need to avoid further excesses against the workers and the local population during such round-ups, as these would not only damage the image of the German police but would also serve to sabotage the required measures and create unnecessary disturbance among the population.[55]

An example of the difficulties the Germans encountered in fulfilling their quotas can be seen from the Brest district. In the summer of 1943 the names of 53 people were published in one of the *rayon* towns by the local authorities, stating that these people were to be deported to work in Germany. However, a local inhabitant recalled that of these only a few were actually transported. Some girls were excused as they had liaisons with the local police, while others bought themselves out with bribes.[56] The District Commissar reported that many people fled on the way to registration or did not turn up at all.[57] One man from near Brest recalled:

> I reported at the school to appear before the medical board for the next dispatch to Germany. I was at that time completely healthy and had nothing wrong with me, but owing to the fact that G. had had a word with someone in the German authorities and given him a 'present' of food and home-distilled vodka, I was given a certificate to say that I was ill. I do not know what diagnosis was indicated in the certificate but I remember that the word '*krank*', that is, ill, was written. So I was released from deportation to forced labour in Germany.[58]

According to a post-war Soviet Extraordinary Commission report, some 2200 people were deported from the Nesvizh district to forced labour in Germany. Detailed records are available in Moscow for more than 150 persons who returned at the end of the occupation. Of these 60.5 per cent were born after 1920, 23.7 per cent between 1911 and 1920 and 15.8 per cent before 1910. Given that some of those recorded were relatives of policemen who left during the retreat or persons arrested and deported to concentration camps for partisan contacts, it can be seen that the majority of those sent for work were born after 1920 and generally were in their late teens.[59]

Deportations increasingly became a part of the harsh system of rewards and punishments employed by the Germans in an attempt to control the local population. Some people arrested for suspected contacts with the partisans were deported with their families for work in Germany; others volunteered to join the police in order to avoid being deported.[60]

Common to many German reports is the recognition that the deportations had proved to be disastrous politically and a boon to the partisans. Typical is the comment of the *Generalkommissar* in Volhynia-Podolia in April 1943, who noted that the forced recruitment of Ukrainian workers for the *Reich* 'is equated by enemy propaganda with exile to Siberia'.[61] In the Brest district it soon became clear that no one wanted to go voluntarily. In particular the initial recruitment started carelessly, with the effect that many peasants and workers simply fled to the forests to avoid being caught.[62] In this way they were being literally driven into the arms of the partisans.[63]

Certainly the effectiveness of the policy was not helped by the manner in which it was implemented. Many of the transports to and from the *Reich* were carried out in unheated wagons. Under these circumstances the number of persons was increased and straw was added in an effort to keep them warm.[64] The Soviets made the most of such treatment in their own counter-propaganda, including personal accounts of the poor conditions experienced in German 'slave labour' camps:

> Germans arrived one day and took me to a foreign country. With me there were some who believed that they would live well in Germany. The Germans had promised this. When I arrived in Germany I was put behind barbed wire. Although the food was very bad, we had to work from dawn until dusk. Many people get sick in Germany and are killed simply because they are sick. I ran away from Germany because I want to carry on living.[65]

It would be wrong to rely solely on Soviet propaganda for an accurate picture of the conditions experienced by the eastern workers (*Ostarbeiter*) sent to Germany. More recent studies have observed that conditions varied according to the type of work place to which workers were assigned. In the personalized circumstances of a small family farm there was scope for more humane treatment. In spite of the regulations, on the farm employer and employee 'sat together at the same dinner table and ate the same meals'; it was in the interests of the farm owners to treat their eastern workers well in order to maintain valuable labour.[66]

Conditions in the factories were generally considerably worse than on the farms. A former French worker in the *Volkswagen* factory in Wolfsburg recalled the conditions of the eastern workers there: 'they were treated very badly by most of their guards and lived in a filthy and miserable state caused by lack of proper clothing, hygiene and nourishment'.[67] Some factory workers even volunteered to work for farmers after hours, as one former *Ostarbeiter* recalls: 'After work farmers came to us and asked us for help. Those who were fit worked for them . . . the farmers fed us very well during the time we worked for them. We received milk, bread and butter from them. In the camp the food was very bad.'[68]

In general the *Ostarbeiter* have been described by German witnesses as being good and adaptable workers, often belying the image projected by Nazi propaganda.[69] At the same time the humiliating treatment of the eastern workers – experienced in terms of wearing distinctive markings similar to the Jews, restricted movement and low food rations – increased their awareness of being third-class citizens compared with the German population. The initial voluntary recruits were especially disappointed at this treatment, as demonstrated by one letter home to Ukraine: 'Dear relatives, we live in barracks, each barrack is fenced in, we sit here as if we were in prison and the gate is locked.'[70]

By December 1943 about 1 800 000 people had been deported from the occupied Soviet territories to work in Germany. In the German factories the main dangers came from Allied bombing and the spread of disease in the overcrowded barracks. This vast labour force helped to keep Germany's war industry going at a time of acute labour shortage. Nevertheless, there was a high cost in terms of the effect on the morale of the eastern population and the growth of partisan strength and support. In the light of the murderous German reprisal policy, some of those deported to Germany returned after the war to find that their families had been killed and their homes destroyed.

In the propaganda war for hearts and minds the Germans may have been victorious on the home front,[71] but they lagged severely behind the Soviets in the occupied territories. The report of the Slonim District Commissar on the mood of the population in the summer of 1942 reflects the rapid deterioration, which occurred as local expectations clearly went unfulfilled:

Generally speaking the political situation is worse than at the beginning of our construction work a year ago. At that time the population was immensely impressed by the forceful impression of the rapid victory march of the German troops and performed willingly and loyally all the tasks assigned to them. Furthermore they had hopes of improved economic conditions. At the beginning they heard that through a loyal political attitude and unstinting work they would have the opportunity to receive their own land according to their performance.[72]

The failure to meet these expectations and the deterioration of Germany's military position meant that, by the end of the occupation, even active collaborators could no longer be relied upon. One former village elder subsequently lamented the lack of diligence amongst those local foremen he appointed in 1943 with the task of exposing partisans and assisting in the collection of foodstuffs for the German Army: 'I must say that they did not carry out my tasks and instructions very well, that they even had to take from themselves... bread and meat for the Germans.'[73]

Only during the latter stages of the occupation did the Germans intensify their own propaganda efforts in an attempt to relieve declining morale amongst local collaborators and in those villages still within the German sphere of influence. Numerous speeches were held and propaganda pamphlets distributed. Particular attention was paid to the *Schutzmannschaft*, where educational topics varied from the 'duties of the Belorussian people in the struggle for the new Europe' to warnings about the dangers of home-brewed vodka.[74] Typical of German propaganda in the summer of 1943 is the following appeal made to the enemy:

> Partisans!
>
> You have been tricked by the Jews and the Bolsheviks and are only the blind instruments of their base and inhuman orders, which are directed against the Russian peoples. Don't believe the Jewish-Bolshevik appeals and their propaganda that this war is being fought by the Germans to enslave Russia or against the Russian peoples...
>
> There where the German Army appears slave labour, hunger and the terror of the *NKVD* vanishes and freedom rules.[75]

Nevertheless the Germans believed that the most effective propaganda was to wipe out those villages which supported the partisans, as word would quickly spread and this would earn the respect of the peasants.[76] However, it was precisely such brutal reprisal attacks which were skilfully exploited by Soviet propaganda:

> The fascistic beasts appeared early one morning in the village of Kraschin and organized a regular slaughter. Barbarically they chased children, women and the elderly into a barn and set it alight burning 150 people. All the inhabitants of this village who could not flee to the forest were killed. The inhabitants of the villages of Lyadki, Novoye Selo, Pogorelka and many other villages of the Baranovichi district were killed by the bloody hands of Hitler's hangmen.[77]

Not unrelated to the issue of Soviet propaganda are the Soviet Extraordinary Commission reports compiled in the period immediately after liberation by the Red Army. After more than fifty years, it is not possible to quantify the precise extent of German plunder and destruction during the three years of occupation. The detailed records compiled by the Soviet Extraordinary Commissions should be treated with some scepticism, as they were compiled by Party officials with a good grasp of Soviet propaganda aims. The detailed inventories of destroyed property were drawn up with the intention of extracting compensation from the Germans. Included in such records are also damages incurred in combat and probably some losses attributable to the activities of the variegated partisan groups. Nevertheless, the figures presented provide the reader with a vivid impression of the enormous scale of the destruction which swept through Belorussia and Ukraine like a hurricane. One local report records, for instance, that:

> in the years of the German occupation more than 1000 hectares of forest were destroyed in the Nesvizh district. The Germans took away to Germany 3000 horses, 15 000 sheep, 6000 cows, 18 000 pigs and 1 200 000 head of poultry, they looted and carried off 500 colonies of bees, 593 machines and items of agricultural equipment, 2400 tonnes of grain, 45 000 tonnes of potatoes, they burnt down more than 1000 dwelling-houses, more than 1000 farm buildings. The total amount of the losses caused to the private economy is more than 164 million roubles. During their rule in Nesvizh district the German fascist invaders demolished and destroyed the towns of Snov and Gorodeya, the villages of Uzhanka, Dalnyaya Gorodeya, Gornaya Gorodeya, Kachanovichi, Ogorodniki, they destroyed fifty to sixty per cent of the very beautiful old town of Nesvizh. These inhabited localities were barbarously destroyed by the Germans during their terrorist air raids and the arson attacks by individual *SS* units. During these more than 3000 people were killed.

The same report goes on to note that the cultural heritage of the district was also erased as the Germans removed all valuables, pictures, sculptures, books and furniture from the ancient castle of Prince Radziwill.[78] Such cultural looting was due to the combined efforts of *Einsatzstab Rosenberg*, established specifically to exploit and catalogue the cultural treasures in the east, together with other German individuals and institutions, which acted on their own initiative. Many items were destroyed beyond repair in the chaos of the retreat in 1944, when inadequate evacuation measures caused precious items to become exposed to the elements.[79] This last image of wanton pillage and destruction completes the picture for the whole occupation.

The forcible deportation of young people to work in Germany and the ruthless exploitation of agricultural and industrial production in support of the German war effort left no doubt as to the vassal status granted to the occupied peoples. German economic policies in practice frustrated most local hopes for effective land redistribution. Political repression was enforced by mounting police terror, carried out with the help of the *Schutzmannschaft*, against the indigenous population. The role of the local police was not only to enforce economic exploitation and the deportation of young people to Germany, but became directed increasingly against the local population in the form of anti-partisan reprisals, once the Jews had been murdered.

The grandiose plans for colonization of the east, which lay behind Hitler's invasion, were pursued primarily in terms of the brutal clearance of local inhabitants from specific areas. Belated attempts to gain popular support through limited economic and political concessions were overtaken by mounting partisan strength. It is only in terms of a detailed examination of partisan warfare in the east that the brutal reality of German occupation and collaboration can be fully comprehended at the local level.

7 Partisan Warfare, 1942–44

The level of civilian casualties suffered in Belorussia and Ukraine during the Second World War was amongst the highest in Europe. Official estimates indicate that the Belorussian Soviet Republic lost approximately one-third of its total population. This was a demographic catastrophe of the first order, comparable in historical terms only with events such as the 'Black Death' or the Thirty Years War. Much of this figure can probably be accounted for by the effects of Soviet deportations, the murder of the Jews, Red Army losses, German deportations and post-war emigration. Nevertheless, a residue of civilian casualties remains, in the realm of several hundred thousand people.[1]

A considerable proportion of the non-Jewish civilian losses were violent deaths, resulting from the intense partisan warfare, which raged especially in Belorussia and the northern parts of Ukraine. The greatest destruction was undoubtedly wrought in the large-scale anti-partisan sweeps by units of the German Army, *Waffen SS* and police, which aimed to render large areas uninhabited. Literally hundreds of villages were razed to the ground never to be rebuilt, as there were virtually no survivors. In some areas rival partisan groups also fought each other or attacked civilians of other ethnic groups, shifting alliances as the overall political situation developed.

In their initial assessment of the partisan situation, the Germans were victims of their own ideology. Their reports in 1941 generally overstated the level of partisan activity amongst a population which remained passive, if not well-disposed towards their new masters. In part the German officials were looking for an excuse to justify their own unprovoked mass murders against a Jewish population which, at that time, had barely started to organize armed resistance.[2] For the majority of the local inhabitants, it was the combination of economic exploitation and political repression, seen most clearly in the treatment of PoWs and the deportations for work in Germany, which served to turn them against the German occupiers.

Under these conditions, continued fierce Soviet resistance at the Front and skilful propaganda provided fertile ground for the Soviet partisan movement in many areas. By the summer of 1942 a small cadre of former Red Army soldiers and Soviet partisan leaders had begun to mobilize and exploit the growing will to resist.[3] The vicious reprisals exacted on whole communities by the German police in turn escalated the partisan conflict, embroiling almost the entire population. By the end of 1943 vast areas of countryside were no longer under German control; their influence was restricted in many areas to the towns and the main lines of communication.[4]

119

The partisan struggle behind the Front, especially in the areas under German civil administration, has received comparatively little attention from western historians.[5] Access to new sources now permits a detailed examination of the nature of this struggle, as experienced by the local population. The recollections of a former partisan from the Mir *rayon* provide a valuable insight into the development of the partisan movement at the local level during the first year of occupation.

In the summer of 1941 retreating Soviet soldiers abandoned their weapons in the River Nieman. These were then retrieved by local inhabitants and hidden, with a view to offering some kind of resistance to the German occupying forces in the future. From an early date the Germans and the local police came regularly to the villages to rob the local people of cattle and other foodstuffs. There were no partisans at this time and no resistance was offered.

During the course of 1942 partisan resistance in the Mir *rayon* began to organize itself. According to our partisan informant from the village of Berezhno:

> In the winter of 1941 to 1942 there was myself and four other activists in the village. We would go to where we had hidden the abandoned Soviet weapons and learn how to handle them. We were afraid that our existence would become known to the Germans and at night we would post two guards on the road outside the village to keep watch, and an additional guard within the village itself. By May 1942 the number of activists within Berezhno had risen to twenty-eight, and this number included five Soviet soldiers, who had retreated and stayed and worked within the village.[6]

According to a German report for the Minsk region, most trouble had been caused during the winter of 1941–42 by a few plundering bandits who were active in the area of Slutsk and Gantsevichi. At the same time the partisans were trying to gain recruits from amongst those PoWs who had been released to work on the *Kolkhozy* (collective farms) and other civilian workers. In March 1942 the partisans began to prepare for their summer offensive. Partisan activity increased once the snow had melted, as it became easier for them to travel unobserved. The partisans also began terrorizing those who worked for the German administration.[7]

It was at about this time that the Germans began to intensify their own counter-measures. For instance, in the spring of 1942 the village of Antoniovo near Mir 'was burned down in an act of reprisal against the partisans and as an act of advertisement to the local population to prevent collaboration [with the partisans]'.[8] Such actions, however, frequently only served to force their opponents into more active resistance: for instance, a Pole from Nesvizh, Josef Marchwinski, fled to the partisans in April 1942, when his neighbour's grand-daughter warned him that the Germans were asking after him. He was fortunate not to be in his own house when a group of Germans and local police came to arrest him. He did not have time to retrieve the arms he had obtained the previous day, but managed to escape over the roof. He recalls that: 'thanks to the fact that we had been warned by the child, we managed to escape the clutches of the Nazi thugs and despite the heavy fire they soon opened on us, we reached the Alba woods about 2km away'.[9] Thus he became a partisan after narrowly escaping arrest.

In May 1942 an order was issued that all former Soviet soldiers were to report to Mir to be re-registered. Our informant in Berezhno recalls:

> The five former Soviet soldiers in Berezhno decided not to go, so we issued them with weapons and they fled to the forest. I suppose it could be said that at this time some form of partisan movement had started. Myself and my fellow activists left in Berezhno stayed and helped on our parents' farms as there was still much work to be done. We ourselves did not flee into the forests until July or August 1942 once the work had been completed.[10]

In other areas, such as Brest, a similar chronology can be observed. An initial nucleus of border guards and former Red Army men went into hiding in 1941 and received passive support from elements of the local population. Then in the summer of 1942 they went over to the offensive against the Germans. For example, on 21 June 1942 a German convoy was attacked on the Brest highway. According to the partisan report four trucks and one car were destroyed, causing considerable German casualties.[11] German loss reports also record the killing of two Gendarmes in the area in late June.[12] Post-war investigative records indicate that severe reprisals were instigated shortly afterwards:

> In the summer of 1942, after the destruction of the German car on the highway, the Germans punished the villages nearby; they shot several people in Zbunin and burned their homes, then they destroyed Smolyar-nya, near Dubitsa station, and then they went on to the village of Leplevka; many people had already fled, but they managed to catch about 10 people and shoot them and they burned about 50 houses.[13]

In September the *HSSPF*, Hans-Adolf Prützmann, issued instructions for officers of the Order Police in Ukraine to avoid unnecessary trips by car due to the recent losses suffered from partisan attacks.[14]

In *Weißruthenien* units of the *Waffen SS* involved in the on-going ghetto 'liquidations' around Vileyka noted in May 1942 that the 'alarming reports about partisans were proving mostly to be exaggerated and were often only a false alarm'.[15] It was a common feature of partisan tactics at this time to spread rumours exaggerating their own strength in order to intimidate their opponents and facilitate their own operations. Shalom Cholawski recalls:

We soon learned, however, that a much more powerful weapon than arms in partisan warfare was the effect rumoured strength created. A necessary precondition to feeding these rumours was to establish a rapport with the population. We worked at creating the illusion of great power. We kindled stories of force and victories. These, in turn, sparked the imaginations of the peasants who exaggerated and distorted them in retelling.[16]

During the summer of 1942, however, actual partisan activity increased considerably. According to one Gendarme: 'the patrols which we carried out around Mir became fewer and they contained more people from the summer of 1942 as the risk from partisans increased'.[17] Following the heavy losses suffered by the Security Police from Baranovichi on 9 June 1942 near Naliboki, a meeting was held at the offices of *Reichskommissariat Ostland* to discuss the mounting threat posed by the partisans. In particular it was noted that the current strength of police manpower was inadequate to cope with the situation.[18]

The German response was to reinforce the *Schutzmannschaft*, in order to combat the growing threat without weakening their forces at the Front. Accordingly from July 1942 to the end of the year, the overall strength of the *Schutzmannschaft-Einzeldienst* was increased from about 30 000 to over 200 000 men.[19] This rapid expansion also changed the nature of the *Schutzmannschaft*; it grew from being a small voluntary organization to one that could only be built up by a form of conscription.[20]

The actual increase in partisan activity can be seen most clearly from an examination of German situation reports at a local level. These began to contain less propaganda and more hard facts: for instance, in late July 1942 a patrol of two Gendarmes and 27 *Schutzmänner* in the Mir *rayon* succeeded in interrupting a raid to collect grain by about 50 partisans in the village of Obryna. During a brief battle the former communist mayor of Yeremichi was killed and subsequently two suspected partisan agents were summarily shot.[21]

At the same time the Germans and local police began to suffer their first losses; compensation claims were processed for the relatives of *Schutzmänner* who fell in battle.[22] For the *Gendarmerie* in Zhitomir the first casualties were registered as a genuine shock in their orders: 'Fate has showed itself also to have a more serious side. Like a bolt from the blue, it has taken away two of our Gendarmes.'[23] It was in response to these losses that the Germans developed their policy of harsh reprisals, which raised the stakes for all concerned.

The Soviet partisans developed a skilful propaganda campaign amongst the population from the winter of 1941–42, exploiting German setbacks at the Front. They spread rumours about German retreats and the recapture of certain cities by the Red Army. Posters were put up on walls in confirmation of these rumours. The posters also included exhortations to join partisan units and threats against those collaborating with the German authorities.[24] Many of the initial attacks were directed against village elders and policemen in the more isolated villages. This in turn made it harder for the Germans to recruit replacements if they were shown to be unable to protect them from the partisans.

It is important to stress the largely spontaneous nature of much initial partisan activity. Former communists and Red Army men hiding in the forests and living off the land provided the impetus for resistance, but many of them were not in contact with Moscow at this time. Likewise in the Minsk ghetto, the initial resistance organization grew up without any orders from 'above'.[25] It was the harsh policies of the Germans which drove even teenagers into active resistance. In Berezhno our former partisan recalls:

> In the forests there were other organized groups from villages such as Sinyavsky Sloboda, Pogorelka and Lyadki. We were based in the Naliboki forest. The first group was called the '*Komsomolsky*'. It was called this because the majority of its members were very young. We numbered 56 people. We immediately started ambushes in areas such as Yeremichi and Turets. We cut telephone wires. Other groups would attack railway lines with mines.[26]

The partisans also established a network of contacts within each village to give them warning about police activities. In a village near Derechin, Slonim district, the wife of a partisan (who herself acted as a courier) recalls that:

> The police could walk freely around the village during the day and obtain food from the villagers, they often visited their relatives in the village. The partisans could only come at night. But they could not be certain that the police had left the village. It might happen that a partisan came into a house and a policeman was staying the night there. So, I would go to a house to find out if there were any policemen there or the house was safe.[27]

Partisan agents within the population were also employed to smuggle weapons and ammunition from the police to the partisans.[28] Some policemen may have played a double game deliberately, as a form of insurance in case the wrong side should win the war. It was not uncommon for former policemen to claim during post-war interrogations that they regularly supplied the partisans with ammunition and information.[29] However, the risk in the event of being detected could mean death not only for the policeman, but also for his family. Children were frequently employed by the partisans as couriers and for the transportation of weapons. Members of the *Komsomol* might be employed for these essentially grown-up tasks.[30]

Clearly the success of the partisans depended heavily on support from the local population. As the overall balance of forces in the war began to shift during the second half of 1942, the strength of the partisans also increased. In this context the actions against the Jews served to augment the forces in the forests determined to offer resistance to the Germans. Several German reports observed this consequence and stressed the need to hunt them down.[31] However, the Jews were by no means always welcomed by the Soviet partisans; Jewish survivors have described the difficulties they encountered in being accepted, especially if they had few weapons of their own.[32] Some were turned away or even killed by anti-Semitic partisan groups. In Volhynia thousands of survivors of the ghetto 'liquidations' were slaughtered by Ukrainian nationalist partisans.[33]

One concern of Soviet partisan leaders was that large groups of unarmed Jewish refugees would act as a drain on resources, which might hinder their efforts to hit back at the Germans. Very few Jews were trained soldiers and many fled to the forests without arms.[34] Thus there was a tendency for some experienced partisans to look down on the Jews as non-fighters. Not untypical was the attitude of Captain Chorny, a Soviet partisan leader south of Baranovichi: 'He sneered at the Jewish fighters, saying that they had given all their gold and silver to the Germans and had worked for them, only to come to the forests at the end, not to fight, but just to save their skins.' He even threatened to shoot every tenth man of a Jewish partisan group for alleged plundering.[35] Only the practical deeds of Jewish partisans were able to overcome these prejudices.

A partisan leader from the Slonim region has put forward a balanced assessment of the performance of the Jewish partisans:

> The partisan group which I led was not less in its heroism and the accomplishment of its tasks than was the organized Russian partisan network. These simple Jews, who didn't know what a rifle was or what war was, in a few months adjusted themselves to the situation and did great things, great things in the sense, that first of all they did not go to the slaughter; and second, they showed the world that the Jews were soldiers – I wouldn't say better than the Russians, but generally similar to the Russians and the soldiers of other nationalities.[36]

Given the hostility shown towards them, making initial contact with the partisans was often decisive for Jews' chances of survival. A group of survivors from the 'liquidation' of the Nesvizh ghetto were lucky to be found by Josef Marchwinski, who had already joined the partisans in April:

> In late June or July, 1942 – I really do not remember when – I returned from a combat mission . . . and as a matter of pure partisan interest called on an acquaintance of mine who lived 2km north of Nesvizh. What

I discovered from him filled me with horror. He said that the day before the Nesvizh police had murdered all the Jews who had been left alive after the first slaughter and in a whisper immediately went on to say: 'I have sheltered 17 people who came to my place during the night in the barn.' He asked me to take them with me because the police could be there at any minute and kill them together with his family. I quickly consulted my entire group and, having obtained their consent, took them with me ... Of those seventeen three subsequently died. The others survived the war.[37]

Another survivor, who escaped from the 'liquidation' of the Lesnaya camp in March 1943, was also 'fortunate to meet up with good people' who showed her some sympathy, when she knocked on their door in the forest with her child. They provided her with food and clothing before she set out again on her chosen path.[38] In the Novogrudok ghetto it was known that a poor Gentile family who lived about 4km outside town, the Hicles (dogcatchers), would take in escaped Jews and assist them in making contact with the Bielski Jewish partisan group. Jack Kagan recounts that:

> Every Jew who managed to escape from the ghetto and reach the Hicles was hidden for a day or two and supplied with food for the journey ahead. The Hicles kept in touch with the Bielski partisans, and they would tell runaway Jews where they might be found. When the Germans later found out about the activities of the Hicles, they killed them and burned their property.[39]

Another group which was known to treat the Jews sympathetically were the Baptists. Shalom Cholawski reports the selfless help he received from this Christian sect:

> Our meetings with the Baptists were reminders of kindness and admiration. They were a religious sect devoted to the Holy Bible and to the messianic mission of the Jewish people. They lived in a different spiritual world from others in the area, and their lives seemed separated from the hatred and murder that surrounded them. The partisans usually aroused respect in the local population, respect for their strength and their weapons. But with the Baptists, it was different. For them, the human being came first. They showed respect toward Jews and our ideals, and they made us feel that it was a privilege for them to be our hosts. Their compassion aroused deep feelings among the Jewish fighters. They provided a refuge and sanctuary for human values.[40]

This was, however, very much the exception to the rule. Most Jewish fugitives had no one to turn to. As one Jew from the Miory area explained to a local peasant: 'it was not only the Germans who wanted to kill us; most of the

Poles and White Russians also wanted to see us dead. And without help from the Gentiles, the Jews could not organize any resistance of their own.'[41]

In order for Jewish families to survive many had to turn to self-help. Jewish family camps were established in the forests. The most famous was organized by Tuvia Bielski, who never turned away any Jews who came to him and who even made efforts to rescue Jews from the remaining ghettoes.[42] In January 1943, the partisan, Possessorski, dressed as a peasant, entered the Novaya Sverzhen camp by bribing the German guard with a bottle of vodka. He made contact with relatives in the underground and entreated the Jews to escape from the camp immediately. As their plan for a break-out was ready, the underground spread the word that the time was ripe. The ensuing escape was largely successful, as has been described by Shalom Cholawski:

> At a signal, the men ran quickly toward the fence. Quietly, they disappeared through a hole and out into the darkness. After some time, they heard a series of shots, but by then they were safely out of reach of any bullets. Some members of the group headed toward the Naliboki forests; the majority toward the Kopyl forests.[43]

However, Jewish chances of survival in the forests were not good, as can be seen from the testimony of one survivor recorded immediately after the war:

> The group which stuck with Possessorski was led by him to the partisan base. The very next day 11 Jews from our group were sent out on domestic operations. Those Jews were ambushed. Eight of them were killed. Several days later there was a German raid on the forest. Several Jews from our group drowned in the marshes. Those who were armed were immediately separated from those who were not. Those who were unarmed were told to go and acquire arms themselves. They were told that the Jews had lots of gold with which they could obtain weapons. Those Jews who did not possess arms were left on the spot and the detachment moved on.[44]

Jack Kagan has also described the hostility of much of the local population towards the Jews:

> The environment in which the Bielski partisans operated was hostile. The Christian population, the peasants and villagers, were deeply anti-Semitic, and detested the Jewish partisans. Sometimes they would even turn the partisans in to the authorities. The Bielskis were forced to retaliate severely, executing informers and burning their property. This was the only way to frighten the others, and teach them that Jewish blood wasn't cheap.[45]

In the winter of 1943 six members of the Bielski partisans managed to capture two Belorussian policemen from Novogrudok when they went home to visit their families in the countryside. They were interrogated and killed after confessing to having participated in the murder of Jews.[46] In another operation motivated by revenge, a group of Jewish partisans under the command of Dr Atlas in the Slonim district took a leading part in an attack with Soviet partisans on the Derechin garrison in August 1942. A number of local policemen were killed.[47]

Detailed reports from the Mir *rayon* reflect a further increase in partisan activity in the autumn of 1942. Many of the attacks were raids upon outlying economic facilities such as mills and estates, which were only weakly defended by the Germans. The partisans' aim was mainly to obtain supplies for themselves or deny agricultural produce to the Germans. Not untypical was a raid on the village of Simakovo near Mir on 10 November 1942. The partisans burned down the *Schutzmannschaft* outpost building, which had recently been abandoned, 14 houses with their outbuildings, seven barns full of produce, the village hall, the school and the church. One calf, six pigs and 13 sheep died in their stalls. Those inhabitants who co-operated with the Germans were beaten and threatened with being shot.[48]

As the partisan units increased their strength, equipment and discipline they went over to direct attacks against German patrols amd outposts. German reprisals were then concentrated against villages believed to be partisan strongholds. A series of brutal actions was conducted by units of German Police Regiment 15 in the Brest region in the autumn of 1942: for instance, at the end of September an action was conducted by one company against the village of Zablotye near Brest. According to the German report 289 people were shot dead, 151 farmsteads were burned down and 700 cattle, 400 pigs, 400 sheep and 70 horses were seized. In addition considerable amounts of corn and agricultural equipment were removed. Only five of the local families were released following interrogation.[49] German correspondence from this area shows that even the Security Police had doubts about the humanity of the methods employed by the Order Police.[50]

Subsequent actions in October and November by the same police regiment revealed a variety of pretexts given for destroying villages or murdering families. The Security Police leader in Brest proposed 'clearing' remaining *khutors* (farmsteads) in one area, as the locals had failed to report any partisans, although it was well-known that partisans were active there.[51] On another occasion it was decided to shoot those families who had members absent, as it was assumed that these persons had left to join the partisans.[52] Another group which was singled out for 'special treatment' (execution) in the Brest area were all persons who had arrived from the east following the Soviet occupation in 1939.[53] In a village near Mokrany a list of persons aiding the partisans was prepared, presumably with the help of local informers, who must have known the likely results of this denunciation.[54]

In the Mir *rayon* one of the most notorious actions was the murder of about 60 members of partisan families by the local police in the village of Lyadki on the morning of 13 January 1943. The considerable evidence available permits a detailed reconstruction of this massacre. The main witness is a man who served as secretary to the Mir police and at the same time was a partisan agent. Other policemen and a number of local inhabitants provide a remarkable degree of independent corroboration.

Over 100 local policemen and about five Gendarmes were concentrated for the action from the posts of the Mir *rayon* with some external support from Baranovichi. They approached the village of Lyadki on foot without encountering any partisans on the way. The police secretary records:

We arrived in Lyadki at one o'clock in the morning. Someone local had pointed out to the police chiefs those houses which were to be occupied by the policemen... One of the commandants ordered the policemen to occupy the houses in groups of five or six policemen to each house. It was ordered not to let anybody out... The policemen occupied only those houses where partisans' families lived, though they had no idea why they were ordered to guard them... I was also ordered to guard one of those houses with several other policemen... That family consisted of one old man and four boys aged from five to 13... We stayed there all night long guarding them and having naps in turns, until daybreak. When there was broad daylight somebody gave an order from the outside to leave the houses and go in the direction of the end of the street towards Turets. I went out of the house I had been guarding all night and when I was at some distance away from it I saw a group of [senior] policemen coming out of another house... They were talking with each other and their conversation seemed suspicious to me. I saw G. pointing to his pistol and I had heard him saying, 'I keep loading it all the time and still I am running out of cartridges.' The rest of the group were also busy with their arms... Then I decided to look in the house from which the [group of] policemen had just exited. There were three or four bodies there, lying randomly, all dressed. They were motionlessly lying in pools of blood, and on the whole they were all wounded in their heads.[55]

In this way the killing squad went to each partisan house in turn and shot the occupants. A survivor of the massacre was hiding behind the stove in his own house when the local police shot his mother and four other members of his family. He noticed that the policemen were drunk when they carried out this atrocity.[56] Another younger survivor of the massacre, whose older brother was a partisan, has given her personal view of what happened:

On 13 January 1943 I was at home with my father, mother, sisters and a small child, when at about 10 o'clock in the morning, the morning was clear, frosty, two policemen arrived. They were drunk, they could hardly stand up and they were cursing, calling us partisan scum. I then crawled on to the stove out of fear, there was another seven-year-old girl there, my cousin's daughter. Before the two policemen burst into the house, another policemen was posted by the entrance. But also before that a woman came to the house and said that they were dealing with partisan families, but for some reason we did not run away. After the policeman was posted at the door, my father sat at the window and saw the two policemen coming to the house. I remember him saying, 'our death is coming.' We were all in the same room ... The two policemen ordered my father, mother and two sisters, one had her child with her, to lie down on the floor. They ordered Nina and me to climb down off the stove, but then [policeman] M. fired at my mother, he shot her in the back and her chest exploded. They must have been firing explosive cartridges. Then they shot my sister, they shot off her right arm, then the child, they shot off his left arm. M. was firing. He asked the other policeman why he was not firing. He replied that he was misfiring. Then M. fired at my younger sister and wounded her. The child was crying and he turned and shot the child in the head, and his brains flew all over the stove. My sister told me later that she was lying on the floor, her mouth was full of blood and she thought she was dying, and then she saw the policemen leaving. Nina and I were on the stove at that time. M. saw us and told [his mate] that we also had to be killed, but the latter said we should be left. When [they] were leaving the house they saw Nina's grandmother, but they did not try to kill her because they were afraid the partisans would hear the shots. When the policemen had left I saw my father getting up from the floor. He was covered in the blood of my sister and the child, but he had not been shot and he was not wounded. My elder sister was mortally wounded and was moaning, she died shortly after. The child was dead. My younger sister was wounded in the side, but she survived. They had killed mummy. My father got up and ordered me to hide under the bed, but I was already too big and could not fit, then I climbed up on the stove again. The grandmother took Nina away. Then I saw through the window four policemen coming towards the house. My father and sister lay down on the floor and pretended to be dead. The policemen had come to check if everyone had been killed. It was the first time I had seen these policemen. They glanced in at the house and immediately left.[57]

Another policeman, now living in the West, tells a very similar story to that of the police secretary, especially with regard to the conduct of the action:

> I along with another policeman was ordered to guard a house in the village of Lyadki to prevent the occupants leaving. We were not told the reason for this, but I knew Lyadki was a strong partisan village. This was on the

evening of 12 January 1943, it was dark, we were inside guarding the house all night... The following morning, it was just getting light, the [senior policemen] came into the house, they were carrying Russian short machine guns with round magazines, one of these men told us to move out. Almost immediately as we left, I heard the sound of gunfire coming from within the house we had just left, it sounded as though the gunshots were coming from different guns, pistols, not rifles or machine guns. I could not see what was going on inside... We joined other policemen in the street, I saw the leading group come out of that house after the shooting had finished and then go into another house further along the road, we were making our way out of the village by now but could still hear gunfire coming from the house they had just gone into. The above mentioned men, who were officers [NCOs] and ordinary policemen whose families had been killed by the partisans, were involved in the shooting of the people inside the houses. The policemen who had been guarding the houses waited on the edge of the village for the others to join them. As we were leaving the village a group of partisans were coming into the village from the other end, I don't think they knew we were there, there was an exchange of fire between us and the partisans which resulted in one or two of them being killed...A couple of cows were stolen from the families who had been shot, I along with other policemen was ordered to take these cows back to Turets.[58]

Some partisans who had spent the night not far away came to the assistance of the village shortly after the shooting started. There was a brief battle between Barnosovo and Lyadki in which the German commander of the motorized *Gendarmerie* platoon from Baranovichi, Lt Steinert, was killed. The Germans even called up air support to help cover their retreat.[59] A local partisan amongst the relieving party has described the scene on his arrival in Lyadki:

The Germans withdrew to Turets. I say the Germans, but these were local policemen, there were only one or two Germans among them. We killed one of the Germans. Our group went towards Lyadki. There was no shooting as the policemen were all in Turets. All the people in the village ran out into the street as they knew what a tragedy had occurred. I went into the last house on the edge of the village and there was a lot of blood there, all the adults had been killed and were lying on the floor, two small children were lying on top, the policemen had shot them. This was the family of the partisans Mikhail and Vladimir Mazheyko. Among those killed were the father, mother, daughter-in-law and two children aged two and four years, and also an old man who had evidently pointed out the partisans' houses to the policemen. In Lyadki I met my mother and sister, who told me how the action happened. An informant pointed out to the policemen the houses of the partisans' families. One policeman was in the house, another stood at the gate so that the group who was carrying out the shootings saw which houses to go to. The shootings were carried out by a special group of policemen – about 15 Belorussians, who were in a state of intoxication . . . That night altogether eight families were killed, about 60 people.[60]

It appears that during the action some mistakes were made and the wrong families were killed. Partial looting took place during the action, but one or two days later the police returned to take away the remaining livestock and property of the village.[61] The partisan agent within the police has summed up succinctly the nature of the perpetrators and the purpose of the action within the overall German strategy:

All those who killed people in Lyadki were real enthusiasts of executions, which was manifested by their behaviour, and besides, they never made a secret out of it. I remember that there was an anxiety among the policemen after those families had been shot, for they were afraid of the partisans' village . . . I think that the action in Lyadki was only a part of the whole strategy of extermination of people, because the Germans, using the police force as their means, tried to impose their power all over. They were strong enough in those cities or other places where they had their garrisons, but if there was a village, for example, that went out of their control they tried to turn it into a dead zone. Subsequently there were other actions against the civilians in the villages of Lyadki, Novoye Selo and Pogorelka.[62]

An estimate of the number of non-Jews killed by the police in the Mir *rayon* during the German occupation lies between 300 and 500 people, many of them women and children.[63]

This detailed account is representative of similar events that occurred throughout Belorussia and Ukraine as the partisan war intensified. The Belorussians have created a memorial to all the villages destroyed during the German occupation at Khatyn to the north of Minsk. On 22 March 1943 the village was burned down and 156 inhabitants killed by the infamous 'Dirlewanger Brigade'. Only three children and one man survived. Official figures state that 209 towns and 9200 Belorussian villages were destroyed. Many of these villages were so completely erased that they were never rebuilt. The official inscription at Khatyn indicates that 2.23 million Soviet citizens were killed on the territory of modern-day Belorussia.[64]

One counter-measure developed by the Germans was to organize large-scale anti-partisan sweeps against areas known to be partisan strongholds. A typical example is 'Operation Hermann', known as the 'great blockade' to the local peasants. This was a large-scale operation conducted in July 1943 not only to track down and destroy partisan groups in the dense Naliboki forest around Volozhin and Novogrudok, but also to gather agricultural products, livestock and forced labourers for deportation, whilst passing through areas largely under partisan control. Local *Schutzmannschaft* units under *Gendarmerie* command participated in the operation, together with mobile units of the *SS* and police (including a Lithuanian *Schutzmannschaft* battalion).[65]

In the concluding German report it was noted that, in accordance with the instructions of the *Führer*, the partisan infested areas had been pacified and evacuated completely. Agricultural products and livestock were collected, while villages, other buildings and everything which could be destroyed, had been destroyed. People capable of work were deported and the remainder handed over to the responsible civil authorities.[66]

What this meant for the affected population can be seen from the recollections of local inhabitants. A man from Pogorelka near the River Nieman recalls that in July 1943 he fled with the other villagers when they saw the Germans and police approaching in line abreast to comb the area:

> The villagers ran towards the River Nieman and the forest to escape. Those who could, swam across the Nieman, others hid in the bushes along the river. There were about 15 people in the group I was in, we were hiding in the bushes. There was a woman with a baby among us, the baby started to cry, and the police, who were nearby, heard it.

As a result they were all discovered. Two men were selected from the group and shot on the orders of the police commandant. The remainder were rounded up and some were deported for work in Germany.[67] In a report compiled by Captain Siegling, the commander of the 57th *Schutzmannschaft* Battalion, which operated together with units of the Mir and Turets police near the River Nieman at this time, it was asserted that partisans were attempting to disguise themselves as harmless peasants.[68]

For the Jews hiding in the Naliboki forest the large-scale sweeps were a particular danger. One survivor recalls:

> on 16 July 1943 a large round-up started in the Naliboki and Volozhin forests ... the round-up started with the woods we lived in. We luckily found out from the peasants that the Germans were approaching. We ran away to the swamps. A few Jews were killed and some were caught. The round-up continued for 5 days in our woods. German tents and medium machine guns were placed along the Nieman river and on the roads. After 5 days they moved deeper into the woods and forests. And we returned to our dug outs.[69]

Jack Kagan, who escaped from the Novogrudok ghetto later in the summer of 1943, claims in retrospect that he was lucky that his escape was postponed at this time. He was unlikely to have succeeded in reaching the partisans whilst the Germans were combing the area in such strength.[70]

As police operations became directed not only against the Jews but also the remainder of the local population, the reliability and motivation of the *Schutzmannschaft* began to decline. The *Gendarmerie* District Leader in Brest complained in August 1942 of the reluctance of the *Schutzmannschaft* in Oziaty and Radvanichi to risk their lives in combat with partisans.[71] Policemen found sleeping at their post were likely to be beaten.[72] The *Schutzmänner* were usually garrisoned in barracks and patrolled in large groups, not only for their own safety but to make it harder for them to desert.

One former police conscript claims that he was viewed with mistrust by the Germans. He was apparently conscripted to the police primarily to prevent him from joining the partisans:

> In 1943 the Derechin garrison police surrounded our village and conscripted young men into the police. They brought us to the Derechin garrison and left us there. They threatened to shoot our families if we tried to escape. They did not trust us. I was posted to guard duties at the mill, in the canteen and other places. They did not take us on actions. If they did, the partisans would have killed us, as it was, I survived. Once, when I was in the police, 32 policemen went on an action, but only 10 returned, the rest got killed. I was one of those whom the Germans did not trust, they suspected I might run away to join the partisans.[73]

Evidence has been found regarding an incident where a group of policemen refused to participate in the shooting of local partisan families. In December 1943 the Polonka garrison, consisting of about 30 men, went on an anti-partisan operation to the village of Teshevla. According to one member of the police, they spread out and surrounded a farm from all sides:

> After a search was carried out an elderly man and woman were brought out of the house, they were the partisan's mother and father. There was no one else on the farm . . . In the farmyard the police commander gave the order, I do not know to whom, to shoot the man and woman, however those persons refused to carry out the order. Then there was an altercation between the commander and the policemen. [The commander] lost his temper and ordered that only the leaders of the police station would shoot them.[74]

The two elderly people were then shot by the police commander, his deputy and the three section commanders who formed the firing squad.[75] A similar example of disobedience involved a local policeman in the Brest area, who announced to his superiors in the autumn of 1942 that, in the event of an escape by a prisoner, he would not shoot as he was a Baptist. After this announcement he was arrested and sent to Brest. His subsequent fate is unknown.[76]

One of the main motives for the policemen involved in reprisal actions was the prospect of the booty to be gained. A former policeman recalls the scene following the shooting of a man as a suspected partisan by the police commander in the Nesvizh *rayon*: 'after the cow shed had caught fire all the policemen, including me, S. and also the rest, rushed and looted the property of the man who had been shot'.[77] In the village of Gumnishchi, Novaya Mysh *rayon*, a woman and her two sons were shot after ammunition was found in their house. 'After the execution of the above-mentioned woman the policemen took her property and then they set fire to the house and pigsty... The policemen took a bicycle, a gramophone and other things.'[78]

The desertion of *Schutzmänner* to the partisans was not infrequent. In this respect it was often easier for those serving close to home, as they had links with people in the partisans who could vouch for them on deserting.[79] However, the consequences for the families of those who switched sides were often catastrophic. As one Nesvizh policeman commented during his own trial:

I did not join the partisans because I was afraid for the fate of my family... When I gave the written undertaking they warned me in the police: 'if you run away from the police to the partisans we will shoot your family and burn down your farm'.[80]

These threats were often made good. Following the desertion of a local policeman from the village of Zhukovichi in the Mir *rayon* in the autumn of 1943, a reprisal action was carried out against the man's family: his mother, younger brother and two sisters (one aged 13 or 14) were all shot by members of the local police.[81]

Another police target was the families of those who left home to join the partisans.[82] Identifying such families was a relatively easy task, if there were local informants inside the village. In such instances it was necessary to hide the family as well, as a former partisan's wife describes:

There were only two partisans in our village: my husband and G. who was single. Usually the partisans' wives went into hiding. My husband and G. left for the partisans on the same day. G. was hiding his mother and his brother from the police in one of the villages in the woods. But Zoloteyevo policemen found G.'s brother and killed him. After that the Germans and the police killed the family of my husband, S., and two partisans. Then the partisans killed a family of a policeman in our village.[83]

In November 1942 the Commander of the Order Police in *Weißruthenien* ordered the fortification of major police posts.[84] Smaller outlying garrisons would be abandoned as they could no longer be held against a sudden partisan attack. As German control of the outlying villages diminished it

became common for policemen to move their families inside the main fortified posts. One policeman asked for a transfer from Polonka to Novaya
Mysh in June 1943, 'because my father, mother, brother and sister had
moved from [the village of] Shpakovtsi to Novaya Mysh for fear of the
Soviet partisans'.[85]

The Germans also organized a variety of self-defence units in the towns
and villages to assist in resisting partisan attacks: for instance, in Turets, Mir
rayon, the *Samookhova* (Home Guard) was recruited in 1943 by conscripting
all men over 17 who were not serving in the police. Most of these men were in
their thirties and forties.[86] They did not go out on patrol, but remained on
guard at night. A particular problem with these improvised self-defence
organizations was the shortage of weapons. A member of a village guard
unit in Chersk, near Brest, remembered:

> once when the deputy village elder came up and asked me how things were.
> I replied that to be on guard unarmed was a terrifying experience. Then he
> produced from his pocket two hand grenades and waving them around
> said: 'You have nothing to be afraid of, we have these to welcome the
> bandits with!'[87]

The main tactics employed by the police were to conduct patrols and ambushes
in an attempt to take the partisans by surprise. Mobile squads, on horseback,
bicycle or with motorized transport, known as *Jagdzüge* (hunting groups), were
formed to permit rapid response to reports of partisan activity. In particular it
was necessary to reinforce posts which came under attack.

The history of the Seilovichi police garrison near Nesvizh in 1943 provides
a good example of growing partisan strength. A first attack by the partisans
was beaten off in May 1943, but a second attack shortly afterwards proved
more successful due to a partisan agent within the police. He managed not
only to disable the police weapons, but also planted a mine which exploded
inside the police station. He then fled to join the partisans. Two days after
this betrayal, his relatives were killed by a police detachment from Nesvizh.
A third attack in September 1943 saw a number of policemen captured, with
several police conscripts being permitted to join the partisans.[88]

Not all Germans remained blind to the reasons for their declining influence. In a report prepared (in early 1942) for the *RSHA* in Berlin four reasons
were given to explain why the initial enthusiasm of the local population
towards the Germans had died away. First, there was the disappointment
of the Nationalists at their frustrated hopes for independence; second, the
notable decline in living standards; third, German setbacks at the Front; and
fourth, the entry of America into the war. The effect on the local population
was an increased reluctance to work for the Germans, a failure to comply
with forced labour regulations and increased support for the partisans,
including acts of sabotage.[89]

The development of the Soviet partisan movement gradually eroded the room for manoeuvre of the civil administration. Although they continued to collect requisitions from all areas, they were unable to assert their own authority.[90] Hans von Homeyer, who visited Ukraine in January 1943, offered his personal comments to *Reichsminister* Alfred Rosenberg as a veteran of the Nazi Party. In his view, there was an urgent need for a change both of policy and personnel. Otherwise the continuing alienation of the population and increasing partisan activity would mean that only a fraction of the food obtained in 1942 for the *Reich* and the *Wehrmacht* would be achieved in 1943: 'To reduce a European people completely to slavery is an impossibility, especially as long as our own forces are tied up.' He had often asked colleagues what they would do if Germany were to be treated in the same manner as Germany treated Ukraine. The answer was 'that we would all join the partisans'. Positive proposals such as land reform or the expansion of schools had always been frowned upon. The population had generally been treated better under the army than by the civil administration.[91]

Rosenberg in turn complained vehemently to *Reichskommissar* Erich Koch in early 1944 that indiscriminate reprisal actions resulted only in a strengthening of partisan forces:

> In the interests of combatting the partisans it appears to be urgently required that a clear distinction be made between members of the partisans and the civilian population. Reprisals based on mere suspicion have according to past experience not in any way reduced the partisan danger. On the contrary numerous reports are available which demonstrate that the reprisals against the civil population in places which were occupied by the partisans soon became known to the population and meant that in future during similar actions the civil population left their homes together with the partisans at the approach of German troops out of fear of reprisals. The consequence of this was an undesirable strengthening of the partisans. It was also often reported that these reprisals against people whose guilt was not proven led not only to a general deterioration in the attitude of the indigenous population, but also among the *Schutzmannschaft* and auxiliaries from the area concerned.[92]

It is mainly in hindsight that representatives of the German police began to acknowledge their own mistakes. For instance, Police Commandant Curt von Gottberg, in Minsk at the time of its evacuation in June 1944, made a detailed report on his experiences during the occupation. He noted that in September 1941, when the civil administration took over from the *Wehrmacht* behind the Front lines, it was assumed that the Soviet system would soon collapse, bringing the war to an end. The small number of partisans initially in evidence had no support from the population at large. The release of PoWs to work on the farms, however, followed by the Jewish and Polish 'actions', all caused men to flee to the partisans. Above all, the poor treatment of the local population was responsible for the development of strong partisan resistance.[93]

As can be seen from such reports, mounting German losses amongst their rear area forces led to increasing demoralization. A senior Gendarme noted in May 1943 that 'of the 500 Gendarmes who arrived with me in the Zhitomir *Generalkommissariat* in November 1941 from Cracov, over 10 per cent have fallen in battle'.[94] The *Schutzmannschaft* also began to suffer heavy losses during the winter of 1942–43. In *Weißruthenien* 268 *Schutzmänner* were killed and 236 wounded between October 1942 and March 1943.[95] Available loss reports prepared by the Commander of the Order Police (*KdO*) in Minsk indicate a marked increase in losses during the summer of 1942 which remained at a high level during the winter of 1942–43, despite German counter-measures, before rising further in the autumn of 1943.[96] By this time the German forces were clearly outnumbered and even outgunned by the Soviet partisan forces.

In this work based primarily on contemporary German and post-war investigative sources it has not been possible to examine the voluminous records of the Soviet partisan organization in detail.[97] In order to understand the development of the Soviet partisan movement, however, it is necessary to look back to the Russian tradition of anarchic peasant uprisings and especially the events of the civil war. During the First World War and revolutionary period partisan groups were frequently formed in the forests by deserters resisting conscription and local peasants opposed to military requisitions. These diffuse partisan groups at times resisted the operations of both Whites and Reds, usually trying to protect local interests against the occupying armies. They survived mainly with the support of local peasants and continued to threaten the security of the revolutionary government in many areas, even after the Whites had been crushed.[98]

Due to these largely anarchic roots, the Soviet authorities were reluctant to plan for partisan resistance in advance; however, they soon recognized its potential importance once the Germans had advanced deep into Soviet territory. In particular, the Communist Party was most concerned to gain central control over all partisan operations. In order to achieve this a Central Partisan Staff was established in Moscow on 30 May 1942.[99] These efforts at organization bore fruit over the following year, as the scattered groups of resistance were gradually brought within a centralized chain of command.[100]

From Moscow's viewpoint, the main aims for the partisan movement were to disrupt enemy lines of communication and gather intelligence about troop locations. This applied especially to the areas immediately behind the Front, where partisan operations were envisaged as acting in direct support of the Red Army. Other long-range objectives were to conduct propaganda work in the occupied areas and inflict maximum economic damage and losses on the Germans. The efforts put into propaganda were considerable: for instance, between November 1942 and the end of March 1943 it is reported that some 8 000 000 leaflets and nearly 2 000 000 newspapers were circulated in the Ukrainian language by the Soviet partisans.[101]

The initial tasks confronting partisan units if they were to survive were to obtain arms and supplies. Weapons were often acquired initially by over-powering Germans or their collaborators caught on their own or in small groups.[102] Care also had to be taken in obtaining supplies, as one former partisan recalled:

> When we first went to the forest to join the partisans we obviously took provisions from our own villages. Survival after that meant that we had to take German provisions. We also had a partisan agent in each of the nearby villages and they would tell us where we could take provisions. That is we used to take it from the local population. We would try to be careful that we didn't leave people with nothing.[103]

The situation of the peasants caught between the conflicting demands for supplies from both the partisans and the Germans was unenviable. A local peasant describes:

> When I was working on the estate, Russian partisans used to come and take foodstuffs, cows, horses and even pigs, bread and cereals and every-thing that they needed. These people were hungry, because they lived in the forest and had to come to the villages to take things. The partisans consisted of former Russian soldiers and local Russian communists. At that time I went a few times to the local market town, taking there ordered supplies (tribute) to the Germans. These deliveries (tribute) consisted of cereals, which I carried on a sledge. Some farmers had to give potatoes to the Germans and others had to give away cows.[104]

Naturally, former partisans have claimed retrospectively that discipline was strictly maintained and that no indiscriminate requisitioning took place: 'The partisans behaved well towards the people, they did not rob them, our group especially behaved well . . . It is not true that the partisans stole, in the event that a partisan was caught stealing they were punished with death. In the forests there were no robber bands.'[105] Nevertheless, there were inevitable conflicts with the local peasants. These were felt particularly by the Jewish partisans, who encountered continuing resentment from the Christian peas-ants.[106] Shalom Cholawski notes that:

> unfortunately, acts of kindness from villagers were less common than hostile actions. On some occasions, our controlled rage against unfriendly peasants suddenly burst forth. The command always regarded these cases

with severity and, at times meted out heavy punishment to those who harmed or offended peasants.[107]

Brutal types were present not only in the police but also among the partisans. A Jewish doctor remembers one partisan notable not only for his bravery, but also his savagery and cruelty:

> The war turned ordinary people into extraordinary ones; in peacetime their potential stayed hidden but in an atmosphere of violence and danger it erupted with a force impossible to predict. This was what had happened to Zhenka. I listened to his tales about the inhumanity and hunger he had experienced in a German prisoner-of-war camp where man, literally ate man and I understood a little of why his hatred for the Germans was so intense and his desire for revenge so savage.[108]

The enforcement of strict discipline could mean the execution of partisans within the group as a result of plundering or other excesses, including rape. Even within the Bielski partisans there were occasions when disobedience or disloyalty had to be made an example of, if the coherence of the unit was to be maintained.[109]

On account of German patrols, the Soviet partisan units had to remain on constant alert. Each unit set up a watch around its base to give advance warning of attack. Guard duty was divided into shifts, usually four hours on and eight hours off. In order to avoid freezing to death in the winter, partisans would often sleep for only four hours at a time.

Nevertheless, in the more permanent bases set up in the forest, an almost normal life with plentiful supplies could be established through hard work. Shalom Cholawski recalls:

> Partisan life in the forests of Orliki was almost appealing: affairs were organized, our shelters were warm and the food was good. Three times a day we had bread, and sometimes we had meat chunks fried in fat or cereal cooked with fat. The fat shielded us from the cold and illness. There was always tea and fried potato *latkes* ('pancakes').[110]

In some ways the large sweeps conducted by the Germans to clear areas of local inhabitants may have helped the partisans, as when they returned to the depopulated areas shortly afterwards they were able to dig up the potatoes left in the ground unharvested by the farmers.[111]

A particular problem for the partisans were louse plagues and other diseases, as well as treatment for the wounded in the unhygienic conditions prevalent in the forest camps.[112] In this respect Jewish doctors were generally accepted in the partisan units on account of their valuable skills. Some women in the forest camps served as nurses.[113] Medical supplies had to be stolen from the towns or were flown in to concealed airfields, such as one which operated deep in the Naliboki forest. The Soviet planes would bring in guns, ammunition, radios, as well as officers and *Politruks*, and sometimes also flew out the wounded.[114]

This direct line of communication helped to consolidate further Moscow's control over the growing Soviet partisan movement. As the Red Army drew closer and the inevitability of a Soviet victory became clearer, Soviet influence penetrated more deeply into each partisan unit and political party affiliation became more important. Independent leaders were purged and their followers split up among separate units.[115]

Occasionally there were surprise encounters within the partisans. One Jewish partisan from Baranovichi was recognized by her former *NKVD* interrogator from the Minsk prison on joining a Soviet partisan unit. She had been arrested by the Soviet authorities for her political activity before the German invasion. After initially deciding to shoot her as a counter-revolutionary spy, she was reprieved by the commander and permitted to stay with the unit for a probationary period. It was commented that she could still be shot at any time if necessary.[116]

The Germans occasionally attempted to gain information about the partisans by sending spies into the forests. When uncovered, these spies, including women, were usually shot.[117] The fear of such agents betraying partisan camps meant that innocent people or political opponents of Moscow could also be shot as 'spies or traitors'. Captured prisoners were treated in a similar manner.[118] Shalom Cholawski describes the fate of a German who was captured 3km from his garrison: 'He began to beg for his life. He showed us the picture of his wife and children. We were not insensitive to this, but we knew the dangers of the road and the impossibility of transporting him back to camp. We shot him on the spot.'[119] Knowledge that such a fate was likely to befall them certainly had a dampening effect on German morale, and a siege mentality developed amongst the occupying forces. Confined mostly to their own strongholds, the vast forests of Belorussia came to represent enemy territory holding unknown dangers. The impressions recorded by a service-man in the German medical corps whilst travelling through Belorussia in the summer of 1943 convey well this fortress mentality:

> the strongpoints on the railway have been converted into little fortresses, about 2pm in Minsk we enter a region of strong partisan danger, every day explosions with railway cars on their side along the whole railway line ... the woods have been cleared for 300 or 400 metres on each side of the rails.[120]

Destroying railway tracks and blowing up trains were amongst the most common forms of partisan attack, aiming to disrupt the German lines of communication, even if only temporarily. A daily report by the *SSPF* in Kazatin on 29 September 1943 noted an explosive mine attack by partisans against a train between Kazatin and Fastov. The train was derailed with nine cars wrecked and the locomotive severely damaged. Five members of the *Wehrmacht* were seriously injured and taken to Kazatin.[121] In addition to the *Gendarmerie* and *Schutzmannschaft*, the Germans also employed further auxiliary police units to guard the railway lines, known in some areas as 'Bahnschutz' (railway protection) units.[122]

In the second half of 1943 the Soviet partisans operating behind the German Central Front conducted a concerted onslaught against the German railway communications. According to partisan records this resulted in more than 200 000 rails being destroyed on the territory of Belorussia between August 1943 and January 1944. Units encompassing more than 70 000 Belorussian partisans participated in these actions.[123] Jewish partisans played an active role in such attacks against the railways and roads.[124] During the summer offensive in 1944 partisan attacks on communications were again co-ordinated to support the advance of the Red Army.

Typical for the rapid expansion of the partisans during the latter part of the occupation was the development of the Voroshilov detachment, which was formed in February 1943 from small local groups and operated in the Brest district. Its initial personnel consisted partly of local people and partly of former Red Army soldiers who had remained in hiding on German occupied territory. The strength of the detachment had risen to 121 by the end of June 1943 when it was subordinated to the Stalin Brigade. Recruitment continued during the summer, bringing the unit's strength up to 337 by 1 September 1943. The new recruits were mostly locals and deserters from the German garrisons, including a number of Cossacks who had deserted *en masse*.

Partisan operations in this area consisted mostly of battles against the German garrisons and attacks on the railway lines. Initially the smaller outlying garrisons were attacked and forced to withdraw such that the Germans could only collect requisitions from the countryside by sending out large armed expeditions. By the autumn of 1943 large-scale attacks were also being mounted against the main German garrisons. By the time of the liberation in June 1944 further groups had been incorporated and the Voroshilov detachment's strength numbered 588 partisans.[125]

Records are available showing the national composition of a variety of partisan units. Figures for the Stalin Brigade consisting of almost 1000 partisans in the autumn of 1943 in the Brest area reveal, for instance, that Jews made up only 3 per cent, compared with Russians 32 per cent, Belorussians 38 per cent and Ukrainians 10 per cent.[126] Some predominantly Jewish formations in the Naliboki forest contained considerably higher proportions of Jews. Records concerning over 8000 partisans active in the Ivenets–Lida area (Naliboki forest) on 1 September 1943 reveal a Jewish proportion of over 12 per cent.[127] This reflected the success of the Jewish family camps in this area. Given that the Germans had probably reduced the Jews to about a tenth of their original population in the area by this time, it can be seen that a large proportion of survivors actively served in the partisans. According to official figures there were some 370 000 Soviet partisans in Belorussia in 1944, of whom about 4 to 5 per cent (or over 15 000) were Jews.[128]

Shmuel Spector has estimated that in Volhynia, of 13 700 Soviet partisans active at the end of 1943 some 14 per cent were Jewish. This higher proportion reflects in part the extreme weakness of support for the Soviet partisans amongst the local Christian population there.[129] Elsewhere in Ukraine the proportion of Jews in the 'Red' partisans was considerably lower. Soviet partisan strength was in any case weaker in Ukraine than in Belorussia. Its main bastions were in the wooded regions of Sumy, Chernigov and Zhitomir within the northern sector of the pre-1939 Soviet borders. A recent estimate put its strength at only some 150 000 partisans and underground agents. Of these Russians and city dwellers were overrepresented compared to the Ukrainian population as a whole.[130]

By 1943 there were large areas behind the German lines effectively under partisan control, where food deliveries were no longer made to the Germans. Instead excess supplies were given directly to the partisans, who also administered their own justice and in places even forcibly recruited the local population into partisan units.[131] In the autumn of 1943 the collapse of German authority was becoming apparent, as the partisans even began to undermine the German administration in the smaller towns. One collaborator recalled after the war: 'I was discharged from my job as headman in the following manner. In autumn 1943 Soviet partisans burned the town, then the inhabitants dispersed to various villages and our agricultural authority collapsed. So I was automatically discharged as there was no one to lead.'[132]

The activities of the Polish Underground in Belorussia and Ukraine during the occupation remain the subject of much controversy. In this work it is not possible to deal with the arguments exhaustively. By presenting a few examples, however, it is intended to demonstrate how different groups of Poles reacted to the situations they faced.

Polish Underground organizations, containing elements from diverse political backgrounds, were established in the eastern provinces during the Soviet occupation and continued to be active under German rule.[133] In many areas their activities remained mainly passive, registering members, passing on information and collecting money and supplies for future use. Indeed many Poles initially accommodated themselves with the German occupation regime, taking consolation in the Soviet defeats. In Belorussia, Poles competed with Belorussians for positions within the German administration. In these local power struggles denunciation was employed by both sides to remove potential rivals.[134]

In the Novaya Mysh *rayon* the local police was heavily infiltrated by the Polish Underground. Several former policemen claimed after the war that they had been recruited to the Belorussian Police on instructions from the Polish Underground. They swore secret oaths of loyalty to General Sikorski and took conspiratorial nicknames. Poles were directed to serve in the *Schutzmannschaft* from 1942 in order to receive military training. The chief of the Novaya Mysh Police, Henryk Zaprucki, was simultaneously a commander in the Polish Underground. Whilst serving with the Germans, Polish policemen attempted to smuggle food, weapons and ammunition to Polish partisan units. During the retreat these *Armija Krajowa* (*AK*) men became split up and some were killed in a battle against the Germans near Slonim after deserting.[135]

Membership of the Polish Underground did not prevent some policemen from participating in German actions against the Jews. The following scene is recalled by a Polish policeman from Novaya Mysh at the end of 1943:

> While we were eating breakfast and drinking vodka the policeman P. came into the house and reported to Zaprucki that the policemen had arrested a Jew and a Jewess. Then Zaprucki said to policeman L., 'Go and deal with them.' L. and P. left the house and we stayed as before. After some time, while we were in the house I heard several single shots, but I did not see who was shooting at whom, but later P. told me and the other policemen that he and...W. had shot the Jews who had been arrested. After the shots L. returned to the house alone and told Zaprucki that the Jews had been dealt with.[136]

Similar anti-Semitism has been recorded among certain Polish partisan groups.[137] The Polish Underground in their reports stressed the indisciplined plundering by so-called 'Jewish-peasant gangs'.[138] At the same time, in areas such as Volhynia, the Poles were more prominent than the Ukrainians in rescue efforts for the Jews.[139]

Some Polish groups actively resisted the Germans, especially following the arrest and murder of members of the Polish 'intelligentsia' in the summer of 1942.[140] However, the Poles also showed great mistrust towards the Soviet partisans, as well as Belorussian, Ukrainian and Lithuanian nationalist forces.[141] In areas such as the Naliboki forest, the Polish Underground formed their own partisan units and there was sporadic co-operation with Soviet partisan forces. In response to German deportations in June 1943 about 40 Poles left their homes in villages near Derevna to join the detachment known as the 'Polish Legion' in the forest.[142] During the course of 'Operation Hermann' in the summer of 1943 the Germans reported that a number of Polish partisans were destroyed, captured or driven westwards into a pocket.[143] At this time the Poles began to complain of being betrayed by their Soviet comrades in arms.[144] Equally, Jewish partisans under Soviet leadership reported being attacked by members of the 'Polish Legion' from September 1943, after the arrival of officers sent by the exile government in London.[145]

As the return of Soviet power to the former territory of eastern Poland became more likely, friction mounted between the Soviet and Polish partisan groups. By the autumn of 1943 these tensions increasingly broke out into open conflict.[146] The Polish government in exile sought to establish its authority within the eastern territories before the advance of the Red Army; Polish reports complained of 'wild looting' by the Soviets against the Polish population, driving them into the towns.[147] One of the local *AK* commanders, who had also been a commander in the police, forbade all contacts with the Soviet partisans. He told his subordinates that 'these were enemies who had to be fought. After the retreat of the Germans, we were to continue fighting in the rear of the Red Army.'[148]

By the end of 1943 the Soviet partisan commanders in turn insisted that the Poles subordinate themselves to the 'legal' pro-Soviet government in Moscow under Wanda Wasilewska. In surprise attacks the leaders of the Polish partisan units were arrested by the Soviets; some were taken to Moscow and others were killed. Captured other ranks of the 'Polish Legion' were disarmed and conscripted into Soviet units.[149]

The Germans were aware of these rivalries and attempted to turn them to their advantage. At the end of 1943 Polish partisans in the Vilnius district opened negotiations with the Germans as they came under increasing pressure from Soviet partisans. The Poles offered to clear the area of Soviet units in return for weapons, medicines, freedom of movement and the ability to recruit in the area. They also sought German support in their on-going struggle for power against the Lithuanians in Vilnius.[150] At the same time some Polish units still fought fierce battles with the Germans and especially their Lithuanian police auxiliaries, who committed excesses against the Polish population.[151] Following the German retreat there began a new period of war against the [Soviet] invaders by the remnant Polish Underground forces which had escaped 'incorporation' into the Red Army.[152]

A number of rival nationalist groups organized partisan activity in Ukraine apart from the communists. Ukrainain Nationalist forces were divided between supporters of Bandera (OUN-B), Melnik (OUN-M) and the partisan leader, Borovets. These groups fought against the Germans, Soviets and Poles with varying degrees of intensity, depending on the changing political situation.[153] In Polesia and Volhynia there were also elements of the Polish Underground movement. The Polish organizations were concerned first and foremost with the protection of their communities against attacks by Ukrainian 'bandits'.[154] In addition there were Soviet partisan units operating in Ukraine, especially within the pre-1939 Soviet borders. The conflicting political aims of these various organizations resulted in frequent fights between rival partisan groups, as well as attacks against the German occupying forces. One reason for the reluctance of Ukrainian units to declare open war on the Germans remained a fear of the consequences for the local Ukrainian population.[155]

Like the Poles, the Ukrainian nationalists also adopted a policy of infiltrating the German police and administration with the aim of gaining weapons and local influence. Subsequently many deserted to the *UPA* (Ukrainian Resistance Army) in the forest; for instance, in March 1943 some 6000 Ukrainian policemen deserted with their equipment following a call from the nationalist leadership.[156]

At the beginning of 1943 detachments of the *UPA* also began to attack Polish villages, massacring the unarmed population. The situation in Volhynia was described in the Polish Underground press in May 1943 as follows:

> Volhynia is the scene of the insane, savage massacre of the Poles. It surpasses all conception. According to information which is not exaggerated, in the three districts of Sarny, Kostopol and Rovno, where the gangs prevail, about 2000 Poles have been killed. Entire Polish villages which did not manage to defend themselves or to flee, have perished. Whole gangs of Ukrainians, sometimes numbering up to several hundred persons, composed mainly of people from the surrounding villages, often led by the militia, surround a village and murder everyone, they burn the buildings, looting what there is. The most gruesome are the squads of 'axe-men', by which the bodies of innocent victims are butchered.[157]

According to a contemporary German report, in May 1943 Ukrainian 'bandits' murdered the Polish population in the village of Horodets, near Sarny, to the last man.[158] The *Generalkommissar* in Volhynia-Podolia noted in June 1943 that:

> Many Polish families were wiped out and whole Polish villages burned down during the reporting period. It should be stressed that the greater part of the Ukrainian population take part in this. Fighting against these partisans is made considerably harder as during the day they play the role of peaceful peasants.[159]

In response the Polish Underground formed self-defence squads in Polish villages. Poles from isolated villages fled to the larger Polish settlements, enjoying German protection in some places.[160]

Subsequently the pattern of massacres gradually spread further to the west, encompassing Galicia by late 1943.[161] Soviet partisan units appeared in Volhynia at this time. These squads were also hostile towards the Polish Underground, attacking detachments of Polish partisans and murdering their commanders. Efforts by the Poles to establish contact and co-operate with the Soviets came to nothing.[162] In the second half of 1943 the Ukrainians, disappointed by the Germans in their expectation of building an independent Ukrainian state, commenced more frequent attacks against German police posts and detachments.[163] The situation in Volhynia has been described by some commentators as 'a war of all against all'; partisan warfare did not cease here with the arrival of the Red Army in 1944.[164]

The unquestioned losers of the partisan conflict were the peasants who lived and worked in the contested areas. Their desperate plight is summed up by the words of the village elder of Okuninovo, south of Baranovichi, who complained:

> We live between the hammer and the anvil. Today we are forced to obey the partisans or they will kill us, tomorrow we will be killed by the Germans for obeying them. The nights belong to the partisans, but during the days we are in no-man's land. Oh, I know the partisans can protect us now, but for how long?

About a year later his village was wiped off the face of the earth. A few survivors brought the terrible news that 290 villagers, including women and children, had been killed. They had been herded into the community hall and burned to death.[165]

Even German reports occasionally reflected some sympathy for the plight of the local peasants. In March 1943 a report on the situation in the Slonim district noted that in the countryside:

> a peasant has no choice but either to be robbed and possibly murdered by the partisans in due course, or to be rounded up for work in the *Reich* or even shot by a German police unit during the 'cleansing' of a partisan-infested area. In this way conditions have been created, which if any sort of comparison is possible, without doubt can only be compared with the conditions of the German peasant during the Thirty Years War.[166]

Nevertheless the pressure from above for German units to submit successful reports about their anti-partisan operations no doubt encouraged the tendency towards indiscriminate reprisals. This was especially true of *Wehrmacht* units and mobile police formations, which were assigned to an area for a short period and did not have time to get to know the local conditions. A former partisan has recalled with regard to German reprisal actions: 'It was difficult to fight against the partisans even for the regular German troops, so often whole villages with all the inhabitants were annihilated, and the Germans and the police would report to the higher command that a certain number of "partisans" had been destroyed.'[167]

The collaborationist local police formations were generally better informed about which villages were actively supporting the partisans. On occasions, however, their attacks against local villages were just as brutal as those conducted by German units. Their participation in killing innocent women and children takes on another quality insofar as they were killing close neighbours, relatives and even former friends. In these actions the dominant role was played by the police volunteers, who had committed themselves to the Germans and received rewards and promotions for their loyalty. These men were clearly the most active, together with a minority of the conscripts who acted from motives of personal revenge.

In general German collective reprisal actions did more to alienate the local population than the more selective attacks of the partisans. This was combined with effective Soviet propaganda campaigns, which appealed to national patriotism as against the destructive self-interest characteristic of German policies. As one Soviet appeal directed towards Nazi collaborators explained: 'The German fights against culture, against progress, he burns our villages, he destroys the weak and old as well defenceless women and children. The question is: why do you serve the German?'[168]

Leon Berk, a Jewish partisan doctor, forcefully rebuts any simple attempt to make a direct comparison between Soviet partisan violence and the aggressive destruction unleashed by the German invasion:

> Under no circumstances can I equate the excesses committed by the partisans with the crimes against humanity committed by Nazi Germany. The killings, however appalling they were, which took place in the forest, were an instinctive defence reaction which, with time, evolved into an orgy of vengeance exacted by free, courageous people against a vicious invader who, in the name of spurious racial superiority, intended the deliberate and systematic destruction of a great nation.[169]

Partisan attacks in the occupied territories increased commensurately with German setbacks at the Front. Forced recruitment into the *Schutzmannschaft* and mutual reprisals against families on both sides intensified the violent struggle, in which innocent civilians often bore the brunt of the casualties. In Belorussia and Ukraine hundreds of villages were razed to the ground.

Even before the German retreat, effective control had been lost over much of the countryside in the 'occupied' east. The most serious consequence of this for the Germans was its effect on morale in the rear areas, which also undermined their ability to resist the Soviet advance. Like the aerial bombardment of Germany, it is impossible to measure precisely the contribution of partisan resistance in the east to Allied victory. Some Soviet historians, like the partisan commanders in their own reports, have tended to inflate the practical significance of the Soviet partisan contribution. Nevertheless, it probably deserves more credit than it has received from many western historians hitherto.[170] When the Red Army drove German forces out of Belorussia and northern Ukraine in 1944, it was with considerable practical and psychological support from their own Soviet partisan forces.[171]

8 Post-War Fates of Collaborators and Survivors

In many respects the story of the local police has remained untold. Mostly uprooted from their homes, the few Jewish survivors engaged themselves in rebuilding their lives; many have been reluctant to burden their children with too much of their difficult past. Their memories have been preserved quietly in Memorial books, memoirs and court depositions. Former policemen have also remained silent about their wartime experiences. Even in the former Soviet Union, the trials of numerous collaborators were quickly overshadowed by a monolithic Soviet historiography, which stressed heroic resistance to the invader and played down the extent of local collaboration. Geography and post-war developments explain how many pieces of the puzzle have been kept secret for the last 30 or 50 years.

As the Red Army advanced westwards in 1943 and 1944, the German civil administration was already disintegrating. For local policemen the fear of Soviet retribution was sufficient to persuade most to leave with the Germans. The story of their retreat and subsequent fate is a largely unknown odyssey that took many to new lives in the West. Those who remained behind or returned after the war, by contrast, generally encountered the full rigour of the Soviet penal system.

Jewish survivors greeted the Soviet liberation with mixed feelings. Joy at driving the Germans from their homeland was tempered by the unprecedented sense of loss in their close-knit communities. Lingering hostility among the local population and the feeling that their home towns had become graveyards encouraged large numbers to emigrate, first to Poland and then, via Germany, Austria and Italy, to Israel and the West.[1] Here they started again from scratch, often with much of the same vigour which had helped them to survive.

For the majority of peasants in Belorussia and Ukraine the renewed change of masters was not as important as the end of the war. The massive destruction of people and property during the German occupation took more than 20 years to make good. Forced labourers returning from Germany were questioned by the Soviet authorities on their return and treated as potential spies; some were also punished for their alleged disloyalty. A comparison of the post-war fates of individual participants helps to explain why much of this story has remained buried for almost 50 years due to the enduring suspicions of the 'Cold War'.

By the spring of 1943 the Germans had begun their retreat from eastern Ukraine and attempted to evacuate the local police units with them. Initially

148

the evacuated policemen were incorporated directly into similar police format-ions further to the rear. For example, the *Schutzmannschaft* in the area of Lipsk in western Belorussia in 1944 contained a large proportion of former *OD* men from the area of Yezerishche north of Vitebsk.[2] A similar pattern can also be found in Ukraine: during the course of the retreat in the autumn of 1943 many policemen from the Kharkov and Kiev regions were trans-ferred to the *Schutzmannschaft* in the Zhitomir area.[3]

As the Front moved further west towards the River Bug, the Germans prepared for the removal of everything of value, to deny its use to the Red Army. According to a military order issued in December 1943 in Ukraine, it was intended to evacuate all men capable of bearing arms between the ages of 16 and 65.[4] Experience had taught the Germans that the Soviets would conscript almost all men of military age into the Red Army. With regard to the local police, orders were issued in February 1943 that in the event of a withdrawal, the local *Schutzmannschaft* was to be retreated under German leadership to prevent desertion to the partisans.[5]

An indication of the extent of German destruction on their retreat can be gained from the Soviet Extraordinary Commission report for the town of Kobryn:

> On their withdrawal they [the Germans] blew up and burned down two brick works, three steam mills, a tannery, a sawmill, a power station, two railway stations, eight railway bridges, two bridges on a highway across the River Mukhovets, two locks on the Dnepr–Bug canal. They destroyed all the railway stock, telegraph and telephone communications and equip-ment, the radio network and a cinema, which they took away with them to Germany.[6]

In the area south of Brest, all the available cattle were rounded up and driven westwards in a large 'trek' together with the local police: for instance, in the village of Lipenki some 50 local inhabitants were rounded up and compelled to escort the cattle on the initial stages of the journey across the River Bug. Most of these escorts managed to slip away or were released to return home a few days later.[7] One local inhabitant recalls: 'I remember a number of people were ordered to take their horses and carts to the town centre where they were loaded up with police, Germans and their belongings and local men were forced to take them over the Bug to escape the advancing Russian Army.'[8]

Given the growing tendency for members of the auxiliary police to flee to the partisans taking their weapons with them, there remained a reluctance to deploy these forces in direct combat against the Soviets, where the oppor-tunity for desertion appeared greatest. Thus in 1944 efforts were made to transfer them to other fronts where manpower was also in short supply.

Retreat paths have been reconstructed for several local police units. From the small police post of about 30 *Schutzmänner* in the town of Gnivan near

Vinnitsa, the fate of 16 members is known. Three were killed in combat with the Russians during the Soviet occupation of the town in March 1944. Ten others remained in the Soviet Union and were punished after the war, at least six following service in the Red Army. These men were ordinary policemen who received sentences from 15 to 25 years, with most serving at least six until the widespread amnesty in 1955.[9] The three senior Ukrainian NCOs all retreated with the Germans and served subsequently in the Air Defence Police (*Luftschutzpolizei*) in Hanover in 1944–45.

A documentary trail has been uncovered which reveals the precise route these three men took to get to Germany. A large number of *Schutzmänner* from the Zhitomir district were amongst a group of 3351 Ukrainian policemen loaded up by rail from a collection point at Kamionka, near Lvov, in April 1944. Many of the unmarried policemen were scheduled to go to Estonia, but the remainder, most with their wives and children, were destined for major cities in the *Reich*, such as Nuremberg and Salzburg. A group of 175 men were sent to Hanover.[10] Those sent to Germany served as air raid wardens, to assist in dealing with the extensive damage resulting from Allied bombing.[11]

Records in the Hanover archives confirm that former Ukrainian *Schutzmannschaft* personnel from Gnivan and other police posts in the Zhitomir region were registered there in 1945.[12] A roster for the police in Hanover from August 1944 includes the names of over 100 former *Schutzmänner*. Many of these men were from the Zhitomir, Poltava and Kharkov districts.[13] After the war, of the three former NCOs from Gnivan, one emigrated to Australia, one to the USA and one to the UK.[14]

A similar retreat path can be reconstructed for Ukrainian and German police personnel from the local posts in the Kirovograd district. According to Soviet trial records, many of the Ukrainian policemen deserted on their retreat westwards. One escaped only a few kilometres from home, another at Tiraspol, north of Odessa and another near the River Dnestr on the Romanian border. Only one of the *Schutzmänner* who was tried by the Soviets remained with his unit all the way through Rumania to Hungary. From here he was transferred to Königsberg to dig trenches and work as a fireman, before being captured by the Red Army.[15]

Documentary evidence indicates that the area around Kirovograd was recaptured by the advancing Red Army in mid-March 1944. By then units of the *Gendarmerie* and *Schutzmannschaft* from Rural Police Commander (*KdG*) Nikolayev were already retreating westwards to the Romanian border. At the end of June 1944 Police Rifle Regiment 38 was formed from these forces, incorporating many ethnic German local policemen and Gendarmes from southern Ukraine.[16]

Not all of the retreated forces were incorporated into Police Rifle Regiment 38. The remaining Ukrainian local police, redesignated as *Hiwis*, were formed into three Police Volunteer Commandos 'Black Sea', with only a few German police officers in command.[17] At the end of August 1944 the collapse of the German position in Romania caused these police formations to retreat rapidly towards Hungary. In early September 1944 elements of Police Rifle Regiment 38 regrouped near the towns of St George and Ill-yefalva in what is now central Romania.[18]

During the retreat Police Rifle Regiment 38 was reduced to battlegroup units named after unit commanders, such as Captain Saurenbach. These units were then reorganized into *SS* Police Regiment 8 by November 1944.[19] Elements of *SS* Police Regiment 8 were located near Budapest in Hungary in November and December 1944.[20] Loss and situation reports at this time indicate that the Regiment was not in good shape. Further loss reports filed from Czechoslovakia in February 1945 indicate that the Regiment had been removed from the line to reorganize.[21] Some men from the Regiment ended up near Stettin in North Germany at the end of the war. From here they attempted to escape westwards, to avoid capture by the Soviets.

The path of retreat taken by many of the Belorussians serving in *Schutzmannschaft* units in early 1944 can also be recreated in some detail. One *Gendarme* from Mir recalls the initial retreat:

> We left Mir on 1 July 1944. It was mid-day. We drove towards Zhukovichi via Usha. When we arrived in Zhukovichi in the evening, we could see that Mir was on fire. It must have been captured or it could have been the *Schnaps* distillery on the Mir estate burning. Our platoon went towards Bialystok. The Mir station travelled alone, together with the 60 to 80 local volunteers and some of the civilian population. I think we met men from other stations in Novaya Mysh.[22]

A policeman, serving then in Novaya Mysh, used the retreat to evacuate his family before merging into the peasantry further west:

> At the end of June 1944 there was the evacuation of the police station and we were taken with our families to the west. We travelled in carts. I don't know what happened to the *Jagdzug*. In the area of Ostroleka I managed to escape together with my wife and [two other families]... We dressed in plain clothes and threw away our arms. We stopped in the region of Ciechanow and started to work on an estate.[23]

On the first stage of the retreat, many former *Schutzmänner* arrived in East Prussia on 'treks' together with their wives and families. Here they were given the option of remaining to work on defence construction and local farms, or of joining the 30 *Waffen Grenadier* Division of the *SS*. Many Belorussian policemen opted for the 30 *Waffen SS* Division, leaving their families behind in East Prussia.[24] The Division was transferred in August from Rosenberg in East Prussia to France by rail, arriving via Dijon in Chalon-sur-Sâone.[25] Max Eibner, the former *Gendarmerie* Captain in Baranovichi, also served as an officer in the 30 *Waffen SS*.[26]

The history of the 30 *Waffen SS* Division as a fighting unit is less than glorious. Soon after their arrival in France (in late August 1944) there was a mutiny, in which some of the Belorussians killed their officers and fled to join the French partisans.[27] As a result part of the remaining personnel of the Division were sent to a punishment camp near Dachau. One former Gendarme recalls:

> At this time...[some *Schutzmänner*] disappeared for 24 hours. We suspected that they had made contact with the enemy. When we were retreating again, there was another mutiny, only in the 10th company. Schmied and Gayda were killed. All the local volunteers, except for about five or ten, escaped into the woods. In Dôle we were loaded on to trains again and transported in the direction of Munich. Here the rest of the local volunteers were sent to a concentration camp.[28]

A former *Schutzmann*, who subsequently returned home from England after the war, has also given his version of this event:

> In France, the soldiers of the 1st company of our junior leaders school killed all their officers and sergeants and went off into the forests and hills to the French partisans. Because of this all our ammunition was taken away and we were given only rifles, but no cartridges for them. We were housed in a concentration camp which was guarded by Germans. We were there for about three weeks.[29]

Of those who went over to the French partisans at this time, one company consisted of runaway policemen from the Mir *rayon*.[30]

Despite this experience, many former local policemen soon found themselves in the front line. From 20 November 1944, the 30 *Waffen SS* Division became involved in fighting in France, just to the west of the River Rhine and close to the Swiss border. Poorly equipped and with no grudge against the western Allies, many former *Schutzänner* were captured on this sector from 21 to 27 November 1944. Hundreds were recorded as missing in action as American tanks overran their positions.[31]

In fact most of these former policemen deserted or surrendered without a fight. The entries in the War Diary of the German 19th Army at the end of November record the dubious contribution of these foreign troops to the defence of the *Reich*: 'The 30 *Waffen SS* Division has become completely unreliable. It partly fires on its own troops.' A more detailed report notes:

> The centre of the Front is seriously endangered by the poor condition of the 30 *Waffen SS* Division and the loss of Galfingue... The Russians of the

30 *Waffen SS* Division run away as soon as an enemy tank appears. Also many deserters in the last few days. A group of captured Russians in Galfingue from the baggage train took up arms against the German troops during the course of a counter-attack.[32]

One former *Schutzmann* subsequently explained his desertion in France on 27 November 1944 in the following words:

> I fled from the Germans during their retreat just at the French border as I was afraid that if I did it earlier they would shoot my family. That is also why I did not run away to the partisans in Ukraine. For example the family of a policeman was shot after he ran away to the partisans.[33]

For some members of the 30 *Waffen SS* Division deserting to the Allies almost seemed like a dream:

> In view of the fact that I was very exhausted I lay down in a hayrick, where I fell asleep... I slept till about mid-day and when I woke up I saw the Americans in the village. I left my weapon and belt in the hay and came out into the street. An American soldier who met me asked me in English 'German?', to which I replied 'Polish'. Then a second American came up to me and began talking to me in Polish, which he spoke well... The American asked me where I came from, to which I replied, from Baranovichi province, and that I was not Polish but Belorussian. This American told me that in two days' time we would all be in the Polish Army.[34]

Many former men of the 30 *Waffen SS* were transferred to the Free Polish (Anders) Army within a month or so and sent to serve against the Germans in Italy in early 1945. After the end of the war, the British became concerned about the attitude of a possible communist government in Italy. The British government decided to bring back to the UK those members of the Polish Army who did not wish to be repatriated to a communist Poland. This measure was also partly intended to assist with the labour shortage in Britain at that time. It is perhaps understandable, however, that most of those who had served with the Germans were reluctant to return to a communist-dominated eastern Europe.

Of the former Polish Army men who came to Britain, some subsequently migrated to Canada, the USA or South America, although the larger part remained in the UK.[35] The nucleus of the Polish Army had been formed from 74 000 men who were released from Soviet captivity and made their way via Persia and North Africa in 1942 to fight against the Germans in the Italian campaign.[36] These men also had a special reason for not wishing to fall back into Soviet hands. They were joined by many men recruited in Europe as deserters from the German Armed

Forces or released from forced labour for the Germans.[37] It should also be remembered that the pre-1939 borders of Poland included much of modern-day Lithuania, Belorussia and Ukraine. Therefore, it was not un-common for persons of these nationalities to be recruited into the Free Polish Army together even with some ethnic Germans born within Poland.

The *Schutzmänner* who escaped to the West included many of the NCOs and local police chiefs. They generally fared much better than the men who remained behind. Investigations were commenced immediately by the Soviet authorities to track down and investigate people who had collaborated with the enemy. Severe punishments were given to those who had sworn an oath to the Germans and borne arms, regardless of their actual activities. In this way many who were only conscripted late in the occupation and participated in anti-partisan patrols faced as much as ten years of penal servitude. A large proportion of the main culprits, meanwhile, managed to avoid punishment through flight.

For some policemen the change of location during the retreat offered the possibility of escaping detection: for instance, one former policeman from Polonka fled with the Germans to East Prussia where he was assigned to work on a farm. Subsequently he was mobilized into the Red Army, from which he soon deserted. He was then caught and sentenced to 7 years' corrective labour for desertion, of which he served three, before entering Poland in 1948 through repatriation.[38] Another man deserted directly to the Soviet partisans in June 1944, before being enlisted and wounded in the Red Army. Like many others, he was not tried until he returned home from military service and was identified by his neighbours.[39]

From the Novaya Mysh police post, where Poles were heavily repre-sented, more than 20 policemen were tried after the war in Poland. It is probable that a similar number were tried in Belorussia, although research efforts have uncovered only about ten Soviet trial files. More than eight local policemen from this district are known to have escaped to the West.

For the larger *Schutzmannschaft* post in the Mir *rayon* a more comprehen-sive analysis of the post-war fates of policemen has been constructed on the basis of extensive research (see Table 8.1). This sample, which includes men recruited towards the end of the occupation, produced the surprising figure of at least one-third ending up in western countries. Of those who remained untraced it is probable that they were killed in the war or remained in the Soviet Union or Poland. The mass desertion of Mir policemen from the 30 *Waffen SS* in France in the autumn of 1944 clearly helps to account for the large numbers in the West. It is remarkable that nearly all the NCOs managed to escape; these men were quite certain of the fate which awaited them if they returned home.

Table 8.1   Post-war fates of members of the Mir *rayon* police

	Schutzmänner	NCOs	Total
Killed in action with partisans	29	–	29
Killed on the way to the partisans	2	–	2
Escaped to the West	93	11	104
Died in a German prison	2	–	2
Remained in the East	75	1	76
No information	128	1	129
Total	329	13	342

Source: WCU 93/1 Appendix II/1–11.

A few former policemen succeeded in bringing their wives out to join them in western countries in the post-war years. More common were acts of bigamy, whereby new marriages were celebrated without an annulment being obtained from partners left in the east. Occasional letters were written to friends and relations in Poland or the Soviet Union. There was a real danger, however, that this would only reveal their whereabouts to the *KGB*, who held files open for a number of years.

Many former policemen found cover amongst the millions of Displaced Persons (DPs) in German camps at the end of the war. More than 600 000 Soviet DPs chose to remain in the West.[40] The majority of former Soviet DPs had been deported to Germany for forced labour. Therefore, it was relatively easy for collaborators to claim that they had worked on their farms until deported by the Germans and had since lost their papers (or obtained forged ones). Despite rules excluding former collaborators from DP status and therefore also access to emigration under UN regulations, many slipped through the net. Effective screening was very difficult given the vast numbers involved. The available records of the Berlin Document Centre and the War Crimes Suspects (CROWCASS) lists contained very little information regarding collaborators from the east.[41] A number of former policemen was undoubtedly amongst the roughly 90 000 European Voluntary Workers who emigrated to Britain between 1945 and 1950.[42] Even the Jewish groups who argued strongly for DP immigration into the USA thereby unintentionally made it easier for some Nazi collaborators from eastern Europe to enter America amongst almost 400 000 DPs who arrived by 1952.[43]

The fate of the remaining civilian population left behind in the Soviet Union was in material terms unenviable. The local economy was in ruins, not least due to the loss of Jewish craftsmen and traders. The Soviet planned economy was able to distribute staple goods with some degree of equity, but any 'luxuries' became the prerogative of those with Party connections. For many the risks of the black market had to be run in order to make some sort of a living.

The tale of a woman from near Derechin, who married a former partisan, reflects the material position of many peasants at the end of the war:

> S. was older than me, but we went out with the same group. I had another boy-friend. But after the war S. returned, poor as a church mouse, he had nothing but an old house which had to be rebuilt. The reason was, that when his family were killed, the police had taken everything, even the clothes from his house, they had even taken the chickens, wrung their necks and threw them on to the carts. I felt sorry for S. and married him.[44]

The post-war experiences of surviving Jews from Belorussia and Ukraine provides an interesting counter-point to that of the local policemen. Many headed west, not in order to escape punishment, but also to put the past behind them. A number of factors influenced their decision to emigrate, not least the hopes they held for emigration to Palestine.

Even during the last days of the occupation there were still dangers for the Jews living in the forests. As the Red Army started its offensive in the summer of 1944 the partisan units were sometimes confronted with German front-line troops fleeing west to escape encirclement. For instance, the Bielski camp in the Naliboki forest was surprised one morning by a large force of German soldiers. Nine partisans were killed as the Germans fired in all directions and threw grenades into the huts. However, the Germans were only passing through and were subsequently counter-attacked by another Soviet partisan unit. Red Army troops arrived the next day hot on the heels of the Germans and were greeted warmly as liberators.[45]

For many partisans the arrival of the Red Army meant conscription into this force and months more of dangerous service pursuing the Germans to Berlin. Many gallant partisan fighters were killed and wounded in achieving final victory. Fearing this outcome, Tuvia Bielski disbanded his force against orders, enabling some men to avoid recruitment by gaining local jobs exempted from conscription. He himself escaped to Palestine via Romania after being denounced to the *NKVD*.[46]

For the Jews returning to their villages from the forests it was a very sad homecoming:

> I remember the day of the emancipation [liberation]. It was a rainy day. We and the two children walked on foot after the waggon. It was a sad day. When we entered our village, I had the feeling that we had to apologize for being alive. Our whole village was just one long street; in the center dwelled the Jews and on the outskirts the Gentiles, the Belorussians, who stood and looked at us as at ghosts who came from another world. They had already reconciled themselves to the fact that no Jewish foot would ever step on the soil of the village.[47]

In Volhynia, the continuing danger from *UPA* partisans encouraged the surviving Jews to concentrate in the larger towns for safety, especially in Rovno where over 1000 survivors initially gathered. According to Shmuel Spector's calculations only about 3500 survived altogether in this area. By the end of the year, however, a movement of survivors into Poland had begun, which continued over the following years until hardly any native Jews remained.[48] In the immediate post-war years citizens of the former eastern Polish provinces were given the option of being 'repatriated' to within the new Polish borders; many Jews were amongst those who availed themselves of this option.[49] For these Jews, however, Poland was only a staging post for destinations in the West. Continuing anti-Semitism in Poland, culminating in the Kielce pogrom in July 1946, when 42 Jews were killed and many others were injured, encouraged survivors to look further afield for a new home.[50]

An impression of the post-war locations of Belorussian Jews can be gained from the available figures for more than 50 Jewish survivors from the Mir *rayon* (see Table 8.2). The majority migrated to Palestine, where they helped in the establishment of the new state of Israel. Apart from Israel, the USA and Canada were the most popular destinations, despite certain obstacles to immigration there. A few also went to South America which, with South Africa and Australia, were the main other regions taking European migrants.[51] Of three Mir survivors who remained in Poland into the mid-1950s, all three had left by 1970, reflecting the difficulties they encountered establishing themselves there.

Table 8.2   Destinations of (traced) Jewish survivors from Mir

Country	Number
USA	8
Israel	32
South Africa	2
Belorussia	3
Canada	9
Russia	1
Denmark	2
Via Poland	(3)
Total	57

Source: WCU 93/1.

A minority of Jewish survivors remained in the Soviet Union. In Novo-grudok, of a Jewish community of some 6000 souls before the war, currently there are only five remaining.[52] Considerable obstacles to the emigration of Soviet Jews persisted up to 1989, despite some relaxations in the 1970s. Here, as elsewhere in eastern Europe, periodic bouts of anti-Semitism encouraged many to abandon part of their Jewish identity. Even the sufferings of Jews in the Holocaust were largely denied by official Soviet propaganda. Inscriptions on the memorial plaques at many Jewish grave sites described the victims simply as 'peaceful Soviet citizens'.[53]

In the initial weeks and months after the liberation a number of Jews were involved both as investigators and witnesses in the process of identifying local collaborators. Witness statements from Jewish survivors have been found in Soviet trial files from the Baranovichi and Brest areas, mostly dating from the period 1944–45. Oswald Rufeisen recalls preparing a detailed statement on his experiences in the police for the *NKVD* in the autumn of 1944.[54] A female survivor from Davidgrodek worked directly as an investigator with the *NKVD* before subsequently asking for permission to emigrate.[55]

A precise figure for the number of persons tried for collaboration in the Soviet Union is not available, but the number certainly runs into tens of thousands.[56] For those districts studied in detail, criminal case files have been found for a majority of persons known to have served with the Germans and who remained in (or returned to) the Soviet Union after the war. Not only local policemen but also members of the 'Home Guard' (*Samookhova*), and especially village elders or those serving in the civil administration, were likely to be punished. The usual sentence was at least 10 or 15 years' hard labour for service with the Germans, with up to 25 years or even death for those convicted of more serious crimes against the state and civilian population. Many were released in the mid-1950s, having served between five and ten years' hard labour.

In 1947 the death penalty was temporarily abolished in the Soviet Union, as it was deemed to be no longer required in times of peace.[57] This meant that some collaborators convicted for murder lived to serve long sentences in Soviet jails. The death penalty was re-introduced, however, by 1950 and a few war criminals were still being executed in the 1980s. For instance, the chief of the local police in Ustinovka near Kirovograd, Mefody Marchik, was uncovered by a local resident who travelled to another town in Ukraine and recognized him on the street. Following a detailed investigation, Marchik was tried and executed in 1958.[58]

An impression of Soviet interrogation methods can sometimes be gained from the complaints of defendants. Individual prisoners complained of psychological pressure, such as repeated night-time interrogations and sleep deprivation designed to induce a confession.[59] Dieter Pohl has identified numerous indications of mistreatment of prisoners during Soviet interrogations.[60] It would not be surprising if some *NKVD* officials gave the former policemen a taste of their own medicine in terms of physical beatings whilst in custody.[61] Often short statements appear to have taken many hours to prepare and are accompanied by unsteady signatures. The almost ritual admissions of guilt found in many cases inspire little confidence in the reliability of such confessions. In most cases examined, however, there appears to be little doubt that the suspects had served the Germans in some form. Often documentary evidence, in the form of captured German service papers (*Personalbogen*), is included with the trial records.

With regard to the statements by local witnesses rather than suspects, errors in the transcripts appear to be more often the result of carelessness or a lack of proper education among the interrogators rather than specific manipulation. In the immediate post-war period trained staff and even paper were in short supply. The levels of proof required by Soviet procedures were not strict and much evidence was in the form of hearsay. Nevertheless, detailed investigations were conducted and some attempt was made to establish the facts, if the offences charged were as much political as criminal in nature. Wearing enemy uniform, swearing an oath and going out on raids were all criminalized, as well as participation in specific crimes.

More detailed records are available for Polish trials from those areas of eastern Poland handed over to the Soviet Union in 1945. Records concerning more than 400 individuals can be examined at the office of the former Polish Main Commission in Warsaw (INRW) for the western districts of Belorussia and Ukraine. Most date from the late 1940s and early 1950s, but a further wave of trials was conducted in the 1960s and 1970s, with a handful of cases thereafter. For both the Soviet and Polish trials, there is a notable improvement in the thoroughness of the investigations and the reliability of the conclusions by the 1960s. In the Polish trials there are instances of persons being acquitted and a more careful assessment of the degree of personal responsibility is evident in the later cases.

As both perpetrators and victims fled to Poland, some war criminals were revealed there as a result of chance encounters. One collaborator from Davidgrodek was recognized on the market square at Klazk in Lower Silesia by a Jewish survivor. Through this man the Polish authorities obtained information which led to the arrest and punishment of a number of senior collaborators from Davidgrodek.[62] A former survivor from Mir also recalls being called to a police station in Poland to assist in identifying local collaborators under arrest.[63]

What has been the attitude of the survivors towards their former tormentors? Not unnaturally considerable bitterness remains with many survivors, who see some of their former neighbours as the willing agents of the Nazis in their brutal murder campaign against the Jews. Partisan memoirs often stress the element of personal vengeance in actions taken against the Germans and local police. The decision of Jews to emigrate was not uninfluenced by the fear that anti-Semitism remained strong amongst the local population. However, the view of many Jews who have assisted with the often vexing legal enquiries can be better summed up in the words of one survivor: 'I feel justice should be done to those criminals who have been caught, and I am upset when it is not done. But I do not have revenge in me. Revenge would change me to being one of them.'[64] This is the same desire for 'justice rather than vengeance' which has inspired Simon Wiesenthal's unremitting investigations from his personal office in Vienna.[65]

Unfortunately, with regard to local police collaborators it is not possible to say that justice has been done. Like the German punitive policies which often struck only the innocent civilians left behind in a 'partisan' village once the perpetrators had left, so the blanket nature of Soviet justice generally caught those least guilty, who had not thought it necessary to flee to the West. Meanwhile the chief collaborators often made it safely to Germany or an Allied PoW camp. Here many were protected from return to the Soviets, due to Allied fears that innocent people might also be punished.

Equally regrettable is the fact that Jewish survivors in Europe at the end of the war encountered much greater obstacles to emigration than other eastern European nationalities. Refugees from the Baltic states, for instance, were viewed as good 'racial stock' by western governments when it came to the selection of immigrants. The advent of the 'Cold War' and the exploitation of war crimes issues for propaganda and espionage purposes by the communist states permitted many collaborators to complete their lives unrevealed in the West. Only after the end of the 'Cold War' was it possible to investigate and uncover a handful of the local police collaborators who were then still alive. These investigations are now reaching their natural conclusion: soon only history can be their judge.

9 Conclusion: Local Collaboration in the Holocaust

There is a growing recognition amongst historians of the need to modify some of the widely received perceptions of how the Holocaust was implemented. Between 1941 and 1943, according to Hilberg's cautious calculations, approximately 2 000 000 Jews were killed within the May 1941 borders of the Soviet Union, primarily by shooting in pits close to their homes.[1] The role played by the *Einsatzgruppen* has become infamous on the basis of their own detailed documentation. However, there was a 'Second Wave' of killings in the summer and autumn of 1942. In the areas under German civil administration in western Belorussia and Ukraine this 'Second Wave' proved more destructive than the first, comprising the elimination of all but a few main work ghettos. The Nazi aim was to cleanse these regions of their Jewish inhabitants: to render them '*Judenfrei*'.[2]

The organization and implementation of the 'Second Wave' in these areas was more thorough than the 1941 actions; it was directed and co-ordinated by the regional *SSPF*s, together with the established posts of the Security Police. In order to carry out this terrible project in the vast eastern expanses considerable assistance was required from units of the Order Police and indigenous collaborators. Not only mobile Order Police and *Schutzmannschaft* battalions were involved; great reliance was also placed on the German *Gendarmerie* and their local police collaborators (*Schutzmannschaft-Einzeldienst*), who formed the police authority in every *rayon* throughout the region.

The participation of the *Gendarmerie* and local police consisted mainly in rounding up the Jews and cordoning off the killing sites in support of the Security Police. Occasionally members of these local units participated directly by pulling the trigger at the pits. However, the *Gendarmerie* and *Schutzmannschaft* were usually left to finish the job afterwards; they searched diligently over the following days for any Jews who had escaped the round-up, murdering those they found: for instance, the Glubokoye Memorial Book records: 'the police did not tire. For days and weeks on end they continued searching for the hidden and fleeing Jews.'[3] A consistent pattern of local police participation has been clearly identified for the regions of Glubokoye, Novogrudok, Polesia, Volhynia and Zhitomir, covering much of the area of Jewish settlement in western Belorussia and Ukraine.

Who were the local collaborators who actively implemented Nazi genocide in the east? In the areas under German civil administration, the active participants came mainly from more than 25 000 men who volunteered for local police service during the first months of the occupation. Of these about 2000 held an NCO rank by July 1942, but many were subsequently promoted in recognition of their services as the *Schutzmannschaft* forces expanded.[4] Their initial motives for joining included revenge against the Soviets and the desire for a regular wage. The nature of the work attracted nationalist activists, ambitious individuals, local hooligans and anti-Semites, even some former criminals. Others were simple peasants who preferred the routine guard duties to hard labour on the land.

The brutal crimes of these local police units have been described in graphic detail within the pages of this book. The wide variety of sources used, including contemporary reports, post-war investigative records and numerous testimonies from Jewish and non-Jewish witnesses, leave no doubt as to the overall pattern. Local police collaborators are described by some witnesses as being more cruel than the Germans in their treatment of the Jews.[5] Many callous acts of slaughter were committed by local policemen against women and children.

Nevertheless certain clear distinctions have to be made within the group of perpetrators. Specific individuals can be identified as 'excessive' killers, who volunteered for 'execution' duties and employed violence for the thrill and sense of power it gave them. These men had no respect for human life. Another significant group were the leaders or local NCOs who issued orders on behalf of the Germans. Not all such leaders were excessively brutal, but they led from the front and were prepared to kill to gain favours and promotion. These main perpetrators were the men most likely to throw in their lot with the Germans and flee to the West; they knew they could expect no mercy on the arrival of the Red Army. The role of the remaining volunteers is less prominent in the sources, with many understandably claiming that they only obeyed orders.

As partisan warfare intensified from the summer of 1942, the Germans increasingly reinforced the ranks of the local police by means of compulsion; they feared that otherwise the young men would join the partisans. These later conscripts proved less willing fighters and were less trusted by the Germans. Some conscripts participated actively in the murders of partisan families, partly out of revenge for losses amongst their own family and friends. Others, however, performed their duties with reluctance, deserting to the partisans when the opportunity arose. Ironically, more of the conscripts remained behind when the Germans retreated; these men endured the harsh punishments applied by the Soviet authorities to any 'collaborators'.

The role of anti-Semitism amongst the active policemen and in the remainder of the population is difficult to assess. Available sources indicate that it was only one amongst several motives which influenced their actions. Other considerations appear to have included personal greed, alcoholism, anti-Communism, careerism, and peer pressure. Both German and local anti-Semitic propaganda was effective in linking the Jews with a supposed 'Judaeo-Bolshevik' conspiracy. This undoubtedly found a receptive audience amongst those who had suffered from Soviet repression. In the former Polish areas the brief Soviet occupation exacerbated ethnic tensions and dissolved social ties due to rapid political and economic change, and especially the effects of Soviet mass deportations. For many Poles the perception of some Jews taking their places as administrators and even policemen was a particular affront. They chose to overlook the fact that Soviet repression affected Jewish businesses, organizations and refugees just as harshly as the Poles.

It remains doubtful, however, that those who participated in Nazi atrocities acted purely from motives of racial hatred. A similar bloodthirstiness and indifference to human life was applied by the local police towards many victims who were not Jews. Gypsies, PoWs, partisan families and even Russians ('easterners') all suffered similar treatment from local police units as 'hostile elements' identified by German policy.

Discrimination against the Jews was an established feature of Russian history. In the late nineteenth and early twentieth century it culminated in violent attacks. During the Russian civil war more than 100 000 Jews were murdered in pogroms conducted predominantly by Polish, Ukrainian and White Guard forces.[6] In times of crisis the Jews had learned to bury their valuables and even take to the woods if necessary to fight the 'pogromchiks'. In times of peace under Polish rule, indigenous anti-Semitism was not sufficient to ignite violent pogroms.[7] Its latent character, however, meant that the Germans encountered few problems in finding sufficient volunteers to assist in the massacres. Other local inhabitants in turn helped themselves to 'ownerless' property, once the Jews had been murdered.

A recurring theme in the recollections of Jewish survivors is the sense of isolation they experienced during the Holocaust. The lack of close ties to the Christians left them with few people to turn to in their time of need. For them betrayal by their neighbours was more disturbing than the hatred of alien Germans with whom they had little direct contact. In a situation where not only local policemen but also some local peasants betrayed Jewish lives for a few kilos of salt,[8] each chance encounter became a matter of life and death. In fact those Jews who survived often received help from several Christians in succession, given at considerable risk to themselves, as most survivors generously acknowledge.[9] It took only one case of betrayal, however, to snuff out the meagre prospects for Jewish survival and resistance.

This element of the perpetrators personally knowing the victims in the small ghettoes of the east lends a gruesome intimacy to the massacres. It does not conform with interpretations of the Holocaust which stress the bureaucratization and impersonalization of mechanized killing.[10] These local massacres in certain respects bear resemblance to the 'ethnic cleansing' of former Yugoslavia, where neighbours were terrorized, expelled and murdered by local militias for motives of nationalistic revenge and personal gain. Since it was not possible for Ukrainians, Belorussians and Poles to establish their own armed forces, many nationalists joined the German auxiliary police with the aim of gaining weapons and training in preparation for struggles yet to come. Of course, the central direction and scale of Nazi genocide as organized by Himmler's police apparatus remains unique to the Holocaust. The incorporation of local forces within this process in the east is deserving of greater recognition. Direct comparisons with more recent 'ethnic cleansing', however, are better suited to the national conflicts which blazed in Volhynia or the Vilnius district in 1943 and 1944. In these areas ancient feuds between Ukrainians, Poles and Lithuanians were re-ignited in the 'power vacuum' which developed as the Red Army closed in.

Without the collaboration of indigenous forces it would undoubtedly have been more difficult for the Germans to implement their plans. One survivor recalls her fear of being recognized when she fled from one massacre to the nearest large town: 'When I escaped to Mir the Jews hid me because they said I had been condemned to death...[as I had] escaped from Turets and since...the policemen from Turets knew me from before they would have immediately recognized me in Mir and killed me right away.'[11]

In this close local environment the reality of the Holocaust was immediately common knowledge. Even the massacres themselves took the form of some macabre ritual, with policemen getting drunk in celebration of their new found wealth and the local Christians sometimes coming 'to watch the "entertainment", which they later described...in minute detail'.[12]

In certain respects the more improvised pogroms, such as those in Mir or Jody in late 1941, demonstrated most clearly the anarchic forces which the Germans had unleashed. At this time there was almost no resistance by the Jews, but without close supervision the eagerness of the local police degenerated into a bloody slaughter on the streets of the town.

The 'Second Wave' was more carefully prepared by the established posts of the Security Police. By the summer of 1942 the Jews were also forewarned; many resisted by hiding in bunkers, attempting to flee or (in some instances) turning on their tormentors with any available arms. The clearing of the ghettoes house by house as witnessed in Slonim or Nesvizh present the most ghastly scenes of the local police rooting out their innocent 'prey'. Many victims were burned alive in the fires that swept the ghettoes. Jews found in hiding, attempting to escape or simply unable to go any further were frequently shot on the spot and left lying in the streets.

The numerical significance of these 'Second Wave' killings, especially in the former Polish areas, should not be underestimated. The initial *Einsatzgruppen* units had passed through quickly in June and July 1941 before the escalation to mass killings took place. According to Shmuel Spector, almost 80 per cent of Jewish deaths in Volhynia came as a result of the ghetto liquidations in the second half of 1942.[13] In the Glubokoye area only a few large-scale actions took place in 1941; most ghettoes were liquidated in the summer of 1942 with only a few specialist workers preserved until 1943. Estimates available for the scale and timing of the actions in Polesia indicate a similar pattern to Volhynia. In the Novogrudok and Minsk regions the combined efforts of the *SS*, Order Police and *Wehrmacht* inflicted greater losses in the autumn of 1941; here too, however, more than 50 per cent of Jewish deaths were inflicted in 1942. The inmates of the few remaining work camps who did not escape were killed or deported in 1943.[14]

In the central Ukrainian regions of Zhitomir, Kiev and Nikolayev, the *Einsatzgruppen* operations supported by the *HSSPF* conducted large-scale actions in most of the major towns in the autumn of 1941. Here a larger proportion of the Jews managed to flee before the German advance, especially from main cities such as Zhitomir and Nikolayev, which had good lines of communications. Nevertheless, numerous actions were conducted in the first half of 1942, directed mainly against the smaller rural ghettoes (as, for instance, in the Zhitomir *Generalkommissariat*). The few remaining rural Jews of the Nikolayev region were also killed at this time. In these actions the local police assisted in rounding up and escorting the Jews to their deaths, as well as in the capture and shooting of Jews found thereafter.

The decision of the German leadership to implement 100 per cent liquidations in most towns in 1942 meant that there was nowhere for surviving Jews to find refuge. They were forced to arm themselves and attempt to survive in the forests. In this way the escaped Jews provided a small but determined impetus to the growing Soviet partisan resistance, especially in Belorussia. The 'Second Wave' came to mean absolute genocide as every Jew hiding in the forest was ruthlessly hunted down with the aid of the local police and peasant informers.

In this way the fate of the surviving Jews became inextricably linked with the evolving partisan struggle. The treatment of PoWs, economic exploitation and deportations to Germany all served to increase dissatisfaction with German rule. Here the *Schutzmannschaft* also played a key role as the instrument of German requisitions and deportation round-ups, together with (often corrupt) local officials. The brutal reputation earned by the *Schutzmannschaft* for beating and robbing local inhabitants did little to enhance the image of the German civil administration.

The nucleus for growing Soviet partisan resistance from the summer of 1942 came from Soviet PoWs, who were driven into the forests by the threat of starvation or being shot. The escape of surviving Jews at this time strengthened the partisan forces, if sometimes they were also robbed and killed by the partisans. Crucial to Jewish survival was access to weapons. What the Jewish partisans lacked in experience and equipment, however, they often made up for in their thirst for revenge. Jewish efforts for survival and resistance deserve recognition for their bravery under the most terrible circumstances.

Once in the forest, the main enemy for the partisans remained the German police and their local collaborators. The continuity of local police participation in murder actions against other sections of the local population apart from the Jews, including the murder of women and children, demonstrates the extent to which the *Schutzmannschaft* served as the willing instrument of German policy. Resistance to German orders and desertion increased, however, especially amongst those forcibly conscripted into the police after the murder of the Jews. Many of the NCOs and volunteers remained loyal to the Germans and escaped with them to the West.

Even after the war, the fate of Jewish survivors and the local police collaborators remained intertwined as the patterns of post-war migration took many towards the same destinations. Failures of international co-operation, as a result of the Cold War, meant that many of the main perpetrators escaped Soviet justice and found refuge in the West. Information regarding their crimes remained mostly concealed until the opening of the archives in the 1990s.

In summary, the 'forensic' analysis of the crimes of the local police using a great variety of new source materials has revealed widespread and active collaboration in the Holocaust. In the predominantly rural districts of Ukraine and Belorussia, at the time of the ghetto 'liquidations' in 1942, the local policemen outnumbered the Gendarmes by between five and ten to one.[15] Other units also participated in the massacres, especially German Order Police and *Schutzmannschaft* battalions for the larger actions; and overall direction lay firmly in the hands of the Security Police, who usually provided the firing squads. Nevertheless, the rounding-up and escorting of large numbers of Jews would have been difficult without the active support of the local police units. Individual local policemen distinguished themselves particularly in the subsequent search for and 'execution' of Jews who went into hiding. As with the German Order Police, there was no shortage of volunteers for the 'Jew hunts' and firing squads.[16]

The willingness of the local policemen to carry out such actions can be seen from a wide variety of sources depicting local policemen acting more or less unsupervised in accordance with German policy. The example of the November 1941 massacre in Mir, examined here in some detail, demonstrates enthusiastic participation in a brutal slaughter conducted on the streets of the town. The numerous eye-witnesses leave no doubt as to the key role played by local police collaborators, who were the only ones clearly able to identify their Jewish neighbours.

A hard core of local police volunteers were amongst the most active participants in shooting Jews found hiding in the ghettoes and forests. In answering the question of how the Holocaust could happen, historians must also take account of collaboration in the east. Local participation in no way diminishes Nazi responsibility for these terrible crimes; however, it became a significant feature in the implementation of the Holocaust in these areas. For many Jewish survivors, the active participation and greed of their neighbours proved especially distressing. In Belorussia and Ukraine it was not only Germans who became 'willing executioners'.

Appendix A: Demography of the Holocaust in the East

Reliable demographic data concerning the Holocaust in the east is especially difficult to obtain. The available census material for Belorussia and Ukraine is presented here to provide an indication of the population of these areas during the 1930s. A number of considerations have to be taken into account in attempting to convert these numbers into an estimate of the Jewish population affected by the German occupation.

The Polish 1931 figures should be increased by about 10 per cent to reflect demographic growth over the following decade. War in 1939 involved the flight of approximately 300 000 Jews from western to eastern Poland; of these probably more than half were amongst those sent to the central and eastern parts of the USSR due to Soviet deportations and other labour projects. Further deductions must be made for the deportation of local inhabitants, recruitment to the Soviet Army and the effects of flight and Soviet evacuation. Evacuation was considerably more effective further east and was proportionately greater from the towns than amongst the rural population. Despite these uncertainties, the 1931 census provides a reasonable base estimate for the number of Jews present in the former districts of eastern Poland on 22 June 1941 (see Tables A.1 and A.2).

The results of the Soviet 1939 census published recently by Mordechai Altshuler (Tables A.3 and A.4) should be treated with the caution appropriate for most Soviet estimates of the Jewish population: that is, the results probably slightly understate Jewish numbers. Nevertheless these detailed figures are most useful, if allowance is also made for subsequent recruitment to the Red Army. The degree of evacuation from the Soviet areas was considerably higher, reportedly exceeding 70 per cent from some large towns in the east. Some of the Jews retreating eastwards were also trapped behind German lines during their flight and therefore might appear as losses in these eastern areas.

According to the available population figures it can be concluded that more than one million Jews were living in 1939 in those areas which came under German civil administration by the end of 1941 (*Weißruthenien*, Volhynia-Podolia, Zhitomir, Kiev and Nikolayev). The 1941 estimates presented here (Table A.5) are intended only as a 'rough guide' to assist in assessing the number of Jews who came under the German civil administration in Belorussia and Ukraine.

How can one estimate the level of Jewish losses? Most available figures for the numbers of persons killed in specific actions constitute estimates made by the Germans, local inhabitants and survivors. These sources must be treated with considerable caution, as numerous examples can be found where they are contradictory and clearly imprecise. A range has been given here to indicate the inevitable uncertainties in the sources. Only a detailed analysis of available information for each location permits a 'rough estimate' to be adduced. The figures presented here are no more than an outline sketch drawn from the many sources referred to elsewhere in this book. They should be viewed sceptically as an initial marker and an inspiration for the more detailed local studies yet to come. A definitive figure for most locations is not to be expected.

The level of Jewish survival for these areas is also problematic, with estimates ranging from 1 to 5 per cent for those trapped by the German occupation. Post-war demographic movements render a precise figure almost impossible. Much work still remains to be done in this field, evaluating and incorporating the newly available Soviet sources into the results of existing research.

Table A.1   Jewish population of Novogrudok province, 1931 census

District	Jews	Total population	% Jewish
Baranovichi	16 074	161 038	9.98
Lida	14 913	183 485	8.13
Nesvizh	8 880	114 464	7.76
Novogrudok	10 462	149 536	7.00
Slonim	12 344	126 510	9.76
Stolpce	6 975	99 389	7.02
Shchuchyn	7 883	107 203	7.35
Volozhin	5 341	015 522	4.62
Total Novogrudok	82 872	1 057 147	7.84

Source: Published results of Polish 1931 census.

Table A.2   Jewish population of eastern Poland, according to adjusted 1931 census figures

District	Jews	Total population	% Jewish
Vilnius	111 000	1 275 900	8.7
Novogrudok	83 000	1 057 100	7.8
Polesia	114 000	1 131 900	10.1
Volhynia	208 000	2 085 600	10.0
Total	516 000	5 550 500	9.3

Note: the western half of the Vilnius district was transferred to Lithuania in 1940; part of Polesia (Pruzhany) was included in Bialystok.
The estimated Jewish population in the former Polish areas which came under German civil administration in Ukraine and *Weißruthenien* during the course of 1941 is 430–470 000. Approximately 540 000 Jews lived in Galicia in June 1941.
Sources: Polish 1931 census results from T. Piotrowski, *Poland's Holocaust*, pp. 346 and 353; D. Pohl, *Nationalsozialistische Judenverfolgung*, p. 9.

Table A.3   Jewish population of Soviet parts of Ukraine, 1939

District	Jews	% Jewish
Kiev	297 409	8.4
Vinnitsa	141 825	6.1
Zhitomir	125 007	7.4
Kamenets-Podolsk	121 335	7.0

Dneprpetrovsk	129 439	5.7
Nikolayev	60 402	5.5
Kirovograd	26 419	2.2
Odessa	233 155	14.2
Moldavia	37 035	6.2
Total (west and central)	1 172 026	
Total	1 532 776	5.0

Source: M. Altshuler, *Distribution of the Jewish Population*, pp. 9–12.

Table A.4   Jewish population of Soviet parts of Belorussia, 1939

District	Jews	% Jewish
Minsk	117 615	9.0
Mogilev	79 739	5.7
Vitebsk	77 173	6.0
Gomel	67 578	7.5
Poles'e	32 987	4.9
Total	375 092	6.7

Source: M. Altshuler, *Distribution of the Jewish Population*, pp. 9–12.

Table A.5   'Rough estimates' for Jewish losses during the First and Second Waves of 1941 and 1942–43 in *Weißruthenien* and Volhynia-Podolia

District	1941 losses	1942–43 losses	1941 estimate
Glubokoye*	5–10 000	40–50 000	60 000
Novogrudok‡	25–35 000	55–75 000	90 000
Minsk†	30–50 000	30–50 000	100 000
Weißruthenien	60–95 000	125–175 000	250 000
Polesia‡	20–30 000	75–85 000	110 000
Volhynia	25–35 000	150–200 000	240 000
Podolia	25–45 000	40–85 000	120 000
Volhynia-Podolia	70–110 000	265–375 000	460 000

* Glubokoye represents the eastern part of the Vilnius district (including Vileyka) not incorporated into Lithuania.
† Minsk does not include eastern parts of the Minsk district under military administration.
‡ Polesia: the northern fringes of the Polish district of Polesia were divided between *Weißruthenien* (Novogrudok) and Bialystok.

Abbreviations for Notes and Archival Sources

AANW	Archive of New Documents, Warsaw
Abt.	*Abteilung* Section
Anl.	*Anlage* Appendix
BA	Federal German Archive (*Bundesarchiv*) Many *Bundesarchiv* documents have recently been transferred from Koblenz to Berlin
BA-MA	*Bundesarchiv-Militärarchiv* Federal German Archive, Military Archive, Freiburg
BDC	Former Berlin Document Center collection
BdO	*Befehlshaber der Ordnungspolizei* Senior Commander of the Order Police
BNAM	Belorussian National Archive, Minsk
Brest Archive	Brest Regional (*oblast*) Archive, Brest
CDJC	Centre for Contemporary Jewish Documentation, Paris
Co.	Company
CSAK	Central State Archive, Kiev
Div.	Division
Dorking	Committal Proceedings in Dorking, England 1996
EM	*Ereignismeldung UdSSR* Events report Soviet Union (*Einsatzgruppen* report)
EWZ	*Einwandererzentrale* German immigration centre
Inf.	Infantry
INRW	Institute for National Remembrance, Warsaw (formerly Polish Main Commission)
KTB	*Kriegstagebuch* War Diary
LSHA	Latvian State Historical Archive, Riga
MGFA	*Militärgeschichtliches Forschungsamt* Military Historical Research Institute
MHAP	Military Historical Archives, Prague
Moreshet	Moreshet Archives, Israel
MRA	Minsk Regional Archive, Minsk
NAW	National Archives, Washington
PAAA	*Politisches Archiv, Auswärtiges Amt*, Political Archive, Foreign Ministry, Bonn
Pol.	Police (Order Police)
PUST	Polish Underground Study Trust, London
Rgt	Regiment
SAL	District Court Lodz, Poland
SAM	Special Archive, Moscow (*Osobi*) (Centre for Historical-Documentary Collections)
SARF	State Archive of the Russian Federation, Moscow
SIU	Special Investigations Unit, Australia
SSA	State Security Archives, Ukraine (formerly KGB)

SSPGF	SS and Police District Leader
Sta	*Staatsanwaltschaft* Public Prosecutor's Office
UKGB	KGB Archives, Belarus
USHMMA	US Holocaust Memorial Museum Archives, Washington DC
Volyn SRA	Volhynian Regional State Archive, Lutsk
WAST	*Wehrmachtauskunftstelle*, Berlin German Armed Forces Personnel Records Office, Berlin
WCU	Metropolitan Police War Crimes Unit, New Scotland Yard
Yivo	Yivo Archives, New York
YV	Yad Vashem Archives, Jerusalem
ZA	Zhitomir *oblast* Archive, Zhitomir
ZSL	*Zentrale Stelle*, Ludwigsburg German Central Office (War Crimes investigation)

Notes

1 The Soviet Occupation of Eastern Poland, 1939–41

1. S. Spector, *The Holocaust of Volhynian Jews*, p. 23; S. Cholawski, *Soldiers from the Ghetto*, p. 14; *The Dark Side of the Moon*, pp. 41–2.
2. B. Pinchuck, *Shtetl Jews*, p. 5.
3. M. Iwanow, 'The Byelorussians of Eastern Poland', p. 257.
4. WCU D8160.
5. J.T. Gross, *Revolution from Abroad*, pp. 71–113.
6. M. Iwanow, 'The Byelorussians of Eastern Poland', p. 264; S. Spector, *The Holocaust of Volhynian Jews*, p. 24; Public Record Office FO 371/23685, pp. 129–72.
7. M. Iwanow, 'The Byelorussians of Eastern Poland', pp. 256–8; A. Skrzypek, '*Die polnische Minderheitenpolitik*', p. 401.
8. M. Iwanow, 'The Byelorussians of Eastern Poland', pp. 260–1.
9. J.T. Gross, *Revolution from Abroad*, p. 4. See especially the results of the 1931 Polish census for the district of Polesia, WCU D9093.
10. J.T. Gross, *Revolution from Abroad*, p. 21.
11. For a brief overview of modern historical knowledge of these events see W.A. Serczyk, '*Die sowjetische und die "polnische" Ukraine zwischen den Weltkriegen*', pp. 211–13.
12. D.R. Marples, 'The Ukrainians in Eastern Poland', p. 237.
13. WCU D8158.
14. WCU D7309.
15. K. Sword, *Deportation and Exile*, p. 4 n. 15; A. Paul, *Katyn: The Untold Story*, pp. 113–14 gives the figure of 4143 Polish officers killed near Katyn and approximately 15 000 in total from three separate camps.
16. J.T. Gross, 'Polish POW Camps', pp. 44–56.
17. S. Spector, *The Holocaust of Volhynian Jews*, p. 24.
18. WCU D7466.
19. J.T. Gross, *Revolution from Abroad*, pp. 79–80 and 96–8.
20. J.T. Gross, *Revolution from Abroad*, pp. 56–61.
21. In the 1930s 'a Polish Jew could not become a civil servant, a municipal employee, a policeman, an officer or a professional NCO': R. Ainsztein, *Jewish Resistance*, p. 181. J.T. Gross stresses that the proportion of Jews serving in the militia remained low, especially in the rural communities: see J.T. Gross, 'The Jewish Community', p. 160.
22. WCU D7809; WCU D7808.
23. *The Dark Side of the Moon*, pp. 74–5; J.T. Gross, *Revolution from Abroad*, p. 163.
24. See BNAM 4-21-1875, April 1940 decision regarding the resettlement of persons living within 800 metres of the border.
25. WCU D8518.
26. J.T. Gross, *Revolution from Abroad*, p. 188.
27. See K. Sword, *Deportation and Exile*, p. ix, who describes one family which experienced deportation to Siberia in four successive generations from 1831 to 1940.

28. Z.S. Siemaszko, 'The mass deportations', pp. 217–35.
29. *The Dark Side of the Moon*, p. 52; J.T. Gross, *Revolution from Abroad*, p. 197.
30. Z.S. Siemaszko, 'The mass deportations', pp. 219–21.
31. WCU D5798-5802; P. Silverman, D. Smuschkowitz and P. Smuschkowicz, *From Victims to Victors*, p. 69 notes that some Jews also avoided arrest and deportation by moving to another town and changing their names.
32. WCU D7309.
33. *The Dark Side of the Moon*, p. 76.
34. Z.S. Siemaszko, 'The mass deportations', pp. 221–4.
35. J.T. Gross, *Revolution from Abroad*, p. 13; Y. Litvak, 'The plight of refugees', p. 67.
36. For example, a file from the immigration centre (*EWZ*) held at the BDC (*BA*) indicates that an ethnic German was only conditionally approved for citizenship in 1944, as he came from a former resettlement area (and should have returned to Germany in 1940).
37. B. Pinchuk, *Shtetl Jews*, pp. 106–8 estimates that approximately 300 000 Jews took refuge in the Soviet zone of occupation; S. Cholawsky, *The Jews of Bielorussia*, pp. 8–9 estimates, however, at least 250 000 for western Belorussia alone.
38. WCU D7852.
39. Y. Litvak, 'The plight of refugees', pp. 66–9.
40. Z.S. Siemaszko, 'The mass deportations', pp. 225–8.
41. J.T. Gross, *Revolution from Abroad*, p. 146; for a brief overview of the various estimates of the numbers deported see K. Sword, *Deportation and Exile*, pp. 25–7: 'most estimates from Polish émigré sources range between 1 250 000 and 1 600 000 altogether'. D. Pohl, *Nationalsozialistische Judenverfolgung*, p. 30 notes that studies based on Soviet sources give lower figures for deportations than the exile Polish data. He suggests that unaccounted population losses due to military conscription, labour recruitment and arrests may be responsible for some of this discrepancy.
42. B. Pinchuk, *Shtetl Jews*, pp. 15–16.
43. S. Spector, *The Holocaust of Volhynian Jews*, p. 17.
44. R. Ainsztein, *Jewish Resistance*, pp. 173–9; B. Pinchuk, *Shtetl Jews*, p. 18.
45. WCU D7852.
46. B. Pinchuk, *Shtetl Jews*, p. 21; see also S. Cholawsky, *The Jews of Bielorussia*, p. 6 on the sense of security offered by the Red Army to many Jews.
47. S. Cholawski, *Soldiers from the Ghetto*, p. 33.
48. B. Pinchuk, *Shtetl Jews*, p. 23.
49. WCU D7810.
50. B. Pinchuk, *Shtetl Jews*, p. 90.
51. S. Spector, *The Holocaust of Volhynian Jews*, p. 38.
52. B. Pinchuk, *Shtetl Jews*, p. 31. This quotation refers to the city of Lutsk.
53. Ibid., p. 131.
54. The figures for Volhynia are that 44 per cent of Jews were engaged in commerce and 40.5 per cent in handicrafts: S. Spector, *The Holocaust of Volhynian Jews*, p. 17. For Minsk see the works in Hebrew of Shalom Cholawski on Belorussian Jewry during the Holocaust.
55. WCU D7308; see also S. Cholawsky, *The Jews of Bielorussia*, p. 15.
56. B. Pinchuk, *Shtetl Jews*, p. 35.
57. S. Spector, *The Holocaust of Volhynian Jews*, p. 31.
58. B. Pinchuk, *Shtetl Jews*, pp. 92–5; I. Grudzinska-Gross and J.T. Gross (eds), *War through Children's Eyes*, pp. 16–17.

59. S. Spector, *The Holocaust of Volhynian Jews*, p. 36.
60. B. Pinchuk, *Shtetl Jews*, pp. 66–8.
61. S. Cholawski, *Soldiers from the Ghetto*, p. 26; B. Pinchuk, *Shtetl Jews*, p. 83.
62. S. Cholawski, *Soldiers from the Ghetto*, p. 37.
63. B. Pinchuk, *Shtetl Jews*, pp. 59–61; L. Berk, *Destined to Live*, p. 19.
64. S. Cholawski, *Soldiers from the Ghetto*, p. 18.
65. B. Pinchuk, *Shtetl Jews*, p. 44; J.T. Gross, *Revolution from Abroad*, p. 227.
66. *The Dark Side of the Moon*, p. 149.
67. B. Pinchuk, *Shtetl Jews*, p. 58.
68. D.R. Marples, 'The Ukrainians in Eastern Poland', p. 239; B. Pinchuk, *Shtetl Jews*, p. 44.
69. J.T. Gross, *Revolution from Abroad*, pp. 63–4 and 223.
70. Ibid., pp. 190–2.
71. D.R. Marples, 'The Ukrainians in Eastern Poland', pp. 236–52.
72. J.T. Gross, *Revolution from Abroad*, p. 4.
73. Ibid., p. 6.
74. Dorking, Y.V. Brazovsky on 19 March 1996, I.L. Yatsevich on 21 March 1996, J. Harkavy on 25 March 1996, Z. Schreiber on 27 March 1996 and L. Abramovsky on 1 April 1996; L. Berk, *Destined to Live*, p. 3.
75. J.T. Gross, *Revolution from Abroad*, pp. 18–21 and 35–9.
76. *The Dark Side of the Moon*, pp. 59–73 and 133.
77. D.R. Marples, 'The Ukrainians in Eastern Poland', p. 239.
78. Ibid., pp. 238–9.
79. See J.T. Gross, 'The Jewish Community', p. 171, n. 27 on the balance of schools in the Lvov district in 1940–41.
80. J.T. Gross, *Revolution from Abroad*, pp. 126–31.
81. B. Pinchuk, *Shtetl Jews*, pp. 74–7.
82. J.T. Gross, *Revolution from Abroad*, pp. 74–87.
83. Ibid., pp. 117–18.
84. Ibid., pp. 120–1.
85. D.R. Marples, 'The Ukrainians of Eastern Poland', pp. 236–51.
86. Ibid., pp. 236–51; B. Pinchuk, *Shtetl Jews*, p. 8; M. Iwanow, 'The Byelorussians of Eastern Poland', p. 263.
87. According to Ainsztein's rough figures, Jews in inter-war Poland made up 25 per cent of communists, but no more than 5 per cent of Jews were communists: R. Ainsztein, *Jewish Resistance*, p. 187. J.T. Gross, 'The Jewish Community', pp. 160–3 uses available figures to demonstrate rather that the Jews were indeed the group that suffered most proportionally from the deportations carried out by the Soviets.
88. Y. Litvak, 'The plight of refugees', pp. 61–2.
89. See C. Madajczyk, *Die Okkupationspolitik*, pp. 186–9; in Konin, for example, 56 leading Poles were murdered by the Germans on 10 November 1939: see T. Richmond, *Konin*, p. 81.
90. K. Sword, *Deportation and Exile*, pp. 13–14.
91. See, for example, R. Overy, *Russia's War*, pp. 47 and 52 regarding the Stalinist purges in the 1930s.
92. D.R. Marples, 'The Ukrainians in Eastern Poland', p. 249.
93. *BA* R 94/17 Situation report of the General Commissar for Volhynia-Podolia, 30.4.43.
94. B. Pinchuk, *Shtetl Jews*, pp. 101–2.
95. Ibid., pp. 117–20; L. Berk, *Destined to Live*, p. 15.
96. B. Pinchuk, *Shtetl Jews*, p. 114.

97. B. Chiari, '*Deutsche Herrschaft*', p. 45 notes that more than 200 000 men born between 1917 and 1922 were called up to the Red Army from the newly occupied territories in 1940.

2 'Operation Barbarossa'

1. WCU D8959.
2. *BA-MA* RH 26-454/5 War Diary No. 1, 22 June 1941.
3. *BA-MA* RH 29-1/4, RH 24-24/72 & RH 26-221/10 War Diary entries, 22 June 1941.
4. *BA-MA* RH 26-221/12B Appendices to War Diary Ia of 221st Security Division, No. 186: Daily Order, 21 June 1941.
5. D. Wolkogonow, *Stalin*, p. 559; G.A. Kumanev, 'The USSR's degree of readiness', p. 203; R. Overy, *Russia's War*, p. 102.
6. A. Dallin, 'Stalin and the German Invasion', pp. 17–18.
7. *BA-MA* RH 26-221/12B War Diary Ia, Appendix No. 186.
8. D. Wolkogonow, *Stalin*, pp. 556–9.
9. J. Barber, 'Popular reactions in Moscow', pp. 1–2; W. Leonhard, *Die Revolution entläßt ihre Kinder*, pp. 79–80; L. Berk, *Destined to Live*, p. 22.
10. WCU D8159, D8626, D8157.
11. The Soviet garrison in the citadel at Brest held out for 28 days until 20 July 1941: P. Kohl, '*Ich wundere mich, daß ich noch lebe*', pp. 28–30.
12. G. Zhukov, *Reminiscences and Reflections*, p. 284; W. Leonhard, *Die Revolution entläßt ihre Kinder*, p. 82.
13. YV 033/2681 note of a conversation with Z.N. Levenbuk made by M.Z. Misko on 22 December 1944.
14. WCU D7812, S282; similar chaotic scenes were experienced by those called up in Lida: *Sepher Lida*, p. VIII.
15. WCU D7852.
16. WCU D8661; see also D9085: 'the seizure of Nesvizh by the German occupiers occurred without a single shot being fired'.
17. M. Lachowicki, *The Victims of Nesvizh*.
18. *BA-MA* RH 24-47/2 War Diary No. 2, XXXXVII *Panzer* Corps Ia, 27 June 1941.
19. *BA-MA* RH 24-26/64 Anl. 55, XXVI Army Corps Order No. 1, 30 June 1941.
20. *MGFA* (ed.), *Das Deutsche Reich und der zweite Weltkrieg. Vol. 4*, pp. 186–7; D. Wolkogonow, *Stalin*, p. 548.
21. *Justiz und NS-Verbrechen*, vol. XIX, pp. 13–14.
22. *BA-MA* RM 7/985 *OKW* Guidelines for Operation Barbarossa, 13 March 1941.
23. *BA-MA* RH 22/155, pp. 304–8.
24. NAW RG 238 NOKW 3357; see also the 'Commissar Order' of 6 June 1941, *BA-MA* RW4/v. 578.
25. See especially the German debate between Alfred Streim and Wolfgang Scheffler about the verbal instructions issued to the *Einsatzgruppen* at Pretsch shortly before the invasion, in P. Longerich, '*Vom Massenmord zur Endlösung*', pp. 254–6.
26. SAM 500-1-25 pp. 13–17 and 391–4 Heydrich Order to *HSSPF*, 2 July 1941 and *Einsatzgruppen* Orders Nos 1 & 2, 29 June 1941 and 1 July 1941.
27. J. Förster '*Das Unternehmen "Barbarossa" als Eroberungs- und Vernichtungskrieg*', pp. 413–47.
28. *BA-MA* RW/v. 43 Notes to the War Diary of *OKW* Chef WFSt, 8 July 1941: 'The *Führer* stressed that he wanted to raze Moscow and Leningrad to the ground.'

29. S. Spector, *The Holocaust of Volhynian Jews*, pp. 64–7.
30. SARF 7021-54-1252, p. 23, M. Schneider on 12 April 1945.
31. *BA* R 58/215 *EM* 40, 1 August 1941.
32. *Memorial Book of Glebokie*, p. 26.
33. Many prisoners were murdered by their Soviet guards as they fled in the chaos of the German invasion. In Lvov these massacres are said to have gone on for a whole week: J.T. Gross, *Revolution from Abroad*, pp. 180–5. On events in Lvov and Sambor, see *BA* R 58/214 *EM* 24, 16 July 1941. Leon Berk estimates that in Lvov some 6000 Jews were killed on the three days from 30 June 1941, as the Germans gave the Ukrainians *carte blanche* to murder them: L. Berk, *Destined to Live*, pp. 26–38. D. Pohl, *Nationalsozialistische Judenverfolgung*, pp. 60–7 notes that the pogroms in Lvov were already under way when the Security Police arrived in the city. T. Sandkühler, *'Endlösung' in Galizien*, p. 117 indicates that of some 2000 Jews taken to the Brygydki prison in Lvov only 80 survived.
34. NAW Nbg. Doc. 180-L, Report of Stahlecker on activities of *Einsatzgruppe A* up to 15 October 1941. On 11 July 1941 Otto Bräutigam, assigned to Rosenberg's Ministry, noted that 'numerous Jewish pogroms were carried out by the Lithuanian auxiliary police (*Hilfspolizei*) with our silent tolerance': see H.-H. Wilhelm, *Die Einsatzgruppe A*, p. 63, n. 40.
35. *BA* R 58/215 *EM* 38, 30 July 1941 and *EM* 47, 9 August 1941.
36. See, for example, *BA-MA* RH 22/227, pp. 9–11; *BA* R 58/214 *EM* 13, 5 July 1941; S. Cholawsky, *The Jews of Bielorussia*, pp. 81–2 and 271–2.
37. S. Spector, *The Holocaust of Volhynian Jews*, pp. 69–71; S. Cholawsky, *The Jews of Bielorussia*, p. 274.
38. *BA-MA* RH 26-252/75, pp. 21–4 Divisional Order No. 10 of 252nd Inf. Div., 16 July 1941.
39. Dorking, Ivan Yatsevich on 21 March 1996; SARF 7021-148-364.
40. *BA-MA* RH 26-403/2 War Diary of *Sich.* Div. 403, 15 August 1941.
41. WCU S325; on a similar check conducted in the village of Yeremichi in August 1941, see WCU D2320.
42. *BA* R 58/214 *EM* 21, 13 July 1941. The screening of the civil prison in Minsk continued into August and September after the departure of the Staff unit of *Einsatzgruppe B*; see also C. Gerlach, '*Die Einsatzgruppe B*', pp. 54–5 who gives the figure of 10 000 victims found in the grave-site after the war on the basis of a Soviet exhumation report.
43. WCU D7812.
44. D. Levin, 'The fateful decision', p. 131; see also K. Segbers, *Die Sowjetunion im Zweiten Weltkrieg*, pp. 167–78.
45. B. Pinchuk, *Shtetl Jews*, pp. 121–2; *David-Horodoker Memorial Book*, p. 61.
46. D. Levin, 'The fateful decision', p. 131.
47. YV M-1/E 2441/2513 David Wolfowicz testimony in Waldstadt on 2 September 1948; see also J. Kagan and D. Cohen, *Surviving the Holocaust*, p. 38.
48. B. Pinchuk, *Shtetl Jews*, p. 121.
49. D. Levin, 'The fateful decision', pp. 140–1; S. Cholawsky, however, estimates only some 10 000 for western Belorussia: see S. Cholawsky, *The Jews of Bielorussia*, p. 80.
50. On this issue see M. Altshuler, 'Escape and evacuation', pp. 77–104.
51. W. Moskoff, *The Bread of Affliction*, pp. 29–35.
52. *Stalin's War Speeches* (London: Hutchinson, n.d.) p. 10 quoted by W. Moskoff, *The Bread of Affliction*, pp. 26–9.
53. W. Moskoff, *The Bread of Affliction*, pp. 26–9.
54. *BA* R 58/215 *EM* 31, 23 July 1941.

55. W. Moskoff, *The Bread of Affliction*, p. 26.
56. *BA R* 58/215 *EM* 31, 23 July 1941.
57. W. Moskoff, *The Bread of Affliction*, p. 28.
58. *BA R* 58/215 *EM* 38, 30 July 1941.
59. *BA-MA* RH 24-27/2 War Diary No. 2 of XXXXVII *Panzer* Corps, 27 June–5 July 1941.
60. *BA-MA* RH 24-27/2 War Diary No. 2 of XXXXVII *Panzer* Corps, 27 June–5 July 1941. Personnel losses from the start of the campaign up to 2 July 1941 17th *Pz*. Div.: 41 officers, 612 other ranks = 4.1%; 18th *Pz*. Div.: 73 officers, 1273 other ranks = 8.4%; 29th Inf. Div. (*mot*.): 56 officers, 970 other ranks = 7.1% of the total strengths including men serving behind the lines. Action-ready combat vehicles on 4 July 1941: 17th *Pz*. Div. 80 of 239 (move-out strength) = 33%; 18th *Pz*. Div. 93 of 320 (move-out strength) = 30%. On the increased Russian resistance encountered by mid-July see also W. Lammers (ed.), '*Fahrtberichte*', p. 24.
61. Manuscript diary of G.S. – I am grateful to Hans-Heinrich Wilhelm and the author for making this material available to me.
62. *BA-MA* RH 24-27/2 War Diary No. 2 of XXXXVII *Panzer* Corps, 30 June 1941.
63. *BA-MA* RH 26-221/12B, *Anl. KTB* Ia 20 June 1941 1 July 1941, *Anl.* 251, 1 July 1941 Special instruction for Corps order: 'increasingly pamphlets are dropped with the message – "desert to us, you will be treated decently, anything else is a lie". These pamphlets have been effective in many places and thereby have saved bloodshed on our side. In order to avoid negating this propaganda, it is necessary that Red Army soldiers who surrender and show the pamphlet are treated as PoWs.'
64. D. Budnik and Y. Kaper, *Nothing is Forgotten*, p. 100 mentions checks for officers, political instructors and Jews amongst Soviet PoWs captured in Kiev in September 1941.
65. Report of Xaver Dorsch to Alfred Rosenberg on 10 July 1941 in P. Kohl, '*Ich wundere mich, daß ich noch lebe*', p. 220.
66. *Memorial Book of Glebokie*, pp. 28 and 31.
67. *BA-MA* RH 26-403/4a *Anl. Sich. Div. Abt.* IIa 1941. 25 July 1941 *OKH* to *Befh. rückw. H. Geb. Nord, Mitte u. Süd.* Order regarding the treatment of enemy civilians and Russian PoWs.
68. WCU D8867.
69. 'Many of the retreating soldiers were captured by the Germans and went into captivity, but I and a few others found work on a farm', WCU D8675.
70. *BA R* 58/215 *EM* 43, 5 August 1941.
71. MHAP A 2-1-3 *KTB* No. 1 of *Pol. Bn.* 322, entry for 31 August 1941 noting expiry of the deadline. See also *BA-MA* RH 26-221/13a, *Anl.* 628. The deadline was initially fixed for 15 August 1941 and was later extended to 31 August 1941, *BA-MA* RH 26-252/75, Corps Order No. 39, 11 August 1941.
72. NAW RG 238 221-L Note of a conference at *Führer* HQ, 16 July 1941; see also R. Headland, *Messages of Murder*, pp. 73–4.
73. NAW RG 238 2718-PS Memo. on discussion with Secretaries of State concerning Barbarossa, 2 May 1941.
74. NAW RG 238 221-L Note of a conference at *Führer* HQ, 16 July 1941.
75. *BA R* 43 II/686a pp. 4–5, *Führer* decree on the administration of the newly occupied eastern territories, 17 July 1941.
76. NAW RG 238 221-L Note of a conference at *Führer* HQ, 16 July 1941; *BA R* 43II/686a *Führer* Decree on Police and security in the newly occupied eastern areas, 17 July 1941.

77. *BA-MA* RW 41/4 Himmler order to *HSSPF*, 25 July 1941 and Order of Daluege, 31 July 1941.
78. This was partly the lesson to be learned from the first weeks of the Polish campaign: see C. Madajczyk, *Die Okkupationspolitik Nazideutschlands in Polen*, pp. 28–9.
79. H. Picker (ed.), *Hitlers Tischgespräche*, p. 137.
80. *MGFA* (*ed.*), *Das Deutsche Reich und der Zweite Weltkrieg*. Vol. 4, p. 461.
81. C. Browning, *The Path to Genocide*, pp. 103–6; C. Browning, 'Hitler and the euphoria of victory', p. 138.
82. *BA* R 58/214 *EM* 10, 2 July 1941.
83. USHMMA RG-53.002M, reel 5 (BNAM) 845-1-6, pp. 54–6 Extraordinary Commission Report for the Nesvizh district, 4 February 1945.
84. WCU S171B, S173C, S97, D3684, S175B, D1766, S87A.
85. Dorking, Ivan Yatsevich on 21 March 1996.
86. WCU D7812.
87. *BA* R 58/215 *EM* 32, 24 July 1941; C. Gerlach, '*Die Einsatzgruppe B*', p. 56 notes the support given by Police Battalion 316.
88. WCU D5949.
89. *BA* R 58/215 *EM* 43, 5 August 1941.
90. YV 033/2681. The events in Gantsevichi are also mentioned in L. Berk, *Destined to Live*, pp. 58–9. This was the first instance in Belorussia when all the Jews were killed – it is dated on 13 August 1941 by S. Cholawsky, *The Jews of Bielorussia*, pp. 87–92. One estimate is that some 3000 Jews were killed, but this source gives the date of 13 September 1941: see S. Wiesenthal, *Every Day, Remembrance Day*, p. 207.
91. *BA* R 58/215 *EM* 32, 24 July 1941.
92. *BA-MA* RH 26-252/75, pp. 21–4 252nd Inf. Div. Ia/Ic. Div. Order No. 10, 16 July 1941.
93. *BA-MA* RH 22/5 *Bfh. rückw. H. Geb. Süd*, 5 August 1941.
94. *BA-MA* RH 26/125-4 XXXXIX Corps Order No. 48, 20 July 1941.
95. SAM 1275-3-662, pp. 3–13 Reports of *FK 675, Abt.* VII to *Sich. Div.* 444, 1 August 1941 & 11 August 1941.
96. SAM 1275-3-662, pp. 3–13 and 30–7 Reports of *FK 675 Abt.* VII to *Sich. Div.* 444, 1 August 1941, 11 August 1941 and 30 August 1941. On the different names given to the militia in the areas under military administration throughout 1941–44 see also F. Golczewski, '*Organe der deutschen Besatzungsmacht*'.
97. *BA* R 94/26 Security Division 454, section VII, Special Order No. 3, 18 August 1941.
98. *BA-MA* RW 41/4 Order of Daluege for Himmler re. security forces, 31 July 1941; and *BA-MA* RH 22/9 Commander Rear Area South *Abt.* Ia, 14 November 1941.
99. SAM 1275-3-662 Reports of *FK 675 Abt.* VII to *Sich. Div.* 444 on 11, 13, 30 and 31 August 1941.
100. SAM 1275-3-662 Reports of *FK 675 Abt.* VII to *Sich. Div.* 444 on 1, 11, 13 and 30 August 1941; *BA-MA* RH 22/5 Commander of Rear Army Area South, *Abt.* VII, 21 July 1941.
101. SAM 1275-3-662, pp. 17–19 and 20a–26 *FK 675, Abt.* VII, to *Sich. Div.* 444 on 14 and 25 August 1941; *BA* R 58/215 *EM* 47, 9 August 1941.
102. SAM 1275-3-662, p. 36 Order of *Abt.* VII No. 7, Commander of Rear Army Area South No. 103/41, 16 August 1941.
103. SAM 1275-3-662, pp. 20a-26 *FK 675, Abt.* VII to *Sich. Div.* 444 on 25 August 1941 and to the interim administration of the Vinnitsa area on 23 August 1941;

on the issue of retaining the *Kolkhoz* system in Belorussia, see also B. Chiari, '*Deutsche Zivilverwaltung*', pp. 76–7.

104. J.A. Armstrong, *Ukrainian Nationalism*, pp. 65–7.
105. For instance, in Ulanov two nationalist activists were permitted to retain their positions once their passes issued by the OUN had been taken from them: SAM, 1275-3-662, pp. 20a–26 *FK* 675, *Abt.* VII to *Sich. Div.* 444, 25 August 1941.
106. NAW T-501, roll 34, frames 203–8 *Sich. Div.* 213 Situation Report, 27 August 1941.
107. Ibid.
108. One source described the popular mood as: 'let the devil rule, but not the Bolsheviks': ZA 1151-1-2, p. 68 OUN report for Troyanov district, 18 August 1941 (German translation).
109. *PAAA* Inl. IIg/431 Activity and situation report No. 2, 14 August 1941.
110. *BA* R 58/215 *EM* 43, 5 August 1941; C. Gerlach, '*Die Einsatzgruppe B*', p. 53.
111. *BA* R 58/214 *EM* 21, 13 July 1941.
112. *BA* R 58/215 *EM* 31, 23 July 1941. A survivor from Baranovichi noted that 'for the first couple of days the Germans were not able to distinguish those who were Jews from those who were not because they thought that all Jews had beards and wore skull caps. For this reason they were simply unable to recognize the Jews': YV 033/2681.
113. YV 033/2681. On additional orders issued by successive military commandants see also *Memorial Book of Glebokie*, p. 34.
114. WCU D7809.
115. S. Cholawski, *Soldiers from the Ghetto*, p. 50; see also YV M-1/E-2441/2513 David Wolfowicz; for a German list of six main prohibitions issued by the mayor in Novogrudok on 26 September 1941 see USHMMA 22.002M, reel 24 (SARF) 7021-81-112, p. 2. According to this proclamation Jews leaving their place of residence without an official permit could be shot immediately by the *Wehrmacht* or Order Police.
116. See, for example, Brest Archive 2135-2-127, p. 3 *OK* Pinsk to *Bürgermeister* of Pinsk, 30 July 1941.
117. *BA* R 58/215 *EM* 31, 23 July 1941.
118. YV 033/2681.
119. *Justiz und NS-Verbrechen*, vol. XX, p. 42.
120. Ibid., p. 41.
121. MHAP *KdoS RFSS* 1/1 *KTB* No. 1 *Kommandostab-RFSS*, 19 July 1941.
122. *Justiz und NS-Verbrechen*, vol. XX, p. 43 Himmler guidelines for the combing of swamp areas by cavalry units, 28 July 1941.
123. MHAP *KdoS RFSS* Report of Fegelein, *SS* Cavalry Brigade 1, Concluding Report, 13 August 1941.
124. MHAP, *KdoS RFSS* Report of Magill, *SS* Cavalry Rgt 2, on the course of the Pripyet action from 27 July–11 August 1941.
125. *Justiz und NS-Verbrechen*, vol. XX, p. 48.
126. See, for example, the Montua order of Police Regiment Centre, 11 July 1941, which states that all male Jews between the ages of 17 and 45 arrested as 'looters' are to be shot: MHAP A 3-1-7, p. 1.
127. Report of Karl Jäger, 1 December 1941, SAM 500-1-25; P. Longerich, '*Vom Massenmord zur Endlösung*', p. 264.
128. R. Ogorreck, *Die Einsatzgruppen*, pp. 176–211; Christian Gerlach has demonstrated that some sub-units of *Einsatzgruppe B* did not begin to implement these orders until later in the autumn, then commencing the complete elimination of the Jewish population in eastern Belorussia: C. Gerlach, '*Die Einsatzgruppe B*', p. 60.

129. *BA-MA* RS 3-8/36 Himmler Order to *SS* Cavalry Rgt 2, 1 August 1941.
130. MHAP *KdoS RFSS* Report of Magill, *SS* Cavalry Rgt 2, on the course of the Pripyet action from 27 July to 11 August 1941.
131. *Justiz und NS-Verbrechen*, vol. XX, pp. 50–8.
132. *BA* Koblenz R 58/215 *EM* 58, 20 August 1941. The 'reason' given for the execution was that a member of the militia in Pinsk had been shot by a concealed sniper. Investigative sources estimate 6–10 000 victims in Pinsk: C. Gerlach, '*Deutsche Wirtschaftsinteressen*', p. 11.
133. Evidence of Jewish survivor witnesses in the case of Ivan Polyukovich, who was tried and acquitted in Adelaide, Australia, 1990–93.
134. *David-Horodoker Memorial Book*, pp. 62–3, 91–3 and 109.
135. *Justiz und NS-Verbrechen*, vol. XX, p. 52; Activity and situation report of the Head of *Einsatzgruppe B* 23 June–13 July 1941, published in P. Klein (Hrsg.), *Die Einsatzgruppen*, pp. 375–86.
136. *Justiz und NS-Verbrechen*, vol. XX, p. 53.
137. MHAP *KdoS RFSS* Report of Magill, *SS* Cavalry Rgt 2, on the course of the Pripyet action 27 July–11 August 1941.
138. *Justiz und NS-Verbrechen*, vol. XX, pp. 50–8. H.-H. Wilhelm, *Die Einsatzgruppe A*, p. 59 describes the same phenomenon for the initial actions in Lithuania.
139. On direct local participation in the 1941 killings see *David-Horodoker Memorial Book*, pp. 91–4, 116 and 123–4.
140. See especially R.B. Birn, '*Zweierlei Wirklichkeit?*', pp. 275–90.
141. *BA-MA* RH 22/227 Commander Rear Army Area Centre report, 10 August 1941.
142. MHAP *KdoS RFSS* Report of Magill, *SS* Cavalry Rgt 2, on the course of the Pripyet action 27 July–11 August 1941.
143. Ibid.
144. Ibid.
145. *BA-MA* RH 22/227 Report of Rear Army Area Group Centre, 20 August 1941.
146. R. Ogorreck, *Die Einsatzgruppen*, p. 222.
147. *BA-MA* RH 22/5 *HSSPF* South Operational Order, 25 July 1941; *BA* R 58/215 *EM* 47, 9 August 1941.
148. A. Angrick, M. Voigt, S. Ammerschubert, P. Klein, C. Alheit and M. Tycher, ' "*Da hätte man schon ein Tagebuch führen müssen*" ', pp. 325–85.
149. MHAP, *KdoS RFSS* Report of Magill, *SS* Cavalry Rgt 2, on the course of the Pripyet action 27 July–11 August 1941.
150. *BA* R 58/215 *EM* 43, 5 August 1941.
151. B. Chiari, '*Deutsche Herrschaft*', pp. 125–6.
152. *BA* R 58/215 *EM* 43, 5 August 1941.
153. *BA* R 58/215 *EM* 33, 25 July 1941. Appendix on the Jewish question in the Belorussian settlement area.
154. H. Guderian, *Panzer Leader*, p. 151.
155. J. Kipp, 'Barbarossa and the crisis', pp. 147–8; *MGFA* (ed.), *Das Deutsche Reich und der Zweite Weltkrieg*, vol. 4, p. 499.
156. A. Dallin, *German Rule in Russia*, pp. 18–19.

3 Mass Killings in the Autumn of 1941

1. Some 44 125 victims (mostly Jews) were reported to have been shot by units subordinate to *HSSPF* South during August 1941, *BA* R 58/217 *EM* 94, 25 September 1941; A. Angrick, '*Einsatzgruppe D*', p. 94 dates the extension of

killings to women and children by this unit to early August; C. Gerlach, '*Die Einsatzgruppe B*', p. 58.

2.   C. Gerlach, '*Die Einsatzgruppe B*', p. 58 stresses this further development, which has received less attention from historians than the extension of killings to women and children. For Lithuania see also W. Scheffler, '*Die Einsatzgruppe A*', pp. 35–6.

3.   For the critique of Arno Mayer's thesis, see C. Browning, *Fateful Months*, pp. 80–1; C. Browning, 'Hitler and the euphoria of victory', pp. 137–45. On Hitler's buoyant mood in early October see R. Overy, *Russia's War*, pp. 127–8.

4.   H.-H. Wilhelm, *Die Einsatzgruppe A*, p. 39, n. 60.

5.   *BA-MA* RH 26-221/13a Commandant *Weißruthenien*, 1 September 1941; RH 22/227 pp. 27–9 Commander of Rear Army Area Centre 10 day report, 1 September 1941.

6.   *CDJC*, CXLVa-8 Report of Gerhard Erren, 25 January 1942; see also NAW NI-441 on the shortage of personnel for the civil administration in Ukraine; B. Chiari, '*Deutsche Herrschaft*', p. 86 on similar problems encountered by the *Einsatzstab Rosenberg* on setting up its offices in Minsk.

7.   BNAM 651-1-1, pp. 12–15 Commandant in *Weißruthenien* situation report, 1–15 October 1941; *CDJC*, CXLVa-8 Report of Gerhard Erren, 25 January 1942: Erren chose to use a number of Tartars in his service as being reliable and standing above most ethnic and religious struggles.

8.   D. Pohl, '*Die Einsatzgruppe C*', pp. 74–5; *BA* R 58/217 *EM* 86, 17 September 1941, p. 18; *ZSL* II 204a AR-Z 136/67, vol. IV and Soviet witnesses, pp. 44–46 and 299–303; I. Ehrenburg and V. Grossman, *The Black Book*, p. 20; Browning, *Ordinary Men*, p. 18 notes that Police Battalions 314 and 45 participated in the execution of several thousand Jews in Vinnitsa in September 1941.

9.   *BA* R 58/218 *EM* 106, 7 October 1941, pp. 17–18.

10. R. Overy, *Russia's War*, pp. 176–7; *BA* R 94/26 Security Division 454 *Abt.* VII, report on visit to *FK* 195 in Kiev, 2 October 1941; *BA* R 58/217 *EM* 101, 2 October 1941.

11. *BA* R 58/219 *EM* 143, 8 December 1941 gives the figure of 15 000; S. Spector, *The Holocaust of Volhynian Jews*, pp. 113–14 puts the number at 18–21 000.

12. *BA* R 58/220 *EM* 155, 14 January 1942.

13. SAM 1275-3-665 *OK* I/253 Krivoy Rog, 15 October 1941.

14. *BA* R 58/219 *EM* 135, 19 November 1941.

15. *BA* R 58/217 *EM* 94, 25 September 1941.

16. C. Gerlach, '*Die Einsatzgruppe B*', p. 59.

17. C. Gerlach, '*Deutsche Wirtschaftsinteressen*', p. 14.

18. Activity and Situation Report No. 7 of the *Einsatzgruppen* published in P. Klein (Hrsg.), *Die Einsatzgruppen*, pp. 245–63.

19. C. Gerlach, '*Die Einsatzgruppe B*', p. 60.

20. *Justiz und NS-Verbrechen*, vol. XIX, p. 796.

21. *Justiz und NS-Verbrechen*, vol. XX, pp. 745–9; on the active participation of local policemen in Jewish shootings in the areas under military administration see also D. Romanovsky, 'Nazi Occupation in Northeastern Belarus and Western Russia', pp. 241–7.

22. *BA* R 58/218 *EM* 124, 25 October 1941; H. Heer, 'Killing Fields', pp. 61–2.

23. Dorking, Prof. C. Browning statement confirmed on 20 February 1996.

24. *BA* R 58/219 *EM* 133, 14 November 1941.

25. BNAM 651-1-1, p. 28 Jedicke to *Reichskommissar Ostland*, 17 October 1941.

26. BNAM 378-1-698, p. 60 Commandant in *Weißruthenien*, 10 October 1941. In Glubokoye the Gypsies were killed in the last months of 1941, *Memorial Book of Glebokie*, p. 44.
27. NAW RG 238 1104-PS Report of District Commissar Carl in Slutsk, 30 October 1941.
28. Soviet Criminal Case against Antanas Impulevicius held at the former KGB archive in Vilnius.
29. NAW RG 238 1104-PS Report of District Commissar Carl in Slutsk, 30 October 1941.
30. *BA-MA* RH 26-707/2 Report of Military Commandant in *Weißruthenien*, 10 November 1941.
31. S. Cholawski, *Soldiers from the Ghetto*, p. 52.
32. WCU D9133.
33. S. Cholawski, *Soldiers from the Ghetto*, pp. 53–4.
34. WCU D9136; see also D9131.
35. WCU D9136.
36. WCU D9135.
37. M. Lachowicki, *The Victims of Nesvizh*.
38. S. Cholawski, *Soldiers from the Ghetto*, p. 55 gives the figure of 585; M. Lachowicki, *The Victims of Nesvizh* puts it at 562.
39. S. Cholawski, *Soldiers from the Ghetto*, p. 56; M. Lachowicki, *The Victims of Nesvizh*; WCU D9136 and D9135; *ZSL* II 202 AR 116/67, pp. 146–53, 444–9 and 549–55.
40. M. Lachowicki, *The Victims of Nesvizh*.
41. WCU D9085.
42. M. Lachowicki, *The Victims of Nesvizh*.
43. *SAL* IV K 79/64, pp. 146–52 undated statement of Josef Marchwinski entitled 'The criminals came from the West'.
44. BNAM 378-1-698, p. 25 Commandant *Weißruthenien*, 3 November 1941.
45. For the investigation into 8./727th Inf. Rgt. see *ZSL* II 202 AR-Z 337/67 (*Sta.* Munich I, 117 JS 2/72) investigation against F. Göbel. On the role of the police see WCU S296: 'The Germans needed the Belorussian police because they were the ones who knew which houses the Jews lived in.'
46. Dorking, Ze'ev Schreiber on 27 March 1996.
47. Dorking, Lev Abramovsky on 1 April 1996.
48. Dorking, Ze'ev Schreiber on 27 March 1996.
49. Dorking, Ivan Yatsevich on 21 March 1996.
50. Dorking, statement of Jacob Lipszyc dated 6 March 1995 accepted in evidence.
51. Dorking, Shmuel Cesler on 28 March 1996.
52. Dorking, Menachem Shalev on 29 February 1996.
53. Dorking, Regina Bedynska on 28 February 1996.
54. Dorking, Lev Abramovsky on 1 April 1996.
55. Dorking, Ze'ev Schreiber on 27 March 1996.
56. Dorking, Boris Grushevsky on 18 March 1996.
57. Dorking, Regina Bedynska on 28 February 1996.
58. INRW SWKsz 72, pp. 158–61.
59. Dorking, Menachem Shalev on 29 February 1996.
60. Dorking, Lev Abramovsky on 1 April 1996.
61. Dorking, Menachem Shalev on 29 February 1996.
62. WCU D7852.
63. WCU D7812.
64. WCU D6249; D6291.

65. *CDJC* CXLVa-8 Report of Gerhard Erren, 25 January 1942.
66. WCU D6291.
67. WCU D7852.
68. WCU D6249; see also *ZSL* 202 AR-Z 228/59 Indictment in the case of Gerhard Erren, p. 4277.
69. *ZSL* II 202 AR-Z 228/59 vol. VI, pp. 6129–34; WCU D6291.
70. WCU D6249.
71. NAW PS-3047 Sönnecken letter 17–20 October 1941.
72. J. Noakes and G. Pridham (eds), *Nazism 1919–45: Vol. 3 Foreign Policy, War and Racial Extermination* Doc. 822, pp. 1098–100 Ehof statement to the Soviet authorities in 1948.
73. NAW PS-3047 Sönnecken letter, 17–20 October 1941; on Borisov see also H. Krausnick and H.-H. Wilhelm, *Die Truppe des Weltanschauungskrieges*, pp. 576–80.
74. J. Kagan and D. Cohen, *Surviving the Holocaust*, pp. 47–9.
75. P. Silverman, D. Smuschkowitz and P. Smuschkowicz, *From Victims to Victors*, pp. 79–83; YV 033/2277.
76. *BA* R 58/217 *EM* No. 86, 17 September 1941.
77. *PAAA* Inl. IIg/117, pp. 165–82 Protocol of Wannsee Conference, 20 January 1942; see also T. Sandkühler, '*Endlösung*', p. 410.
78. D. Pohl, *Nationalsozialistische Judenverfolgung*, pp. 338–42.
79. M. Lachowicki, *The Victims of Nesvizh*; see also S. Spector, *The Holocaust of Volhynian Jews*, pp. 127–37 for similar problems regarding food and water supplies encountered in the Volhynian ghettoes at this time.
80. WCU D9136; D9088; D9129.
81. USHMMA RG-53.002M, reel 5 (BNAM) 845-1-6, pp. 54–6 Extraordinary Commission Report for the district of Nesvizh, 4 February 1945.
82. *Memorial Book of Glebokie*, p. 29.
83. *BA-MA RH* 23/225 *Korück* 582, autumn 1941.
84. C. Streit, 'Partisans – Resistance – Prisoners of War', pp. 272–4.
85. A.F. Vysotsky *et al.*, *Nazi Crimes in Ukraine*, pp. 162–3.
86. Ibid., pp. 149–50.
87. Extract from the notes of the Head of the General Staff of the 18th Army on the treatment of Soviet PoWs from the meeting in Orsha on 13 November 1941. Published in W. Wette and G. R. Überschär (eds), *Der deutsche Überfall auf die Sowjetunion*, pp. 308–9.
88. *BA* R 58/219 *EM* 128, 3 November 1941.
89. R. Headland, *Messages of Murder*, pp. 135–45.
90. T. Schulte, *The German Army*, pp. 181 and 190–1; C. Streit, '*Die Behandlung der sowjetischen Kriegsgefangenen*', pp. 160–72; W. Wilenchik, '*Die Partisanenbewegung im Weißrußland*', p. 209. C. Gerlach, '*Deutsche Wirtschaftsinteressen*' estimates some 700 000 Soviet PoWs were killed by the Germans in Belorussia.
91. C. Streit, 'Partisans – Resistance – Prisoners of War', pp. 272–4; see also T. Schulte, *The German Army*, pp. 180–210; D. Pohl, *Nationalsozialistische Judenverfolgung*, p. 112; J. Noakes and G. Pridham (eds), *Nazism 1919–45: Vol. 3*, p. 909.
92. On the development of this policy see NAW RG 238 Nbg. Doc. 180-L Stahlecker report, Appendix on partisan warfare dated 29 September 1941.
93. BNAM 378-1-698 pp. 11–12 Commandant in *Weißruthenien*, 16 October 1941.
94. WCU D9330.
95. PUST memoir of Jaroslaw Gasiewski (Polish language).
96. WCU D8875.

97. A. Dallin, *German Rule in Russia*, pp. 426–7 gives the official figure of some 67 000 escaped Soviet PoWs.
98. WCU D8855.
99. 'It should be attempted to release Ukrainian prisoners of war to their home areas following a brief examination, provided that these areas have already been occupied by the German Armed Forces', *BA* R 58/215 *EM* 37, 29 July 1941. On 25 July 1941 Himmler instructed that Belorussian PoWS were not to be released as yet, although other PoWs, such as Ukrainians, could be recruited for the auxiliary police units (*Schutzmannschaften*): *BA-MA* RW 41/4; see also *BA-MA* RH 26-454/5 *KTB* No. 1, 4 September 1941.
100. A. Dallin, *German Rule in Russia*, p. 413.
101. WCU D5676.
102. SAM 1275-3-665 *OK* I/253 Krivoy Rog to *FK* 246, 15 October 1941. See also *BA* R 58/216 *EM* 94, 25 September 1941: 'In by far the majority of cases the scattered Russians who have not yet been caught by the *Wehrmacht*, in so far as they are not officers or politically tainted elements, have reported to the collective farms for work and have fitted in without hostile activity. Often individual saboteurs and inciters to partisan group formation have been weeded out from among these soldiers.'
103. W. Wilenchik, '*Die Partisanenbewegung in Weißrußland*', pp. 150–8; C. Streit, 'Partisans – Resistance – Prisoners of War', p. 265.
104. H. Smolar, *The Minsk Ghetto*, p. 35.
105. WCU D8002; W. Wilenchik, '*Die Partisanenbewegung in Weißrußland*', p. 168.
106. *WAST* Loss reports for I. and II. Battalions, 727th Infantry Regiment from summer 1941 to summer 1942.
107. C. Streit, 'Partisans – Resistance – Prisoners of War', pp. 267–8.
108. *BA-MA* RH 22/230 War Diary appendix, Commander Rear Army Area Centre report, 5 February 1942.
109. BNAM 655-1-1, pp. 12–15 and 31 Commandant in *Weißruthenien*, 19 October 1941 and 13 November 1941.
110. *BA-MA* RW 30/103 (NI 441) Report of Prof. Seraphim, 29 November 1941.
111. N. Tec, *Defiance*, pp. 147–8.
112. H.-H. Wilhelm, *Die Einsatzgruppe A*, p. 45. Wilhelm goes on to note that the main cause for the German defeat was the military superiority of the Red Army.
113. C. Streit, 'Partisans – Resistance – Prisoners of War', pp. 267–8.
114. H. Heer, 'Killing Fields', pp. 57–77.
115. NAW PS 3667 Report of *Hauptkommissar* Baranovichi, 10 March 1942.
116. C. Gerlach, '*Die Wannsee-Konferenz*', p. 9; for a more general criticism of Heer's polemical approach see also B. Chiari, '*Deutsche Herrschaft*', p. 12.
117. BNAM 378-1-698 Commandant *Weißruthenien* Order No. 24, 24 November 1941.

4 Local Police Organization, 1941–44

1. D. Pohl, *Von der 'Judenpolitik' zum Judenmord*, p. 144 notes that in the Lublin district the *Gendarmerie* had an important function in German rule due to the rural nature of the area. This is equally true of the territories further east under civil administration: see J. Matthäus, ' "*Reibungslos und planmäßig*" ', pp. 254–74; M. C. Dean, 'The German *Gendarmerie*, the Ukrainian *Schutzmannschaft* and the "Second Wave" of Jewish Killings' pp. 168–92.

2. SAM 1323-2-267 Report of Daluege on strength and operations of the Order Police in 1942, 1 February 1943. The strength of the *Schutzmannschaft Einzeldienst* is given at 223 787.
3. WCU D8011. One former policeman recalled of another that he 'heard that his mother advised him to become a policeman as their food was assured'.
4. WCU D8724.
5. *BA* R 94/7 *Schutzpolizei* Brest report, 12 October 1942.
6. KGB Regional Archive, Grodno (UKGB) Case 59, Archive File No. 20777 V.A.K. on 6 October 1944.
7. WCU D7341.
8. *Justiz und NS-Verbrechen*, vol. XVIII, pp. 100–5; excerpts from the statements of August Meier of *KdS* Kiev made in September/October 1959, published in H.-H. Wilhelm, *Rassenpolitik und Kriegführung*, p. 234.
9. *Justiz und NS-Verbrechen*, vol. XVIII, pp. 100–5.
10. The former *KGB* building in Vinnitsa, which was the *NKVD* headquarters before the war, was used by the German Security Police during the occupation.
11. H.-H. Wilhelm, *Die Einsatzgruppe A*, p. 310, n. 9 gives the strength of *KdS Weißruthenien* on 1 February 1942 as 122 men, including 15 *Staatspolizei*, 11 *Kripo*, 5 *SD*, 37 *SS* reservists and 36 drivers; S. Spector, *The Holocaust of Volhynian Jews*, p. 60.
12. ZA 1182-1-26, p. 104 Overview of the structure of the Security Police in the *Generalkommissariat* Zhitomir; see also M.C. Dean, 'The German *Gendarmerie*, the Ukrainian *Schutzmannschaft* and the "Second Wave" of Jewish Killings', pp. 176–80.
13. N. Tec, *In the Lion's Den*, p. 85.
14. ZA 1465-1-1, p. 9; see also Brest Archive 995-1-7, p. 181 *KdS Weißruthenien*, Baranovichi post to *SS*PGF Baranovichi, 11 August 1942. Order to arrest, interrogate and, if necessary, to shoot named suspects, passed on by the *SS* PGF to be carried out by the *Gendarmerie* post in Mir on 14 August 1942.
15. ZSL 204 AR-Z 334/59 Vol. V, p. 1153.
16. *BA* R 94/8 District Commissar Brest situation report for May–June 1943, 24 June 1943.
17. *BA* Berlin R 19/266, pp. 5–11 Strengths and locations of the *Schutzmannschaft* Battalions, 1 July 1942.
18. See R. B. Birn, *Die Höheren SS- und Polizeiführer*, pp. 79–115. Ruth Birn stresses the role of the *HSSPF* as a steering and co-ordinating office created by Himmler, in order to be flexible and ready to act against emerging threats as necessary.
19. Brest Archive 995-1-11, p. 33 *Jagdzug* I to *SSPF Weißruthenien*, 17 February 1944. *Jagdzug* I fought a short battle with neighbouring cossacks who were also serving with the Germans.
20. LSHA 1444-1-8 Orders of National Labour Defence Battalion; K. Stang, *Kollaboration und Massenmord*, pp. 146–8.
21. WCU D2138; *BA* R 70/22 1 April 1943.
22. *ZSL* II 204 AR-Z 163/67 Vol. II, pp. 311–24 J.K.K. on 14 February 1969 and M.D.K. on 19 February 1969.
23. C. Browning, *Ordinary Men*, pp. 3–25, 44–8.
24. *ZSL* UdSSR 412 – the originals can be found in SARF 7021-148-2. Police Battalion 310 was redesignated III (Battalion)/Police Regiment 15 from 1 August 1942 (see *ZSL* UdSSR 411).
25. C. Browning, *Ordinary Men*, pp. 5–6; the personal details of *Gendarmerie* officials were obtained primarily from *ZSL* 2 AR-Z 16/67 and II 202 AR-Z 228/59.

26. USHMMA RG 53.002M, reel 5 (BNAM) 658-1-2, pp. 77–8 *Erkennungsmarken Verzeichnis Gend. Zug* 1/3 Rechitsa.
27. *ZSL* 2 AR-Z 16/67 Vol. VIII W.L. on 13 May 1970.
28. *BA* R 19/464, pp. 83–6 Express letter of *RFSS*, 26 September 1941.
29. *ZSL* 2 AR-Z 16/67 Vol. VIII W.R. on 30 July 1969.
30. BNAM 378-1-698, p. 27. Military Commandant *Weißruthenien* Order No. 21, 10 November 1941.
31. WCU 93/1 Appendix IV/9 E.F. on 11 October 1966.
32. ZA 1182-1-8, p. 114; ZA 1182-1-10, p. 26.
33. *BA-MA* RH 23/228 Commander Rear Army Area Centre, section VII, Regulations for the *Ordnungsdienst*, 27 November 1941.
34. *BA-MA* RH 26-221/21 Appendices to War Diary Ia, p. 317 Commandant of *FK* 528 (V) in Rogachev, 13 September 1941.
35. *ZSL* 2 AR-Z 16/67 Vol. X, pp. 1977–2013 Max Eibner on 13 June 1973.
36. ZA 1182-1-3, p. 59 *Generalkommissar* to *Gebiets-/Stadtkommissar* in Kazatin, 3 December 1941. Encloses letter of *Reichskommissar* dated 8 December 1941.
37. BNAM 370-1-1262, pp. 147–58 Lecture by Klepsch at the District Commissars' meeting on 10 April 1943 mentions the dismissal and replacement of Polish national personnel within the *Schutzmannschaft* in Baranovichi town.
38. WCU D9084; see also D8661 and S135B which indicate that some Polish policemen were retained.
39. WCU D6104.
40. WCU S119A. In Latvia and Lithuania the first local recruits to the auxiliary police responded to appeals in the press and on radio. See also ZA 1151-1-21, pp. 65–6 Appeal for voluntary enlistment into the *Schutzmannschaft* in Ukraine, 21 February 1942.
41. MRA 685-1-2.
42. WCU S101A. On the voluntary nature of service in the Mir district see also D7308.
43. Dorking, Oswald Rufeisen on 22 February 1996.
44. Ibid.
45. USHMMA RG 53.002M, reel 5 (BNAM) 658-1-1 p. 84 *KdO Befehl* 6/42, 18 February 1942. In Brest individual policemen were sometimes granted release from service at this time for health or family reasons, see *BA* R 94/6 Report of *Stadtkommissar* Brest, 12 January 1942.
46. USHMMA ZA 1151-1-3, p. 27.
47. INRW SWGd 75 pp. 737–8 K.K. on 9 September 1969 at own trial. On the bribing of doctors see also *UKGB* Brest Archive File No. 2905, Criminal Case 69, pp. 16–18 N.L. on 13 September 1944.
48. WCU D7341.
49. WCU D9565 *Rottwachmeister* G.R. was taken on as an ethnic German from the *Schutzmannschaft* unit Brest-Land. For the Kirovograd district see SSA Kirovograd, statement of A.A.G. on 13 June 1947 in own trial.
50. SAM 1323-2-255, pp. 22–3 *KdG* Zhitomir, 23 September 1942.
51. WCU D4858.
52. Published in translation by M. Cooper, *The Nazi War against Soviet Partisans*, pp. 176–8.
53. SARF 7021-348-164 Recommendations for promotion with personal details for members of the *Schutzmannschaft* in the Baranovichi district, 1943 44.
54. WCU S110.
55. WCU S119A.
56. INRW SWSz 77, pp. 1736–71 Court evidence of J.R. on 22 January 1971.

57. WCU D2478.
58. ZA 1182-1-3, p. 58 *KdG* Zhitomir, Command Order 4/41, 8 December 1941; ZA 1151-1-21, pp. 65–6 General Commissar Zhitomir to District and Town Commissars re. recruitment for the Ukrainian *Schutzmannschaft*, 24 February 1942; ZA 1182-1-3, p. 16 Document dated 12 August 1943.
59. WCU D8875; see also ZA 1182-1-35, p. 69 *KdO* Zhitomir order on 24 May 1943 exempting families of *Schutzmänner* from deportation to Germany.
60. WCU D8011.
61. WCU D6950; S296.
62. WCU D8011.
63. WCU S135B.
64. WCU S296.
65. WCU S120B; see also S119A.
66. *BA-MA* RW 41/4 *RFSS* order on security formations in the newly occupied eastern territories, 31 July 1941.
67. ZA 1182-1-17, p. 132 *Gendamerie* Captaincy Order 5/41; ZA 1182-1-3, p. 154 *KdG* Zhitomir, Section Berdichev, 12 February 1942.
68. WCU D4858.
69. *BA* R 94/7 *Gendarmerie* District Leader Brest, 8 November 1942.
70. Two of the automatic weapons used by the partisans were the PPSH and PPD guns: see the photograph in L. Berk, *Destined to Live*, p. 184.
71. BNAM 370-1-1262, pp. 147–58 Lecture by Klepsch at the District Commissars' meeting on 10 April 1943.
72. ZA 1182-1-35, p. 224 *Gendarmerie* post Pogrebichi, 9 March 1943; ZA 1182-1-5, p. 86; ZA 1182-1-17, p. 20 *KdG* Zhitomir re. oaths to be taken by the *Schutzmannschaft*, 19 September 1942; INRW SWB 272, pp. 42–57 W.G. on 7 September 1966; Brest Archive 995-1-6 p. 1 *Gendarmerie* Captaincy Baranovichi re. taking of oaths, 22 October 1942. Many policemen from the Baranovichi district accordingly took their oaths in November 1942: see Brest Archive 995-1-5.
73. Regarding the 'Travnikis', see H. Grabitz, '*Iwan Demjanjuk zum Tode verurteilt*', pp. 176–82. Frau Grabitz notes that most 'Travnikis' were recruited from amongst Soviet PoWs, indicating a degree of compulsion given the death rates in these camps.
74. See, for example, Brest Archive 995-1-3.
75. USHMMA (ZA) 1151-1-21, pp. 65–6 *Generalkommissar* Zhitomir to *Gebiets-und Stadtkommissare* re. recruitment for the Ukrainian *Schutzmannschaft*, 24 February 1942; ZA 1182-1-17, p. 15 Orders concerning unlimited service for *Schutzmannschaft*, 28 September 1942, 24 October 1942 & 2 November 1942. ZA 1182-1-3, pp. 113–15 *KdG* Economic office, 28 July 1943; BNAM 370-1-1262, pp. 147–58 Lecture by Klepsch at the District Commissars' meeting on 10 April 1943; SIU 5776/0 Y.Z.K. on 31 January 1950.
76. ZA 1182-1-23, pp. 533–4 Preliminary Service instructions for the *Gendarmerie* of the *Generalkommissariat* Zhitomir issued by *KdG* Zhitomir, 15 January 1942; ZA 1182-1-3, pp. 17 and 44 Service instructions for the *Schutzmannschaft* of the occupied eastern districts and Head of Order Police, 12 February 1943 – Decorations and awards for members of the *Schutzmannschaft*.
77. Dorking, Oswald Rufeisen on 21–28 February 1996.
78. *ZSL* 2 AR-Z 16/67 Vol. X, pp. 1977–2013 M.E. on 13 June 1973; WCU D7852; WCU D9885; S. Spector, *The Holocaust of Volhynian Jews*, p. 134; *BA* R 94/6 *SSPF* Brest report, 15 March 1942; *Memorial Book of Glebokie*, p. 50.
79. WCU S119A; S135B.

80. Dorking, Oswald Rufeisen on 22 February 1996.
81. *UKGB* Brest Archive File No. 3396, pp. 66–8 interrogation of I.S.K. on 18 August 1945.
82. INRW SWGd 72-3 pp. 44–8, 157–64 and 282–4; WCU D9344; SARF 7021-83-14 pp. 4–7.
83. WCU D9081.
84. INRW SWB 253, pp. 185–7 S.B. on 21 February 1963.
85. N. Tec, *In the Lion's Den*, pp. 107–9.
86. SIU 5776/0 I.V.K on 18 February 1950 and A.A.N. on 13 December 1949.
87. WCU D7560.
88. SIU 5776/0 G.I.K. on 20 December 1948. The witness was beaten by the Head of the police with the handle of his revolver for asking for some water. He was told: 'there's some water for you, take that, you Bolshevik, tell us where the partisans are'.
89. WCU S173C; D2488; D1402; D1855.
90. WCU D9084.
91. *Memorial Book of Glebokie*, p. 34.
92. CSAK 3676-4-317, pp. 67–87 Report of *HSSPF* Ukraine for March 1942. This incident probably took place during the action on 12 February 1942 in Brailov: see *ZSL* II 204a AR-Z 135/67 Vol. III, pp. 575–6. See also SAM 1323-2-228, pp. 11–12 *KdG* Zhitomir, Vinnitsa Captaincy order 16/42, 20 July 1942, which mentions two *Schutzmänner* from Brailov convicted for plundering.
93. *BA* R 94/17a Situation Report for the *Generalkommissariat* Kiev for the beginning of 1943, section 8 Police.
94. *BA* R 94/6 City Commissar Brest report, 26 November 1941.
95. WCU S171B.
96. Dorking, Boris Grushevsky on 18 March 1996. One of the police cohorts described them as follows: 'the first volunteers were just normal lads, my friends, they did not have any special reason for joining the police', S119A; for another cohort in similar vein see S296.
97. *ZSL* 2 AR-Z 16/67 Vol. VI, pp. 1056–9 W. G. on 21 March 1969.
98. *Memorial Book of Glebokie*, p. 139 'the names of the Police have already been listed. All of them, as was mentioned above, actively helped the Germans in their wild murderous deeds.'
99. BNAM 3500-4-263 Partisan interrogation of Ivan Iosefovich Varenik recruited to the police in November 1942.
100. ZA 1182-1-17, p. 57 *SS* and Police District Leader Kazatin: rank badges required for the *Schutzmannschaft*, 18 January 1943; ZA 1182-1-17, p. 83 *Gendarmerie Zug* III/13 Kazatin: clothing available, 14 August 1943.
101. *BA* R 19/122, pp. 129–36 *HSSPF* Ukraine report listing strengths of *Gendarmerie* and *Schutzmannschaften*, 25 November 1942; ZA 1151-1-43, p. 15 survey report by *Generalkommissar* Zhitomir, 1943.
102. BNAM 389-1-3, pp. 139–40 *KdG Weißruthenien* to *Gend*. Captaincy in Baranovichi, 4 November 1942; B. Chiari, '*Deutsche Herrschaft*', p. 337 Strength of the *Schutzmannschaft* in Baranovichi, 29 June 1944.
103. *BA* R 94/7 Brest *Gendarmerie* report, 8 November 1942; *BA* R 94/8 Brest *Gendarmerie* report, 5 December 1943.
104. SAM 1323-2-228, pp. 3–4 *KdG* Zhitomir to *Gendarmerie* District Leader Ruzhin, 1 June 1942.
105. *BA* R 94/8 District Commissar Brest section II report, 19 February 1943.
106. *BA* R 19/333, p. 15 *RFSS* order on police jurisdiction in the newly occupied eastern territories, 19 November 1941.

107. J. Steinberg, 'The Third Reich Reflected', p. 462.
108. WCU S273 and S325. This unit was probably part of the *Samookhova* self-defence force, detached to act as personal guards for the *Gebietskommissar*'s office in Slonim.
109. *BA* R 94/8 *Gendarmerie* District Leader Brest, 4 February 1943.
110. WCU D4355 Interrogation of K.R. 9 September 1947; WCU D6913.
111. ZA 1182-1-17, pp. 123–5, 128 and 150. *BdO* Ukraine Guidelines for training of the *Schutzmannschaft*, 9 April 1943. *RFSS* order on training and schooling of the *Schutzmannschaft* in local posts, 19 August 1942. *KdG Zhitomir, Vinnitsa Captaincy to Gendarmerie* District Leaders, 10 August 1942.
112. *UKGB* Minsk Archive File No. 14687, Criminal Case 36551, pp. 22–4 Interrogation of M.R. on 2 October 1951.
113. ZA 1182-1-17, p. 129 Guidelines for the Training of the *Schutzmannschaft* in the area of *BdO* Ostland and Ukraine. I. Political education and direction.
114. *UKGB* Grodno Criminal Case 1030, Archive File No. 20394, pp. 114–22; see also P. Silverman, D. Smuschkowitz and P. Smuschkowicz, *From Victims to Victors*, pp. 84 and 98 which notes the existence of a night-watch made up of the fathers of policemen in Jody by the winter of 1941–42. This is probably identical with the *Samookhova* (self-defence) organization which operated in support of the police.
115. WCU records indicate that at least four Tartars served in the Nesvizh *rayon* police and three in the various Slonim police units; see also S325.
116. *BA* R 94/7 *Gendarmerie* District Leader Brest report, 5 December 1942.
117. WCU D7341.
118. This interpretation is hammered home by D. J. Goldhagen, *Hitler's Willing Executioners*, pp. 279–80.
119. C. Browning, *Ordinary Men*, pp. 159–89.
120. N. Tec, *In the Lion's Den*, p. 89.
121. Dorking, Oswald Rufeisen on 21–28 February 1996.
122. *ZSL* 202 AR-Z 16/67 Vol. XI, O.R. on 14 March 1966.
123. Dorking, Oswald Rufeisen on 21–28 February 1996.
124. C. Browning, *Ordinary Men*, pp. 159–89.
125. WCU D8607, D408, D4767; YV 03/3567 Testimony of Esther Marchwinski.
126. WCU S135A.
127. WCU D7341.
128. N. Tec, *Defiance: The Bielski Partisans*, p. 53; F. Golczewski, '*Entgegen dem Klischee*' gives several examples of Ukrainian policemen helping Jews; S. Spector, *The Holocaust of Volhynian Jews*, p. 134.
129. Dorking, Oswald Rufeisen on 21–28 February 1996.
130. *David-Horodoker Memorial Book*, pp. 31–2 and 54–8.
131. B. Chiari, '*Deutsche Herrschaft*', pp. 197–8.

5 The Ghetto 'Liquidations' of 1942–43

1. G. Robel, '*Sowjetunion*', p. 557; S. Cholawsky, *The Jews of Bielorussia*, pp. 70–3 and 150; S. Spector, *The Holocaust of Volhynian Jews*, p. 186; on the organization of the 'Second Wave' see also R. Hilberg, *The Destruction of the European Jews*, vol. 1, pp. 368–90.
2. *ZSL* II 204a AR-Z 135/67 Vol. I, pp. 253–9, 260–6 and Vol. II, p. 552; 204a AR-Z 137/67 Vol. I, pp. 88–94 and 227. See 204 AR 56/67, Vol. I, p. iv, statement of W.

R. dated 18 December 1961 on the central co-ordinating role of the Security Police during a similar 'sweep' in the Pinsk area.

3. ZSL II 204a AR-Z 135/67, Vol. I, pp. 253–9 on the involvement of the *Organization Todt*. On the role of the *Gebietskommisariat* see Vol. III, pp. 552–5 Concluding Report.

4. Regarding Hungarian participation, see *ZSL* II 204a AR-Z 188/67 Vol. I, pp. 221–55 and II 204a AR-Z 135/67 Vol. III Concluding Report pp. 570–1. For the Slovakian units see, for instance, the collection on Slovakian military occupation duties in Ukraine, which has been transferred to the Slovakian archives from Prague. I am grateful to Dr Balasch, MHAP, for this information.

5. See, for example, *Justiz und NS-Verbrechen*, vol. XIX, p. 332 on the orders to shoot escaping Jews issued to the *Gendarmerie* and *Schutzmannschaft* prior to the liquidation of the Mizoch ghetto in mid-October 1942.

6. T. Piotrowski, *Poland's Holocaust*, pp. 153–4 and 221–3 draws attention to the active participation of local police units in Belorussia and Ukraine on the basis of published sources. The book, however, generally presents a Polish nationalist view of events and is weakened by its unfortunate treatment of the issue of 'Jewish collaboration'.

7. NAW RG 238, 1104–PS Report of *Gebietskommissar* Carl 30 October 1941 and accompanying correspondence and 3257-PS Seraphim Report 29 November 1941 with covering letter dated 2 December 1941; LSHA 1026–1–3, pp. 251–61 Burckhardt Memorandum.

8. SAM 1323–2–267 Daluege Report on the Order Police in 1942.

9. NAW RG 238 1104–PS Report of District Commissar Carl in Slutsk, 30 October 1941.

10. See Chapter 3 above.

11. BNAM 3500–2–38, pp. 533–5.

12. Dorking, Oswald Rufeisen on 27 February 1996.

13. N. Tec, *In the Lion's Den*, pp. 89–95.

14. WCU D9145.

15. Dorking, Oswald Rufeisen on 22 February 1996.

16. Ibid.

17. YV 016/159 Ester Gorodejska (in Polish) on 9 August 1945.

18. Dorking, Oswald Rufeisen on 21–28 February 1996; WCU S19D, D7573; D5548; D8607; D9154; D9153; D9147.

19. I have personally visited these and other grave – sites in the Mir *rayon* in connection with my work for Scotland Yard.

20. S. Spector, *The Holocaust of Volhynian Jews*, p. 119; *BA* R 94/7 District Commissar Report for the Brest District, 24 March 1942.

21. Circular of District Commissar Traub to mayors and village elders, Novogrudok, 6 March 1942. Published in J. Kagan and D. Cohen, *Surviving the Holocaust*, pp. 156–7.

22. *BA* R 94/6 City Commissar Brest reports, 23 December 1941 and 25 March 1942.

23. S. Spector, *The Holocaust of Volhynian Jews*, pp. 118–19; in Manevichi the Jews continued to live in the same houses as before and no specially fenced off area was created as in Vladimir-Volynsk: see WCU A.S.S. 26 January 1989.

24. Volyn SRA, Lutsk, R-2-1-8B, p. 148 General Commissar Order, 23 March 1942.

25. WCU S20C, D8376.

26. S. Cholawski, *Soldiers from the Ghetto*, p. 62.

27. Ibid., p. 59.

28. *Memorial Book of Kobrin*, p. 386; *Memorial Book of Glebokie*, p. 51.

29. Dorking, Oswald Rufeisen on 21–28 February 1996, p. 21.
30. INRW, AGK SWB 231, pp. 24–30.
31. Activity and situation report No. 11 of the *Einsatzgruppen* for 1–31 March 1942, published in P. Klein (Hrsg.), *Die Einsatzgruppen*, p. 308 reports 2007 Jews shot in Baranovichi; USHMMA RG 53.002M, Reel 6 (BNAM) 845–1–206 Extraordinary Commission report for Baranovichi, 1 January 1945 gives the figure of 3400; *Encyclopaedia of the Holocaust*, pp. 147–8 indicates 2300.
32. *ZSL* II 204a AR-Z 136/67, Soviet material, pp. 44–6 Extraordinary Commission Report for Vinnitsa in 1944, pp. 299–303 statement by Soviet witness L.S. and Vol. IV, pp. 927–35 German statement dated 17 March 1971; A.F. Vysotsky *et al.*, *Nazi Crimes in Ukraine*, p. 149 indicates that 10 000 civilians were gathered in the Vinnitsa stadium and all but 1000 were shot.
33. NAW RG 238 3257-PS Seraphim Report, 29 November 1941 with covering letter dated 2 December 1941; BA-MA RW 30/145.
34. SAM 369–1–29, pp. 24–5 Secret Field Police Note (*RSD*); G. Jukes, *Hitler's Stalingrad Decisions*, pp. 9 and 43.
35. SAM 1323–2–230 Schmidt to Rattenhuber, 12 January 1942. In 1991 the site of Hitler's bunker, just north of Vinnitsa, was little more than an overgrown concrete hole in the ground. On the formation of the *RSD* see P. Hoffmann, *Hitler's Personal Security*, pp. 29–43.
36. On the events in Gnivan see *ZSL* II 204a AR-Z 136/67; SIU evidence taken in the case of Nikolay Beresovsky; A.F. Vysotsky *et al.*, *Nazi Crimes in Ukraine*, pp. 162–3. According to M. Altshuler, *Distribution of the Jewish Population*, Gnivan had 361 Jews in 1939.
37. *ZSL* II 204 AR-Z 128/67 (Ruzhin), II 204a 135/67 (Brailov, Litin and Khmelnik) and II 204a AR-Z 138/67 (Illinzi, Lipovets and Pliskov).
38. *BA* R 6/310, p. 17 Report of *Generalkommissar* Zhitomir for month of May, 3 June 1942.
39. *ZSL* II 204a AR-Z 188/67 Vol. I, pp. 229–31 A.N.W. on 2 June 1953.
40. ZA 1182–1–6, p. 163 *Gendarmerie* post Samgorodok, 31 May 1943.
41. ZA 1182–1–36, p. 30 *Gendarmerie* District Ruzhin to *Gendarmerie* Captaincy in Vinnitsa, 14 June 1942.
42. ZA 1151–1–9, p. 1 *KdG* Zhitomir Order 18/42, 6 June 1942.
43. *Justiz und NS-Verbrechen*, vol. XVI, pp. 346–8. An escape attempt by some Jews resulted in all escapees being shot.
44. ZA 1182–1–36, pp. 235–8 SS and Police District Leader Ruzhin, 5 November 1942.
45. *ZSL* USA Film 7, Heft Ord. No. 26, Bild No. 611–2 (NO 5655); on local police involvement in the ghetto liquidations in the Kamenets-Podolsk district see also I. Ehrenburg and V. Grossman, *The Black Book*, pp. 529–39.
46. Y. Arad, 'The Holocaust of Soviet Jewry', pp. 30–1.
47. *Encyclopaedia of the Holocaust*, p. 798 contribution of S. Spector on the fate of the Jews in Kherson; see also M. Gilbert, *The Holocaust*, p. 353 on the killing of rural Jews in the Kherson district.
48. SSA Kirovograd, statement of G.K.K on 3 April 1946 in own trial.
49. This summary of events in Ustinovka has been compiled from statements in Soviet trials from the 1940s and 1950s. In spite of some discrepancies about dates and numbers, these testimonies appear to be reliable concerning the overall pattern of events. See SSA Kirovograd, A.A.G. on 20 March 1947 and 1 April 1947 in own trial; G.K.K. on 19 February 1946 and 3 April 1946 in own trial; F.F.S. on 1 March 1958 and I.K.K. on 13 February 1958 in File No. 4419.

These accounts can also be compared with the additional evidence collected by the SIU in the case of H.W.

50. Analysis of evidence prepared by John Ralston of the SIU in the case of H.W.; see also *Landgericht* Cologne Verdict 104–28/97 in the case of Ernst Hering, pp. 43–9.

51. *Unsere Ehre heißt Treue*, pp. 237–9 *SS Uscharf*. Lipps *Außenstelle* Vileyka to Burgdorf, 27 May 1942.

52. BNAM 370–1–483, p. 15 Report of District Commissar Glubokoye, 1 July 1942.

53. I. Aron, *Fallen Leaves*, pp. 34–5.

54. BNAM 370-1-483 p. 15 Report of District Commissar Glubokoye, 1 July 1942. On the Jewish actions in this region see also *ZSL* 202 AR-Z 37/60 which mentions the active participation of the Belorussian police in these actions. The dramatized account in I. Aron, *Fallen Leaves* has several further references to escapees from Miory. See also INRW SOGz 43, SOO1 24, SAWr 10 and 127 for references to the arrest and shooting of Jews in the Braslav area. A list of communities affected in this wave is given also in *Memorial Book of Glebokie*, p. 66.

55. *Memorial Book of Glebokie*, p. 70.

56. *Unsere Ehre heißt Treue*, p. 241; *BA* R 58/697, pp. 168–78 Report from the occupied eastern territories No. 9, 26 June 1942.

57. WCU D6104.

58. INRW SWB 221, p. 115 M.P. on 23 January 1964; p. 41 E.L. on 20 June 1963: one local resident of Novaya Mysh witnessed a policeman taking 3 Jewish children to the forest the day after the mass execution. He heard shots and saw the policeman returning alone.

59. INRW SWSz 69–78.

60. *Unsere Ehre heißt Treue*, p. 242 *Gruppe Arlt* report, Minsk 3 August 1942.

61. *ZSL* 202 AR-Z 228/59 Indictment in the case of Gerhard Erren, pp. 4314–24.

62. WCU D7809.

63. WCU S282.

64. *ZSL* 202 AR-Z 228/59, pp. 4322–41; WCU D7809.

65. *ZSL* 202 AR-Z 228/59, p. 4305. *Unsere Ehre heißt Treue*, p. 242 *Gruppe Arlt*, Minsk 3 August 1942 reports 4000 victims; N. Alpert, *The Destruction of Slonim Jewry*, p. 160 gives the figure of 12 000 Slonim Jews prior to the action.

66. *ZSL* 202 AR-Z 228/59 pp. 1823–6 & 4344.

67. *CDJC* CDXXXVI-46 Report of Slonim *Gebietskommissar*, 26 September 1942.

68. S. Cholawski, *Soldiers from the Ghetto*, pp. 57–8.

69. M. Lachowicki, *The Victims of Nesvizh*.

70. *UKGB* Criminal Case 35930, Archive File No. 902, pp. 99–102 I.A.N. on 5 June 1950, pp. 96–8 M.F.K. on 7 June 1950 and pp. 171–3 in which the Soviet investigators conducted a crime scene visit to check out the evidence of the above two witnesses, concluding that they both had a clear view of the march route as described in their statements.

71. S. Cholawski, *Soldiers from the Ghetto*, p. 67.

72. M. Lachowicki, *The Victims of Nesvizh*.

73. S. Cholawski, *Soldiers from the Ghetto*, p. 68.

74. USHMMA RG 53.002M, reel 4 (BNAM) 389-1-3, p. 66 *KdS Weißruthenien* to *Gendarmerie*, 11 May 1942.

75. *ZSL* 202 AR 133/81, pp. 32–5 A.A.G. on 17 October 1979; on the concentration of all Nesvizh district police see also pp. 36–8 A.I.T. on 19 October 1979 and M. Lachowicki, *The Victims of Nesvizh*. On the participation of Lithuanians,

probably auxiliaries of the Security Police, see WCU D9132, D9129 and *UKGB* Minsk Case 2006, archive no. 1592.

76. For the concentration of forces for the action in Stolpce in September 1942 see Brest Archive 995-1-4, p. 233 Schultz report, 3 October 1942. On the concentration of the police for the action in Nesvizh see WCU D9087 and *UKGB* Minsk Case 36551, Archive File No. 14687, pp. 111–2 N.A.K. on 8 May 1948.

77. *ZSL* 202 AR 133/81, pp. 25–38 A.A.G. on 17 October 1979; on the orders to shoot escapees see also A.K.A. on 16 October 1979 and A.I.T. on 19 October 1979. S. Spector, *The Holocaust of Volhynian Jews*, p. 176 mentions shoot to kill orders received prior to the ghetto round ups in Volhynia.

78. M. Lachowicki, *The Victims of Nesvizh*.

79. S. Cholawsky, *The Jews of Bielorussia*, p. 190.

80. M. Lachowicki, *The Victims of Nesvizh*; S. Cholawski, *Soldiers from the Ghetto*, pp. 68–70.

81. *ZSL* 202 AR 133/81, pp. 32–5 A.A.G. on 17 October 1979.

82. M. Lachowicki, *The Victims of Nesvizh*; S. Cholawsky, *The Jews of Bielorussia*, pp. 190–1.

83. *UKGB* Minsk Archive File No. 14687, Criminal Case 36551. Another witness heard from other policemen in the cordon that they also shot people trying to escape: see *ZSL* 202 AR 133/81, pp. 21–4 F.I.P. on 8 October 1979. S. Spector, *The Holocaust of Volhynian Jews*, p. 177 also refers to alcohol consumed by the local police during the 'liquidation' actions.

84. S. Cholawski, *Soldiers from the Ghetto*, pp. 69–70.

85. *ZSL* 202 AR 133/81, pp. 21–4 F.I.P. on 8 October 1979.

86. WCU D8661. This Jewish survivor lived in Minsk after the war and visited the family occasionally in Nesvizh.

87. WCU D9083.

88. *UKGB* Minsk Archive File No. 1592, Criminal Case 2006.

89. *ZSL* 202 AR 133/81, pp. 32–5 A.A.G. on 17 October 1979.

90. *UKGB* Minsk Archive File No. 20309, pp. 18–20 F.I.P. on 13 March 1945.

91. *ZSL* 202 AR 133/81, p. 325 A.I.T. on 19 October 1979. See also *UKGB* Archive File No. 616 pp. 75–6, trial of A.I.T. on 5 November 1945, in which he says that the police opened the door before firing at the Jewish woman.

92. M. Lachowicki, *The Victims of Nesvizh*.

93. Dorking, Oswald Rufeisen on 23 February 1996.

94. WCU Oswald Rufeisen interview on 1 & 5 March 1995.

95. *ZSL* 2 AR-Z 16/67 Vol. I, pp. 70–2 D.R. on 7 February 1967.

96. *ZSL* 2 AR-Z 16/67 F.B. on 8 February 1967.

97. Brest Archive 995-1-7, pp. 211–12 Hein Report, 20 August 1942.

98. *ZSL* 2 AR-Z 16/67 Vol. VIII, W. G. on 24–5 July 1969.

99. *ZSL* 2 AR-Z 16/67 Vol. VI, pp. 1146–55 E.F. on 13 March 1969.

100. *Sta.* Oldenburg 2 JS 138/68 Vol. I, pp. 60–2 A.F. on 14 February 1969; *ZSL* 2 AR-Z 16/67 Vol. VI pp. 1146–55 E.F. on 13 March 1969, Vol. VIII, W.G. on 24–5 July 1969.

101. *UKGB* Grodno Criminal Case 35133, Archive File No. 696.

102. *ZSL* 2 AR-Z 16/67 Vol. VI, pp. 1146–55 E.F. on 13 March 1969.

103. Brest Archive 995-1-7, p. 237 Report of Captain Eibner, 26 August 1942.

104. Brest Archive 995-1-7, pp. 211–12 Hein Report, 20 August 1942.

105. *UKGB* Grodno Criminal Case 35133, Archive File No. 696.

106. Brest Archive 995-1-4, p. 304 Schultz report, 18 October 1942.

107. *Unsere Ehre heißt Treue*, p. 242 *Gruppe Arlt* report, Minsk 3 August 1942. See also WCU D1647 & D1685.

108. *BA* NS 19/1772 Himmler to Berger, 28 July 1942. Also quoted by R. Hilberg, *The Destruction of the European Jews*, Vol. I, p. 368.
109. *BA* NS 19/1757 Himmler to *HSSPF* East Krüger, 19 July 1942. This was codenamed 'Operation Reinhard'.
110. NAW RG 238, T-175, roll 235 Report from the occupied eastern territories No. 5, 29 May 1942 gives the figure of 326 000 Jews for Volhynia-Podolia.
111. INRW Zbior Zespolow Szczatkowych Jednostek SS i Policji – Sygnatura 77. This valuable source was located by S. Spector, *The Holocaust of Volhynian Jews*, p. 173. The documents appear to be Polish transcripts of German originals, which may have been partially destroyed or even smuggled out by the Underground. Efforts to trace the original documents have proved unsuccessful.
112. *ZSL* 204 AR-Z 393/59 Vol. II, pp. 173–94 Wilhelm Rasp on 18 December 1961. This testimony illustrates well the difficult nature of legal evidence as a source. While there is no reason to doubt the detailed description of numerous actions by Rasp, which in part incriminates himself, his self-exculpatory comments on attempting to save Jews must be treated with more care. Also details of numbers killed, places and dates need to be checked carefully against other sources, which generally corroborate him, although revealing some discrepancies. Rasp's statement should be read carefully in conjunction with Spector's work and contemporary German documents.
113. *ZSL* 204 AR-Z 393/59 Vol. II, pp. 173–94 Wilhelm Rasp on 18 December 1961. On resistance during the Lakhva ghetto liquidation see Y. Suhl (ed.), *They Fought Back*, pp. 165–7 and S. Cholawsky, *The Jews of Bielorussia*, pp. 193–8.
114. INRW Zbior Zespolow Szczatkowych Jednostek SS i Policji – Sygnatura 77, p. 7 *Generalkommissar* Volhynia-Podolia to *Reichskommissar* Ukraine, 25 August 1942. This happened subsequently (for instance, in Lakhva and Ivanovo): see *ZSL* 204 AR-Z 393/59 Vol. II, pp. 173–94 and 418–19 W. R. on 18 December 1961 and 14 May 1962.
115. *BA* R 6/243, pp. 20–2.
116. INRW Zbior Zespolow Szczatkowych Jednostek SS i Policji – Sygnatura 77, pp. 8–9 *Generalkommissar* Volhynia-Podolia to Security Police outposts in Brest, Pinsk, Starokonstantinov & Kamenets-Podolsk, 31 August 1942. On the disregard for the continuing demand for Jewish labour see also S. Spector, *The Holocaust of Volhynian Jews*, p. 173.
117. See, for example, *BA* R 94/6 City Commissar Brest report, 27 August 1942.
118. S. Spector, *The Holocaust of Volhynian Jews*, p. 178. On the disposal of Jewish property see, for example, Brest Archive 195-1-300, p. 11 *Gebietskommissar* Brest to all *rayon* Heads, 14 November 1942.
119. *ZSL* 204 AR-Z 393/59 Vol. II, pp. 173–94 W.R. on 18 December 1961. R. mentions that on the first day of the action in Pinsk the deputy *Gebietskommissar*, E., was attacked by a Jew and shot him dead with his pistol.
120. S. Spector, *The Holocaust of Volhynian Jews*, pp. 179–80. On the participation of the local militia in such round-ups see also D. K. Huneke, *The Moses of Rovno*, pp. 55–6.
121. S. Spector, 'The Jews of Volhynia', 164–5. M. Gilbert, *The Holocaust*, p. 467 gives the figure of 300 escapees during the round-up.
122. ZA 1182-1-6 p. 163; *ZSL* 204a AR-Z 135/67; *ZSL* UdSSR 245c, pp. 281–2.
123. J. Noakes and G. Pridham (eds), *Nazism 1919–45*, Vol. 3, Doc. 823, pp. 1100–1, Nuremberg Document PS-2992. Also published in Martin Gilbert, *The Holocaust*, pp. 476–8. For the full story of Graebe's rescue attempts see D. K. Huneke, *The Moses of Rovno*.

124. SARF 7021-148-2 Saur report 29 October–1 November 1942; *ZSL* 204 AR-Z 393/59 Vol. II, pp. 173–94 W.R. on 18 December 1961.
125. SARF 7021-148-2, p. 346 9. Company/Pol. Rgt 15 weekly report, 1 November 1942.
126. *BA* R 94/7 *Gendarmerie* District Leader Brest monthly report, 8 November 1942. 20 000 Jews were 'resettled' in Brest on 15–16 October 1942.
127. WCU D9298; D9297.
128. AANW 202/III/7 t. 1, p. 187 Polish Underground Report 252/A-1, 17 December 1942. On the active role of the local police in the subsequent clear-up actions see also S. Spector, *The Holocaust of Volhynian Jews*, p. 176.
129. *UKGB* Brest Archive File No. 350, pp. 27–30 interrogation of accused G.P.S. on 12 January 1946.
130. On the disposal of Jewish property see B. Chiari, '*Deutsche Herrschaft*', pp. 266–70; see also *Memorial Book of Glebokie*, p. 67.
131. ZA 1151-1-138 Official Publication of the *Generalkommissar* in Zhitomir, p. 12; ZA 1182-1-6, p. 171 *Gebietskommissar* Kazatin to *Gendarmerie* post, 15 May 1942.
132. INRW SWO 12, statement of A.W.
133. SARF 7021-148 3, p. 7 *SSPF* Volhynia-Podolia order, 25 October 1942; *Memorial Book of Glebokie*, p. 68.
134. *BA* R 94/7 *Gendarmerie* District Leader Brest, 8 November 1942.
135. Soviet allegation in the Australian case of I.P.
136. Original to be found in Slonim Historical Museum.
137. C. Browning, *Ordinary Men*, pp. 121–32.
138. ZA 1182-1-36, pp. 275–8 and p. 214: *SS*PGF Ruzhin monthly report for October, 5 November 1942 and monthly report for September, 4 October 1942; ZA 1182-1-6, p. 165 *SS*PGF Kazatin to *SD* Berdichev, 13 March 1942.
139. INRW SwSz 68 statement of accused F.N.
140. Brest Archive 995-1-4, p. 396.
141. WCU S119A.
142. *UKGB* Brest File No. 3431.
143. SARF 7021-148-2 p. 347 11./Pol. Rgt 15 report for period 8–14 November 1942.
144. *BA* R 94/8 *Gendarmerie* District Leader Brest, 4 February 1943.
145. *BA* R 94/7 *Gendarmerie* District Leader Brest, 8 November 1942; see also SARF 7021-148-2, p. 345 Report of 10. Co./Pol. Rgt 15, 26 October 1942.
146. *BA* R 94/7 *Gendarmerie* District Leader Brest, 5 December 1942. See also SARF 7021-148-2, pp. 390-1 9./Pol. Rgt 15 report on 15 October 1942 which indicated that the local population was actively involved in seizing escaped Jews.
147. UKGB Minsk File on A.S., pp. 19–22 P.P.D. on 12 April 1950; see also D. Budnik and Y. Kaper, *Nothing is Forgotten*, p. 101 on denunciation and looting in Kiev.
148. *Memorial Book of Kobrin*, pp. 391–2.
149. Dorking, Oswald Rufeisen on 23 February 1996.
150. Dorking, Regina Bedynska on 28 February 1996. On the round-up of Poles in Mir see also Oswald Rufeisen on 23–8 February 1996 and *ZSL* 2 AR-Z 16/67 Vol. VIII, W. G. on 24–5 July 1969.
151. A. Galinski, 'The extermination of the Polish intelligentsia in the summer of 1942 in the Novogrodek area (problems of investigation)', pp. 188–9. This is an article in Polish received from Mr Galinski at the Lodz branch of the Polish Main Commission in 1993. SARF 7021-81-102, pp. 99–101 Soviet Extraordinary Commission Report for Nesvizh, 4 April 1945.

152. A. Galinski, 'The extermination of the Polish intelligentsia', p. 188.
153. A. F. Vysotsky *et al.*, *Nazi Crimes in Ukraine*, pp. 156–7; 270 mental patients were killed on 28 October 1941, *BA* R 58/219 *EM* 135, 19 November 1941. On the development of the gas van see M. Beer, '*Die Entwicklung der Gaswagen*', pp. 403–17.
154. WCU D9317.
155. Re. Khoiniki see the *ZSL* case against Ermoltschik (Krüger) and the OSI case against Basil Artishenko; C. Ashman and R. J. Wagman, *The Nazi Hunters*, p. 308.
156. S. Spector, *The Holocaust of Volhynian Jews*, pp. 173–4.
157. *ZSL* II 202 AR-Z 228/59 pp. 6624-44 G. R. on 25 November 1964.
158. *BA* R 19/121, p. 655 *KdG* Zhitomir strength on 15 June 1942: 3709 *Schutzmänner* and 766 Gendarmes; *BA* R 19/122 *KdG* Lutsk on 25 November 1942: 9553 *Schutzmänner* and 954 Gendarmes; S. Spector, *The Holocaust of Volhynian Jews*, p. 175. By 1943 the ratio had exceeded ten to one, see SAM 1323-2-267 Report of Daluege on strength and operations of the Order Police in 1942, 1 February 1943. At this time 5860 men of the *Schutzpolizei* and 9093 Gendarmes were responsible for 223 787 members of the *Schutzmannschaft Einzeldienst*.
159. C. Browning, *Ordinary Men*, p. 128.
160. WCU J.L. on 8 September 1988.
161. S. Spector, 'The Jews of Volhynia', p. 160.
162. PUST No. 2792 Memoirs of Lt Mikolaj Balysz (Zagloba); S. Spector, *The Holocaust of Volhynian Jews*, pp. 238–43.
163. WCU I.K. on 8 September 1988.
164. *ZSL* 202 AR-Z 228/59.
165. WCU V.N.K. on 27 January 1989.
166. WCU N.S.L. on 28 January 1989.
167. L. Berk, *Destined to Live*, p. 79; on the strength of family loyalties see especially S. Cholawsky, *The Jews of Bielorussia*, pp. 153, 223–4 and 299–300.
168. Brest Archive 995-1-7, p. 237 Report of *Gendarmerie* Captain Eibner, 26 August 1942; see also S. Cholawsky, *The Jews of Bielorussia*, pp. 85, 151–2 & 201–8.
169. P. Goldstein in *Hoscha Memorial Book* (in Yiddish), pp. 71–2, quoted by S. Spector, *The Holocaust of Volhynian Jews*, p. 164.
170. *BA* R 94/7 *Gendarmerie* District Leader Brest, 6 October 1942.
171. *ZSL* 204 AR-Z 369/63 Vol. I, pp. 213–16.
172. WAST loss reports: E. K., a member of *Reiterabteilung I*, committed suicide in October 1942 in Tomashovka, shortly after the Jewish action in this town. A Gendarme from the Brest district, J. L., committed suicide in 1945.
173. *BA* NS 19/2566, pp. 51–2 Report No. 51 of *RFSS* Himmler to Hitler on results of partisan warfare 1 September 1941 to 1 December 1942. Quoted also by R. Hilberg, *The Destruction of the European Jews*, vol. I, p. 390.
174. *Encyclopaedia Judaica*, vol. 15, p. 7 about 2000 Jews from the Sadki ghetto were murdered in June–July 1942; *BA-MA* RH 22/203 FK (V) 239 report of 17 June 1942 mentions a Jewish action at Lokhvitsa near Poltava on 12 May 1942; *CDJC* Paris, CCCLVIII-2 Extraordinary State Commission Report on the murder of the Jews of Kislovodsk in September 1942 by *Einsatzgruppe D*.
175. C. Gerlach, '*Deutsche Wirtschaftsinteressen*', p. 19 estimates that about 20 000 Jews in Minsk, Lida and Glubokoye were killed or deported in late summer 1943; USHMMA RG 53.002M, Reel 6 (BNAM) 845-1-206, pp. 49–50 *KdS Weißruthenien* order on the action in Slutsk, 5 February 1943 and p. 153 Extraordinary Commission report for Glubokoye, 23 January 1945; the Minsk ghetto was liquidated on 21 October 1943: H. Smolar, *The Minsk Ghetto*, p. 143.

6 Local Administration and Exploitation, 1941–44

1. *UKGB* Minsk, Archive File No. 1677, Criminal Case 34307.
2. Ibid.
3. Ibid.; see also Archive File No. 19165 which contains similar evidence.
4. B. Chiari, '*Deutsche Herrschaft*', p. 113.
5. Ibid., pp. 116–21; W. Wilenchik, *Die Partisanenbewegung in Weißrußland*, pp. 234–5.
6. T. Mulligan, *The Politics of Illusion and Empire*, p. 63; J. A. Armstrong, *Ukrainian Nationalism*, pp. 67–70. The OUN Melnik faction held a number of leading positions in the Zhitomir district.
7. A. Dallin, *German Rule in Russia*, p. 87.
8. T. Mulligan, *The Politics of Illusion and Empire*, p. 64.
9. A. Dallin, *German Rule in Russia*, p. 102.
10. B. Chiari, '*Deutsche Herrschaft*', pp. 59–62.
11. Graebe's boldness almost backfired on him when American interrogators refused to believe that he could cross Europe using his own train without being a spy or a senior Nazi official: D. K. Huneke, *The Moses of Rovno*, pp. 121 and 160.
12. B. Chiari, '*Deutsche Herrschaft*', pp. 71–2.
13. *UKGB* Brest Archive File No. 154-H, Case No. 6, pp. 11–12 E. E. on 18 April 1946.
14. A. Dallin, *German Rule in Russia*, p. 352.
15. B. Chiari, '*Deutsche Herrschaft*', p. 115.
16. Ibid., pp. 74–5.
17. T. P. Mulligan, *The Politics of Illusion and Empire*, pp. 93–105; B. Chiari, '*Deutsche Herrschaft*', pp. 140–2; A. Dallin, *German Rule in Russia*, pp. 344–51; J. A. Armstrong, *Ukrainian Nationalism*, pp. 86–7.
18. J. A. Armstrong, *Ukrainian Nationalism*, p. 117; NAW RG 238, T-175, roll 235 *Meldungen aus den besetzten Ostgebieten* No. 7, 12 June 1942.
19. *BA* Berlin R 94/4b Press release of *Reichskommissar* Koch on 21 June 1943; on the dispute between Koch and Rosenberg regarding the closure of all schools above primary level in the autumn of 1942 see T. Mulligan, *The Politics of Illusion and Empire*, pp. 65–6.
20. B. Chiari, '*Deutsche Herrschaft*', p. 211.
21. USHMMA RG 53.002M, reel 5 (BNAM) 655-1-3, pp. 21–59 *Tätigkeits- u. Lagebericht der Einsatzgruppe B* 15 November–15 December 1942.
22. School buildings were taken over by the police (for example, in Seilovichi near Nesvizh): see *UKGB* Minsk Archive File No. 1919, Criminal Case 35324, pp. 36–7 and in Yeremichi, see WCU D7557; B. Chiari, '*Deutsche Herrschaft*', p. 225.
23. B. Chiari, '*Deutsche Herrschaft*', pp. 56–7; H.-H. Wilhelm, *Die Einsatzgruppe A*, pp. 423–4 also detects a flight from reality amongst the occupying forces from 1942 onwards.
24. B. Chiari, '*Deutsche Herrschaft*', p. 76.
25. NAW (BDC) SSO Carl Zenner; on the role of Jewish partisans in the attack on Kossovo see L. Eckmann and C. Lazar, *The Jewish Resistance*, p. 154.
26. USHMMA RG 53.002M, reel 3 (BNAM) 389-1-1 *KdO* Minsk Daily Order No. 10, 8 July 1942 and Order No. 14, 1 July 1943.
27. USHMMA (ZA) 1151-1-36 *Reichskommissariat Ukraine* order, 21 July 1942.
28. N. Tec, *In the Lion's Den*, p. 105; *Memorial Book of Glebokie*, p. 60 indicates that the liaison of a German with a Jewish girl in Glubokoye had fatal consequences

for the girl and other Jews. See also H.-H. Wilhelm, '*Hitlers "Europäische Neuordnung"* ', p. 293.

29. USHMMA RG 53.002M, reel 4 (BNAM) 389-1-7, p. 12 Report on incident concerning *Oberwachtmeister* Otto Werner at Starzyna post, 8 April 1944. On similar instances of alcoholism in the east see also D. Pohl, *Von der 'Judenpolitik' zum Judenmord*, p. 41.

30. *Memorial Book of Glebokie*, p. 116 notes Germans trading in stolen goods with the Jews in contravention of their own laws. Of course, if caught the punishment for the Jew was likely to be much more severe.

31. *BA* R 94/4b Press release of *Reichskommissar* Koch, 21 June 1943.

32. J. Winter and J.-L. Robert (eds), *Capital Cities at War*, pp. 494–6.

33. *BA* R 94/7 District Commissar Brest report, 24 February 1942.

34. *BA* R 94/6 *SSPF* Brest report, 15 August 1942.

35. H. Smolar, *The Minsk Ghetto*, p. 18 notes that the Jews in Minsk began to barter clothes and household utensils with the peasants right from the start of the occupation; USHMMA RG 53.002M, reel 5 (BNAM) 655-1-3, pp. 21–59 *Tätigkeits- u. Lagebericht der Einsatzgruppe B* 15 November–15 December 1942; USHMMA (ZA) 1151-1-36 *Generalkommissar* Zhitomir order, 30 January 1943.

36. *BA* R 94/7 Brest District Commissar Agricultural section report, 22 October 1942. On the high level of barter with local peasants and smuggling into the ghettos in spite of the regulations, see S. Spector, *The Holocaust of Volhynian Jews*, pp. 133–4.

37. *BA* R 94/8 District Commissar Brest report on the labour situation in May 1943, 24 May 1943.

38. USHMMA RG 53.002M, reel 5 (BNAM) 658-1-3, p. 180 *KdG* Zhitomir order 23/43; see also B. Chiari, '*Deutsche Herrschaft*', p. 191.

39. B. Chiari, '*Deutsche Herrschaft*', p. 122.

40. ZA 1182-1-36, p. 277 *SS* and Police District Leader Ruzhin, monthly report for October 1942 which mentions members of the *Gendarmerie* escorting cattle transports.

41. *BA* R 6/310, pp. 30–2 report of the *Generalkommissar* Zhitomir on food supplies and agriculture policy, 3 June 1942.

42. *BA* R 94/5 Instructions and official circular of the *Generalkommissar* Nikolayev – Section for Food supplies and Agriculture. Order of the *Generalkommissar* Nikolayev, 21 August 1942.

43. WCU D7559.

44. O. Figes, *A People's Tragedy*, p. 46.

45. SSA Vinnitsa Case of I.V.K. and three others, pp. 120–1 K.I.K. on 15 March 1950.

46. *UKGB* Brest Archive File No. 7627 V.I.G. on 31 August 1947.

47. A. Dallin, *German Rule in Russia*, p. 83.

48. CSAK 3206-2-193, pp. 8–9; ZA 1465-1-6, pp. 133–4 Ordinance issued by *Reichskommissar* Koch against breach of contract, poaching of workers and overpayment of wages, 20 December 1942.

49. WCU D8670.

50. *BA* Berlin R 94/7 Brest District Commissar Agricultural section report, 22 October 1942.

51. NAW R 238, T-175, roll 235 *Meldungen aus den besetzten Ostgebieten* No. 13, 24 July 1942. *BA* R 6/310, pp. 33–6 Report of *Generalkommissar* Zhitomir on labour policy, 3 June 1942 indicates that 40 000 people had been deported from *Generalkommissariat* Zhitomir by this date.

52. ZA 1452-1-2, p. 62 *SS* and Police District Leader in Ruzhin to the *Gendarmerie* posts of Ruzhin District, 30 January 1943. On the unscrupulous methods used for forcible recruitment see also W. Wilenchik, '*Die Partisanenbewegung im Weißrußland*', pp. 204–5.

53. Forced recruitment was organized by age groups, as can be seen from the lists of people who returned from work in Germany compiled by the Soviet Extraordinary Commissions: see, for example, SARF 7021-54-1336 and 1252.

54. ZA 1511-1-1, p. 32 *SS* and Police District Leader in Korosten to all *Gendarmerie* posts, 31 May 1943.

55. ZA 1511-1-1, p. 32 enclosed in order of *SS* and Police District Leader Korosten to all *Gendarmerie* posts, 17 June 1943; see also ZA 1182-1-23, p. 521 *Reichskommissar* to *HSSPF* Prützmann in Kiev warning him to avoid excessive beatings of local inhabitants, 12 August 1942.

56. WCU D9229.

57. *BA R* 94/8 District Commissar Brest report for May 1943, 24 May 1943.

58. *UKGB* Brest Archive File No. 466 vol. 3, pp. 198–202 I.G.M. on 3 January 1991.

59. USHMMA RG-53.002M, reel 5 (BNAM) 845-1-6, pp. 54–6 Extraordinary Commission Report for the district of Nesvizh, 4 February 1945; SARF 7021-81-123 deportation records for the Nesvizh *rayon*.

60. J. Schlootz (Hrsg.), *Deutsche Propaganda in Weißrußland*, p. 55; SSA Vinnitsa Case of I.S.K. and three others, pp. 42–4 A.A.N. on 13 December 1949.

61. *BA R* 94/17 Situation report of the General Commissar for Volhynia-Podolia, 30 April 1943. See also *BA* Berlin R 6/307 Situation report for *Generalkommissariat* Nikolayev in May 1942.

62. *BA R* 94/7 District Commissar Brest – Labour Office report, 25 November 1942.

63. *BA R* 94/8 District Commissar Brest situation report for May–June 1943, 24 June 1943; see also U. Herbert, *Fremdarbeiter*, p. 165.

64. *BA R* 94/7 District Commissar Brest – Labour Office report, 25 November 1942.

65. USHMMA RG 53.002M, reel 5 (BNAM) 655-1-3, pp. 26–7 German translation of Russian propaganda pamphlets.

66. K. Heuer, '*Die Region: Definitionsversuche, Aufgabenstellungen, Beispiele und Erfahrungen*' in F. Dorn, K. Heuer (Hrsg.), '*Ich war immer gut zu meiner Russin*', p. 48.

67. K-J. Siegfried, *Das Leben der Zwangsarbeiter*, p. 174.

68. F. Dorn, S. Rupp and A. Sahn, '*Die verlorenen Jahre in Deutschland: Annäherungen an die Geschichte der Zwangsarbeit aus dem Erleben der Leidtragenden als Aufgabe der evangelischen Erwachsenbildung*' in F. Dorn and K. Heuer (Hrsg.), '*Ich war immer gut zu meiner Russin*', p. 217.

69. K.-J. Siegfried, *Das Leben der Zwangsarbeiter*, p. 172.

70. U. Herbert, *Fremdarbeiter*, p. 161 quoted from *BA R* 41/269.

71. R.E. Herzstein, *The War that Hitler Won*, pp. 21–2.

72. *CDJC* CDXXXVI-46 Report of District Commissar Slonim (Erren) on 26 September 1942.

73. *UKGB* Brest Archive File No. 23552, Criminal Case of K.M.B. and M.E.N., pp. 47–8 M.E.N. on 20 November 1945.

74. BNAM 370-6-48 German propaganda reports and material from the Baranovichi district in 1943.

75. BNAM 370-6-48, p. 100 German propaganda appeal to the partisans.

76. *BA R* 94/7 Report of District Commissar Brest – Agricultural section.

77. BNAM 370-6-48, p. 41 German translation of Soviet propaganda pamphlet from 1943. On the action in Lyadki see Chapter 7.
78. USHMMA RG-53.002M, reel 5 (BNAM) 845-1-6, pp. 54–6 Extraordinary Commission Report for the district of Nesvizh, 4 February 1945.
79. B. Chiari, '*Deutsche Herrschaft*', pp. 84–96; on German cultural looting see also L.H. Nicholas, *The Rape of Europa*, pp. 185–201.

7 Partisan Warfare, 1942–44

1. B. Chiari, '*Die Büchse der Pandora*', pp. 1–2; B. V. Sokolov, 'The Cost of War', pp. 171–2 estimates some 16.9 million irreversible civilian casualties for the USSR in the Second World War. He stresses that this estimate includes victims of Soviet deportations, reprisals against collaborators, combat losses, deaths from cold, hunger and illness as well as the effects of German genocidal policies and anti-partisan repression. C. Gerlach, '*Deutsche Wirtschaftsinteressen*', gives figures of 376 362 persons deported to Germany and 340 000 peasants and refugees as victims of German anti-partisan operations in Belorussia.
2. In this respect see especially the orders of the German Commandant in *Weißruthenien* in the autumn of 1941, USHMMA RG 53.002M, reel 2 (BNAM) 378-1-698. S. Spector, *The Holocaust of Volhynian Jews*, pp. 274–5 stresses the small scale and ineffectiveness of Soviet partisan efforts in 1941.
3. 'In July 1942 the Germans estimated that the stragglers and escaped PoWs made up 60 per cent of the total partisan strength': E. Ziemke, 'Composition and Morale', p. 144.
4. *BA* R 94/8 District Commissar Brest, 16 October 1943. He estimated that by this time one-third of the territory in his district was controlled by the partisans; see also S. Cholawsky, *The Jews of Bielorussia*, p. 53.
5. In English see J. A. Armstrong (ed.), *Soviet Partisans in WWII* and M. Cooper, *The Nazi War against Soviet Partisans*, both of which concentrate mainly on the areas under military administration. Most useful is W. Wilenchik, '*Die Partisanenbewegung in Weißrußland*'.
6. WCU D9145.
7. *BA* R 6/27, p. 57 Minsk report on the partisan situation, 1 June 1942.
8. Dorking, Oswald Rufeisen on 23 February 1996.
9. *SAL* IV K 79/64, pp. 146–52 Josef Marchwinski, 'The criminals came from the West'.
10. WCU D9145.
11. BNAM 3500-4-305, p. 20 Partisan report dated 21 June 1942.
12. *WAST* loss reports for *Gendarmerie* forces in Volhynia-Podolia.
13. INRW SWGd 73, pp. 292–3 L.F.N. on 18 June 1968.
14. *ZSL UdSSR* 412, *Bild* 565–6 *BdO* Ukraine order, 9 September 1942.
15. *Unsere Ehre heißt Treue*, pp. 237–9 Activity report of *SS Uscharf*. Lipps in Vileyka, 27 May 1942.
16. S. Cholawsky, *Soldiers from the Ghetto*, p. 111.
17. *ZSL* 2 AR-Z 16/67, Vol. VIII W. L. on 13 May 1970.
18. On the attack on 9 June 1942 see Chapter 5 above; *BA* R 6/354 Meeting of senior staff in *Reichskommissariat Ostland* on 16 June 1942.
19. *BA* R 19/266 Strength of the *Schutzmannschaft*, 1 July 1942; SAM 1323-2-267 Report of Daluege on strength and operations of the Order Police in 1942, 1 February 1943. The strength of the *Schutzmannschaft Einzeldienst* is given at 223 787.

20. See Chapter 4 above.
21. Brest Archive 995-1-4, p. 169 *Gendarmerie* post Mir report, 23 July 1942. For further details on this incident see INRW SWKsz 43.
22. SARF 7021-148-365, p. 8 *KdG Weißruthenien* order, 6 July 1942.
23. USHMMA RG 53.002M, reel 5 (BNAM) 658-1-2, p. 65 *KdG* Zhitomir Order 3/42, 5 May 1942.
24. *PAAA* Inl. IIg/431, 226721-42 Activity and Situation Report No. 10, 1–28 February 1942.
25. S. Spector, *The Holocaust of Volhynian Jews*, p. 277; H. Smolar, *The Minsk Ghetto*, p. 35.
26. WCU D9145.
27. WCU D719A.
28. *UKGB* Minsk Archive File No. 2018, Criminal Case 35371. In post-war trials many of the accused claimed to have assisted the partisans in this way; often it proved difficult to verify these claims on the basis of witnesses and partisan records.
29. See for example *UKGB* Minsk Archive File No. 902, Criminal Case 35930 and Archive File No. 1631, Criminal Case 35994.
30. B. Chiari, '*Deutsche Herrschaft*', p. 202.
31. See for example *BA* NS 19/2715 Experience and evacuation report of v. Gottberg, 31 August 1944; *BA-MA* RW 30/27, p. 52 Armaments Commando Minsk Partisan Report for period 13 May–24 June 1942; W. Wilenchik, '*Die Partisanenbewegung in Weißrußland*', p. 253 n. 533.
32. W. Wilenchik, '*Die Partisanenbewegung in Weißrußland*', p. 250; S. Spector, *The Holocaust of Volhynian Jews*, pp. 288–9 and 352.
33. S. Spector, *The Holocaust of Volhynian Jews*, p. 256.
34. USHMMA RG 53.002M, reel 4 (BNAM) 389-1-5, p. 4 *Gendarmerie* post Starzyna report on 2 February 1944 mentions a camp of about 700 Jews with families which had only about 70 weapons; S. Spector, *The Holocaust of Volhynian Jews*, pp. 284–5.
35. L. Eckmann and C. Lazar, *The Jewish Resistance*, pp. 151–2; see also S. Cholawski, *Soldiers from the Ghetto*, p. 143.
36. L. Eckman and C. Lazar, *The Jewish Resistance*, p. 234.
37. *SAL* IV K 79/64, pp. 146–52 Josef Marchwinski, 'The criminals came from the West'.
38. T. Richmond, *Konin: A Quest*, p. 308.
39. J. Kagan and D. Cohen, *Surviving the Holocaust*, p. 58.
40. S. Cholawski, *Soldiers from the Ghetto*, p. 166. On the role of the Baptists as rescuers in Volhynia, see S. Spector, *The Holocaust of Volhynian Jews*, pp. 243–4.
41. I. Aron, *Fallen Leaves*, p. 79; on the anti-Semitism of the peasantry in this area see also *Memorial Book of Glebokie*, p. 69.
42. N. Tec, *Defiance*, pp. 45 and 90–1; on Jewish civilian camps see also S. Spector, *The Holocaust of Volhynian Jews*, pp. 278–82 and 327–38 and L. Smilovitsky, 'Righteous Gentiles, the Partisans, and Jewish Survival', p. 317.
43. S. Cholawski, *Soldiers from the Ghetto*, p. 137. Some 200 Jews managed to break out during the Novaya Sverzhen escape. Shortly afterwards the remaining Jews in Stolpce were shot: see USHMMA RG 53.002M, reel 4 (BNAM) 389-1-4, pp. 22–4 *Gendarmerie* post Stolpce reports on 30 January 1943 and 5 February 1943. On the escape see also YV 03/3876 Testimony of M. Jalowsky and 016/168 Testimony of Bert Manta: it is clear that not all Jews were ready to escape and many feared the consequences.

44. YV 016/168 Testimony of Bert Manta.
45. J. Kagan and D. Cohen, *Surviving the Holocaust*, p. 66; see also N. Tec, *Defiance*, pp. 97 and 103. W. Wilenchik, *Die Partisanenbewegung in Weißruß-land*, pp. 251–2 argues that in the Nieman-Shchara region (Naliboki forest) the Jewish partisans had better relations with local Belorussian peasants due to German favouritism towards the Poles.
46. J. Kagan and D. Cohen, *Surviving the Holocaust*, pp. 89–90.
47. L. Eckmann and C. Lazar, *The Jewish Resistance*, pp. 53–4; S. Cholawsky, *The Jews of Bielorussia*, p. 247.
48. Brest Archive 995-1-4, p. 407 *Gendamerie* post Mir report, 13 November 1942. The same file contains a number of similar reports for the Mir district: for instance, the Usha estate was attacked on 23 and 30 October 1942 and the Obryna estate on 25 & 31 October 1942 (see 995-1-4, pp. 296, 324–5 and 332).
49. SARF 7021-148-2, pp. 342–3 11. Co./Pol. Rgt 15 report, 30 September 1942.
50. SARF 7021-148-2, p. 133 9. Co./Pol. Rgt 15 Special report, 28 September 1942.
51. SARF 7021-148-2, p. 147 Security Police Brest to *KdS* Rovno, 5 October 1942.
52. SARF 7021-148-2, p. 344 11. Co./Pol. Rgt 15 report, 9 October 1942.
53. SARF 7021-148-2, p. 363 9. Co./Pol. Rgt 15 weekly report on 8 November 1942 and 7021-148-3, p. 21 *SSPF* Volhynia-Podolia Operational Order No. 6 on 5 October 1942.
54. SARF 7021-148-2, p. 148 Security Police Brest to *KdS* Rovno, 14 October 1942.
55. WCU D7341.
56. *UKGB* Grodno Archive File No. 1078, Criminal Case 34821, pp. 94–6.
57. WCU D3619.
58. WCU S119A.
59. SARF 7021-148-316, pp. 3–4 Report to *KdG* Minsk on battle with bandits at Lyadki on 13 January 1943 mentioning death of *Gendamerie* Lt Steinert, 16 January 1943. On the shooting of a German officer see also the relevant partisan reports in BNAM 3500-4-263. These reports also mention the presence of a German aeroplane which strafed the village of Lyadki shortly afterwards.
60. WCU D3622.
61. WCU D7341; *UKGB* Grodno Archive File No. 1078, Criminal Case 34821, p. 46.
62. WCU D7341.
63. WCU 93/1; SARF 7021-81-102, p. 98 Extraordinary Commission report for the Mir district indicates that of 6500 residents of the town of Mir pre-war, only 1850 remained in 1945. A similar level of civilian losses, mainly due to the activities of the German police and their collaborators, can be found for the districts around Brest, see BNAM 4290-2-25, pp. 11–12.
64. P. Kohl, '*Ich wundere mich, daß ich noch lebe*', pp. 106–9.
65. BNAM 370-1-1880 Operational Order for 'Operation Hermann', 7 July 1943.
66. BNAM 370-1-1880 Combat report for 'Operation Hermann', 20 August 1943. Among the recommendations was a request for mosquito nets which were necessary for sleeping outdoors. For an overview of the reported results of several such large-scale 'operations' including 'Hermann' see J. Schlootz (Hrsg.), *Deutsche Propaganda in Weißrußland*, p. 45.
67. WCU D1768; see also D3589 and Dorking, Valentina Keda on 18 March 1996.
68. *BA* BDC SSO Hans Siegling Combat report on 'Operation Hermann', 20 July 1943.
69. YV 016/159 Ester Gorodejska (in Polish) 9 August 1945. For the Jewish perspective on 'Operation Hermann' see also N. Tec, *Defiance*, pp. 108–25.

70. J. Kagan and D. Cohen, *Surviving the Holocaust*, p. 174.
71. SARF 7021-148-2, pp. 57–8 *Gendarmerie* District Leader Brest report, 22 August 1942.
72. INRW SWB 272, pp. 17–22 F. M. on 15 August 1957.
73. WCU D720.
74. INRW SWB 253, pp. 54–9.
75. Ibid., pp. 63–6.
76. *UKGB* Brest Archive File No. 6258, Criminal Case 1230, pp. 19–23 N.S.K. on 13 April 1945.
77. *UKGB* Minsk Archive File No. 5324, Criminal Case 35496, pp. 57–62 M.S.R. on 17 May 1949.
78. INRW SWB 254, p. 374 S.M. on 9 July 1965.
79. *UKGB* Brest Archive File No. 3977, Criminal Case 18, pp. 30–4 P.V.T. on 26 February 1947.
80. *UKGB* Minsk Archive File No. 2018, Criminal Case 35371, evidence of P.A.M. at own trial on 3 February 1949.
81. INRW SWKsz 73, pp. 322–6 D.F.M. on 12 January 1969.
82. See, for example, INRW SWB 256, p. 128 J.C. on 11 May 1962.
83. WCU D719A.
84. USHMMA RG 53.002M, reel 4 (BNAM) 389-1-3, p. 124 *KdO Weißruthenien* order on the creation of fortified police posts, 11 November 1942. An aerial photograph of Mir taken in 1944 shows clearly the earth-work fortifications constructed during the latter part of the occupation.
85. WCU D4355.
86. *UKGB* Grodno Archive File No. 20394, Criminal Case 1030, pp. 114–22 A.V.K. on 21 July 1949.
87. *UKGB* Brest Criminal Case 3632, pp. 41–4 I.V.L. on 19 July 1948.
88. *UKGB* Minsk Archive File No. 1631, Criminal Case 35994.
89. *PAAA* Inl. IIg/431 Activity and situation report No. 10, 28 February 1942.
90. B. Chiari, '*Deutsche Herrschaft*', p. 58.
91. *BA* R 6/15, pp. 108–21 Letter of Hans von Homeyer to *Reichsminister* Rosenberg, 15 October 1943. On the better treatment received from the *Wehrmacht* in comparison to the police and civil administration see also A. Dallin, *German Rule in Russia*, p. 73, n. 1.
92. *BA* R 6/354, p. 144 Letter of *Reich Minister* for the Occupied eastern Territories to *Reichskommissar* Koch, 6 March 1944.
93. *BA* NS 19/2715 Experience and evacuation report of v. Gottberg, 31 August 1944.
94. *BA* Dahlwitz-Hoppegarten ZB 984 Complaint about lack of promotion, 24 May 1943. See also USHMMA (ZA) roll 3 1151-1-138 which indicates the high losses among the *Gendarmerie* in *Generalkommissariat* Zhitomir during the winter of 1942–43.
95. BNAM 370-1-1262, pp. 147–58 Colonel Klepsch lecture on the *Schutzmannschaft*, 10 April 1943.
96. This is the impression gained from the losses of the *Schutzmannschaft* recorded in the daily orders of *KdO* Minsk from the summer of 1942 to autumn 1943. USHMMA RG 53.002M, reel 3 (BNAM) 389-1-1.
97. The opening of the former Soviet archives, especially the vast collections of partisan documents previously held mostly in the former Party archives, will doubtless lead to a considerable re-evaluation of Soviet partisan warfare on the basis of a more critical reading of these sources. I have examined only a tiny sample of this material in connection with investigations into events in specific areas.

98. On partisan warfare during the revolutionary period see, for example, O. Figes, *A People's Tragedy*, pp. 417, 569, 599–600, 662 and 768.
99. S. Spector, *The Holocaust of Volhynian Jews*, p. 283.
100. W. Wilenchik, '*Die Partisanenbewegung in Weißrußland*', pp. 151 and 262–3.
101. O.A. Zarubinsky, 'The "Red" Partisan Movement in Ukraine', p. 408.
102. S. Spector, *The Holocaust of Volhynian Jews*, p. 310.
103. WCU D9145.
104. WCU D8675.
105. INRW SWGd 76, pp. 956–67 A.G. on 11 June 1970.
106. J. Kagan and D. Cohen, *Surviving the Holocaust*, pp. 66–7.
107. S. Cholawski, *Soldiers from the Ghetto*, p. 166.
108. L. Berk, *Destined to Live*, p. 130.
109. On partisan excesses and indiscipline see also BNAM 3705-1-11.
110. S. Cholawski, *Soldiers from the Ghetto*, p. 131.
111. I am grateful to J. Kagan for bringing this detail to my attention. He has found records reporting the massive stores of potatoes collected by the Soviet partisans in the Naliboki forests. See also USHMMA RG-02 133 'From the Lida Ghetto to the Bielski Partisans', Liza Ettinger, p. 52. She was sent to the deserted town of Naliboki to harvest potatoes for the partisans.
112. S. Spector, *The Holocaust of Volhynian Jews*, p. 128; see also N. Tec, *Defiance*, pp. 170–5.
113. L. Berk, *Destined to Live*, pp. 116–24 was nevertheless treated with considerable suspicion on first joining the partisans; S. Spector, *The Holocaust of Volhynian Jews*, pp. 263–4, 321, 326 and 330.
114. J. Kagan and D. Cohen, *Surviving the Holocaust*, p. 86; L. Eckman and C. Lazar, *The Jewish Resistance*, p. 231; W. Wilenchik, '*Die Partisanenbewegung in Weißrußland*', pp. 279–82.
115. S. Cholawski, *Soldiers from the Ghetto*, pp. 168–9; W. Wilenchik, '*Die Partisanenbewegung in Weißrußland*', p. 290.
116. L. Eckmann and C. Lazar, *The Jewish Resistance*, pp. 220–3 testimony of Sarah Rubinowitz-Schiff.
117. S. Cholawski, *Soldiers from the Ghetto*, p. 97.
118. B. Chiari, '*Deutsche Herrschaft*', p. 296.
119. S. Cholawski, *Soldiers from the Ghetto*, p. 112.
120. BNAM 3500-2-43 quoted by B. Chiari, '*Deutsche Herrschaft*', p. 79; on German demoralization see also H. Smolar, *The Minsk Ghetto*, p. 138.
121. ZA, 1182-1-29, p. 60. *SS*PGF Kazatin, daily report for 29 September 1943 on 30 September 1943.
122. ZA 1182-1-26, pp. 121–31.
123. W. Wilenchik, '*Die Partisanenbewegung in Weißrußland*', p. 285.
124. Moreshet A 118 Testimony of Chaim Rabinowitz and A 120 Report on heroism of Miriam Gilimovski; H. Smolar, *The Minsk Ghetto*, p. 133; YV M-1/E 1000/892 Testimony of E. M. Melamed.
125. BNAM 3500-4-305 p. 41 and 3500-4-321, pp. 92–106.
126. BNAM 3500-4-305 records for the Stalin Brigade, 1942–4.
127. J. Kagan and D. Cohen, *Surviving the Holocaust*, pp. 186–7. These figures include, of course, the predominantly Jewish units of Bielski and Zorin.
128. W. Wilenchik, '*Die Partisanenbewegung in Weißrußland*', p. 277; L. Smilovitsky, 'Righteous Gentiles, the Partisans, and Jewish Survival' p. 318. Some registered partisans joined only at the very end of the occupation for opportunistic reasons.
129. S. Spector, *The Holocaust of Volhynian Jews*, p. 323.

130. O. A. Zarubinsky, 'The "Red" Partisan Movement in Ukraine', pp. 404–13, gives figures for 12 286 'Red' partisans operating in five units within Ukraine. Of these Jews were only 1.6 per cent, Russians 37 per cent and Ukrainians 46 per cent; see also J. A. Armstrong, *Ukrainian Nationalism*, pp. 94–102.
131. W. Wilenchik, '*Die Partisanenbewegung in Weißrußland*', pp. 224–8.
132. *UKGB* Brest Criminal Case 23552, pp. 39–42 M.Y.N. on 3 November 1945.
133. B. Chiari, '*Deutsche Herrschaft*', pp. 290–1; S. Spector, *The Holocaust of Volhynian Jews*, p. 257.
134. B. Chiari, '*Deutsche Herrschaft*', pp. 282–6.
135. INRW SWSz 77, pp. 1697–1713 W.W. in January 1971, pp. 1736–71 J.R. court evidence in January 1971 and pp. 1840–4 B.L. on 24 March 1971.
136. INRW SWSz 69, pp. 96–7 B.B. on 24 November 1962.
137. See, for example, H. Werner, *Fighting Back*, p. 155; YV E/459 Testimony of Jacob and Bella Grynshteyn; B. Chiari, '*Deutsche Herrschaft*', p. 293 n. 1309; S. Spector, *The Holocaust of Volhynian Jews*, pp. 260–8 notes that in Volhynia while some Jews were protected by or served in the Polish Underground, others were killed by Polish partisans.
138. PUST Bulletin for Ministry of Interior, 26 August–10 October 1942.
139. On Polish rescue efforts in Volhynia see Spector, *The Holocaust of Volhynian Jews*, pp. 248–51.
140. PUST Account of Stefan Janski who served ten years in Soviet labour camps after the war.
141. On Polish resistance to Lithuanian actions against the Polish majority in the Vilnius area see B. Chiari, '*Deutsche Herrschaft*', p. 292.
142. USHMMA RG 53.002M, reel 4 (BNAM) 389-1-4, p. 52 *Gendarmerie* post Stolpce report on 11 June 1943.
143. BNAM 370-1-1880 Operational Order for 'Operation Hermann' on 7 July 1943 and Combat Report on 20 August 1943.
144. PUST Account of Jaroslaw Gasiewski.
145. S. Cholawski, *Soldiers from the Ghetto*, p. 162; B. Chiari, '*Deutsche Herrschaft*', pp. 293 and 299–303; INRW SWZG 20 – 6, Vol. V, p. 958 Indictment against Zdzislaw Nurkiewicz, commander of the 'Polish Legion'. The *AK* adopted an increasingly hostile stance to the Soviets after the death of General Sikorski in the summer of 1943: S. Spector, *The Holocaust of Volhynian Jews*, p. 261.
146. USHMMA RG 53.002M, reel 4 (BNAM) 389-1-5, p. 4 *Gendamerie* post Starzyna report on 2 February 1944 relates the story of Jan Haschtila, a Polish partisan who was twice captured by the Soviets and managed to escape.
147. B. Chiari, '*Deutsche Herrschaft*', p. 294.
148. INRW SWB 231, p. 66 J. J. on 28 August 1946.
149. PUST Account of Jaroslaw Gasiewski; YV E/459 Testimony of Jacob and Bella Grynshteyn; WCU D8675; B. Chiari, '*Deutsche Herrschaft*', pp. 293–4. On the conflict between the Polish Underground and the Soviet forces, especially the 'incorporation' of Polish units into the Red Army on 'liberation', see also K. Sword, *Deportation and Exile*, pp. 143–51.
150. *BA* R 6/369 Report of *Gebietskommissar Wilna-Land*, 18 January 1944. On alliances with the Germans see also B. Chiari, '*Deutsche Herrschaft*', pp. 299 and 304–5; W. Wilenchik, '*Die Partisanenbewegung in Weißrußland*', pp. 260–1.
151. PUST Account of Stefan Janski; B. Chiari, '*Deutsche Herrschaft*', p. 297; on Lithuanian excesses see *BA* R 6/356 *Reichskommissariat Ostland* report, 11 May 1944.
152. PUST No. 2792 Memoirs of Lieutenant Mikolaj Balysz (Zagloba), the former *AK* commandant in Kovel.

153. For a somewhat apologetic account of Ukrainian resistance to the Germans see W. Kosyk, *The Third Reich and Ukraine*. A more balanced account, documenting as far as possible the relationship between the OUN-M and the OUN-B, is given in J. A. Armstrong, *Ukrainian Nationalism*. MHAP *Einsatzgruppe Schultz* report, 12 May 1943: according to the interrogation of a captured Ukrainian partisan, the efforts of the Ukrainian partisans in Volhynia were directed firstly against the Poles, then the Russians, but they also aimed finally at driving out the Germans in order to establish their own state.

154. For the reports of the Polish Underground organization see the Bulletins held at PUST and *AANW* 202/III/7–8.

155. J. A. Armstrong, *Ukrainian Nationalism*, p. 104.

156. MHAP, *Einsatzgruppe Schultz* reports, 12 May 1943 and 19 May 1943; PUST Recollection of Major Zolocinski on wartime activities of Lieutenant Colonel Oliwa (Jan Wojciech Kiwerski), *AK* commander in the Volhynian region; S. Spector, *The Holocaust of Volhynian Jews*, p. 269; J.A. Armstrong, *Ukrainian Nationalism*, pp. 102, 106 and 115 dates the beginning of Ukrainian desertion to the start of German reprisals in the autumn of 1942.

157. PUST Recollection of Major Zolocinski on wartime activities of Lieutenant Colonel Oliwa (Jan Wojciech Kiwerski).

158. MHAP *Einsatzgruppe Schultz* reports, 1943.

159. *BA* R 94/17 Situation report of the *Generalkommissar* for Volhynia-Podolia, 30 April 1943.

160. PUST No. 2792 Memoirs of Lt Mikolaj Balysz (Zagloba); S. Spector, *The Holocaust of Volhynian Jews*, pp. 258–60.

161. D. Pohl, *Nationalsozialistische Judenverfolgung*, p. 376 gives estimates of the number of Poles killed in this 'ethnic cleansing' ranging from 10 000 to over 100 000, although the actual death toll probably lies somewhere between these two figures. M. Terles, *Ethnic Cleansing in Volhynia and Eastern Galicia*, p. 61 gives the figure of over 100 000 victims.

162. PUST Recollection of Major Zolocinski on wartime activities of Lieutenant Colonel Oliwa (Jan Wojciech Kiwerski).

163. PUST No. 2792 Memoirs of Lieutenant Mikolaj Balysz (Zagloba).

164. S. Spector, *The Holocaust of Volhynian Jews*, pp. 271–2; J.A. Armstrong, *Ukrainian Nationalism*, p. 116.

165. L. Berk, *Destined to Live*, pp. 128–9.

166. BNAM 370-1-487, pp. 102–7 Political situation report for the Slonim district, 21 March 1943.

167. WCU D717.

168. Yivo Occ/E3a/Bar. 15.

169. L. Berk, *Destined to Live*, p. xvii.

170. M. Cooper, *The Nazi War against Soviet Partisans, 1941–44*, pp. xii–xiii notes the scathing view of Sir Basil Liddell Hart and others, including 'recent' estimates of only 15–20 000 German casualties inflicted by the Soviet partisans; J.A. Armstrong (ed.), *Soviet Partisans in WWII*, pp. 38–9 was 'inclined to conclude that from the narrow standpoint of winning the war the whole partisan effort was dubious'; E.M. Howell, *The Soviet Partisan Movement*, pp. 209–11 described Soviet partisan success as 'limited'. All three commentators, however, concede that the Soviet partisans undermined German morale and succeeded in turning the local population against the Germans in many areas under occupation.

171. W. Wilenchik, '*Die Partisanenbewegung in Weißrußland*', pp. 287–8; S. Spector, *The Holocaust of Volhynian Jews*, p. 339; E.M. Howell, *The Soviet Partisan Movement*, pp. 201–2.

8   Post-War Fates of Collaborators and Survivors

1. USHMMA RG-02.078*01 Testimony of Ida Shkolnik from Glubokoye, who comments that when she returned from the forest she found only burned homes: 'the whole town was like a ghost town'. She subsequently came to America in 1949 with her husband after four years in an Italian refugee camp; M. Wyman, *DP: Europe's Displaced Persons*, p. 59 indicates that by December 1945 some 3000 Jews from Eastern Europe were crossing into the western zone of Germany each week; L. Dinnerstein, *America and the Survivors*, pp. 109–12; M. Gilbert, *Israel*, p. 147.
2. Brest Archive 995-1-3, vols 1 to 3.
3. MHAP *HSSPF Rußland Süd* 3, 4 & 8.
4. *BA* R 6/15, p. 135 Order by Commandant of rear Army district 585, 25 December 1943.
5. ZA 1182-1-35, p. 70 *HSSPF* Ukraine order re. local *Schutzmannschaft*, 9 February 1943.
6. Brest Archive 514-1-336, pp. 3–5 Extraordinary Commission Report for the Kobryn district, 11 January 1945.
7. *UKGB* Minsk Archive File No. 154–H, pp. 41–2 I.K.Y. on 18 August 1946.
8. WCU D9780.
9. SSA Vinnitsa – Criminal files regarding ten former policemen from Gnivan were examined here on behalf of the SIU in November 1991.
10. *BA* R 19/326, pp. 24–9 *KdO* Zhitomir reports, 6 April 1944 and 7 May 1944.
11. See *Befehlsblatt des Chefs der Ordnungspolizei*, No. 39, 30 September 1944 on ranks for Ukrainian *Schutzmänner* in the *Luftschutzpolizei* and also *BA* R 19/307, pp. 159–61 *RFSS* order on 15 March 1944, re. training and integration of Ukrainians transferred to the air defence and fire protection police.
12. Inhabitant registration (*Einwohnermeldeamt*) records (including original house books) and driving licence records were examined in Hanover in relation to investigations conducted by the SIU.
13. *WAST Erkennungs-Marken Verzeichnis* for the police administration in Hanover, 7 August 1944.
14. For further details see Australian committal proceedings in the case of Nikolai Beresovsky in Adelaide in 1992. The war crimes case against Beresovsky was dismissed on the grounds of insufficient evidence. Defence counsel conceded, however, that Beresovsky had served in the Ukrainian *Schutzmannschaft* in Gnivan during the war.
15. SSA Kirovograd – a number of Soviet Criminal Case files from the Kirovograd region were examined by the staff of the SIU in 1991 and 1992.
16. *BA* R 19/333, pp. 139–40 Order re. dissolution and reformation of *BdO* Black Sea on 25 August 1944. Amongst the units listed are *Schutzpolizei* commands from Nikolayev, Dneprpetrovsk and Krivoy Rog and also *Gendarmerie* units from the Nikolayev, Dneprpetrovsk and the Crimea regions. *BA* R 19/330, pp. 63–8 Establishment of Police Rifle Regiment 38, 24 June 1944.
17. *BA* R 19/333, pp. 139–40 Order re. dissolution and reformation of *BdO* Black Sea, 25.8.44; *BA* R 19/339, pp. 46–51 Concluding report of retreat of Black Sea 1, 2, and 3 from Romania, 9 January 1945.
18. *BA* R 19/339, pp. 46–51 Concluding report of retreat of Black Sea 1, 2, and 3 from Romania, 9 January 1945; *BA-MA* RH 24/72–48 Situation map of LXXII Corps, 7 September 1944; *BA* R 19/339, pp. 22–3 Retreat of staff train of Black

Sea 2, 18 September 1944. See also the Loss reports for the Police Rifle Regiment 38 from *WAST* in August and September 1944.

19.   *BA-MA* RH 24/72-48 Map of LXXII Corps, 16 November 1944; Loss reports for the Police Rifle Regiment 38 from *WAST* in August and September 1944 and for *SS* Police Regiment 8 in November 1944.

20.   *BA-MA* RH 24/72-46, p. 587 Secret report on visit to Dunafoldvar, 13 November 1944; RH 24/72-48 Map of LXXII Corps positions, 16 November 1944; *WAST* loss reports for *SS* Police Rgt 8 in November 1944; *BA-MA* RH 24/72-46, p. 609 Report on visit to Combat Group Kesseo, 14 November 1944; RH 24/72-45, p. 956; RH 24/72-49 Map of LXXII Corps positions, 11 December 1944.

21.   *BA-MA* RH 24/72-45, p. 981 War Diary of LXXII Corps, 13 December 1944; see also Loss reports at *WAST* for *SS* Police Rgt 8.

22.   *Sta*. Oldenburg 2 JS 138/68, Vol. I, pp. 92–101 V.E.M. on 13 March 1969.

23.   INRW I Zh Kpp 50/93 W.W. on 5 August 1994.

24.   *UKGB* Archive File No. 14687, Criminal Case 36551, pp. 149–53 A.G.S. on 18 September 1951; see also SARF 7021-81-123, pp. 87–8 which is a deportation record given by the same woman (A.G.S.), who married a Nesvizh policeman and left with the police on 26 June 1944 for East Prussia.

25.   *ZSL* 2 AR-Z 16/67 Vol. VI, pp. 1146–55 E.F. on 13 March 1969; *BA-MA* RS 3-30/2, 30 *Waffen Grenadier Div.* (russ. No. 2) report, 31 August 1944.

26.   *ZSL* 2 AR-Z 16/67 Vol. VI, pp. 1146–55 E.F. on 13 March 1969; *BA* (Hoppegarten) Order Police File for Max Eibner from former *Staatssicherheitsdienst* archives.

27.   *BA-MA* RS 3-30/9 Div. Order No. 3, 27 August 1944; USHMMA RG 53.002M, reel 4 (BNAM) 359-1-1, p. 39 *Waffen Grenadier* Rgt of the *SS* 75 (russ. No. 4), report on 3 January 1945 re. *Hauptmann der Schutzpolizei* Peterson killed in France in August 1944.

28.   *ZSL* 2 AR-Z 16/67 Vol. VI, pp. 1146–55 E.F. on 13 March 1969.

29.   *UKGB* Brest Arch. File No. 8670, Criminal Case 36409, pp. 122–30 I.G.L. on 27 June 1951.

30.   *UKGB* Minsk Archive File No. 14687, Criminal Case 36551, pp. 13–19 M.R. on 17 May 1948.

31.   *WAST* Loss reports for 30 *Waffen Grenadier Div. der SS* in November 1944.

32.   *BA-MA* RH 20-19/129, p. 222 War Diary of 19th Army, 26 November 1944 and RH 20-19/136, p. 177 Appendices to War Diary of 19th Army, Report of Commanding Officer High Command Eifel, 26 November 1944.

33.   INRW SWGd 76, pp. 942–50 M.K. on 10 June 1970. For details of his desertion see *WAST* Loss report for M.K. on 27 November 1944 from *Waffen Grenadier* Rgt of the *SS* No. 76 Schallstadt, 6 December 1944.

34.   *UKGB* Brest Archive File No. 8670, Criminal Case 36409, pp. 122–30 I.G.L. on 27 June 1951.

35.   By 1952 approximately 90 000 Poles remained in the UK as civilians, *War Crimes: Report of the War Crimes Inquiry*, pp. 36–7; by this date 10 487 ex-Polish soldiers had entered the USA from the UK: L. Dinnerstein, *America and the Survivors*, p. 286.

36.   K. Sword, *Deportation and Exile*, p. 86.

37.   Some 50 000 members of the Free Polish Army had served previously in the German Armed Forces, see *War Crimes: Report of the War Crimes Inquiry*, p. 37.

38.   INRW SWB 253-9, F.B. on 21 February 1963.

39.   *UKGB* Brest Archive File No. 7627 Case of V.I.G. and K.K.R. tried in 1947; see also SSA Vinnitsa Cases of I.V.K. tried in 1950 and A.A.N. tried in 1949.

40. B. V. Sokolov, 'The Cost of War: Human Losses for the USSR and Germany', p. 169.
41. *War Crimes: Report of the War Crimes Inquiry*, pp. 38–40; L. Dinnerstein, *America and the Survivors*, pp. 192–4; D. Cesarani, *Justice Delayed*, pp. 85–92.
42. *War Crimes: Report of the War Crimes Inquiry*, p. 36.
43. L. Dinnerstein, *America and the Survivors*, pp. 123–4, 198 & 286. Jews made up about 16 per cent of DP immigrants.
44. WCU D719B.
45. J. Kagan and D. Cohen, *Surviving the Holocaust*, p. 91. For a similar description of a battle with retreating Germans on 6 July 1944 see L. Smilovitsky, 'Righteous Gentiles, the Partisans, and Jewish Survival', p. 316.
46. N. Tec, *Defiance*, pp. 201–2.
47. L. Eckman and C. Lazar, *The Jewish Resistance*, p. 233.
48. S. Spector, *The Holocaust of Volhynian Jews*, pp. 359–61.
49. J. Kagan and D. Cohen, *Surviving the Holocaust*, pp. 97–8.
50. T. Richmond, *Konin*, p. 244; L. Dinnerstein, *America and the Survivors*, pp. 108–9; M. Gilbert, *The Holocaust*, pp. 816–19.
51. L. Dinnerstein, *America and the Survivors*, p. 285 gives the main destinations for DP resettlement by the IRO from 1 July 1947 to 31 December 1951 as the USA 302 000; Australia 176 000; Israel 136 000; Canada 112 000; and the UK 104 000. Other destinations included South America, France and Belgium.
52. J. Kagan and D. Cohen, *Surviving the Holocaust*, p. 243.
53. J. Kagan and D. Cohen, *Surviving the Holocaust*, pp. 242–3; D. Budnik and Y. Kaper, *Nothing is Forgotten*, pp. 127–8. In recent years efforts have been made to remedy this insensitivity.
54. Dorking, Oswald Rufeisen on 27 February 1996. Unfortunately, despite repeated requests to the relevant archives, no copy of this valuable document has been located.
55. *David-Horodoker Memorial Book*, p. 114.
56. In Estonia 19 000 trial files of collaborators have been preserved. I am grateful to Carl Modig of the USHMM for this information.
57. Record of the USSR Supreme Soviet, No. 17 1947; D. Pohl, *Nationalsozialistische Judenverfolgung*, p. 391.
58. SSA Kirovograd Case of Mefody A. Marchik tried in 1958.
59. *UKGB* Brest Archive File No. 466 and WCU D9000.
60. D. Pohl, *Nationalsozialistische Judenverfolgung*, p. 391.
61. Direct evidence of this is understandably less easy to find in the official records; see, for example, *UKGB* Minsk Archive File No. 1150, Criminal Case 35220, pp. 173–80 A.M.G. appeal on 27 March 1955.
62. *David-Horodoker Memorial Book*, pp. 121–5.
63. Dorking, Lev Abramovsky on 1 April 1996.
64. Quoted by T. Richmond, *Konin*, p. 267.
65. Simon Wiesenthal's office in Vienna should not be confused with the Simon Wiesenthal Centre based in Los Angeles, which uses his name but operates independently.

9 Conclusion: Local Collaboration in the Holocaust

1. R. Hilberg, *The Destruction of the European Jews*, pp. 1201–20.
2. *BA* R 6/310, p. 17 Report of *Generalkommissar* Zhitomir for month of May, 3 June 1942; *BA* R 6/307, p. 92 Report of *Generalkommissar* Nikolayev for month

of July 1942; INRW Zbior Zespolow Szczatkowych Jednostek SS i Policji – Sygnatura 77, pp. 8–9 *Generalkommissar* Volhynia-Podolia to Security Police outposts in Brest, Pinsk, Starokonstantinov and Kamenets-Podolsk 31 August 1942.

3. *Memorial Book of Glebokie*, pp. 67–9.
4. *BA* R 19/266 Strength of the *Schutzmannschaft*, 1 July 1942. These break down for the rural *Schutzmannschaft* as follows: *Weißruthenien* 251 NCOs/3528 men; Volhynia-Podolia 581/7639; Zhitomir 335/3808; Kiev 312/4262; Nikolayev 482/4071; a total of 1961 NCOs and 23 308 men in these regions. To these should be added more than 2000 additional *Schutzmänner* serving under the *Schutzpolizei* in the major towns. Not included are the men of the *Schutzmannschaft* battalions (33 270).
5. *David-Horodoker Memorial Book*, p. 126.
6. M. Gilbert, *Israel*, p. 49; O. Figes, *A People's Tragedy*, pp. 676–9; Y. Arad, 'Peculiarities of the Holocaust', p. 260 gives the figure of 150 000.
7. One local peasant commented that his Jewish neighbours were not respected as they were viewed as cunning and cheating, if no acts of violence were committed against them under Polish rule, WCU D7559.
8. S. Cholawsky, *The Jews of Bielorussia*, pp. 138 and 198.
9. See, for example, *Memorial Book of Glebokie*, pp. 152–61.
10. See especially Z. Bauman, *Modernity and the Holocaust*, pp. 88–106.
11. WCU F.B. on 12.95. Similar concerns are recorded by the Jews of Jody following the massacre there: see P. Silverman, D. Smuschkowitz & P. Smuschkowicz, *From Victims to Victors*, p. 83.
12. P. Silverman, D. Smuschkowitz and P. Smuschkowicz, *From Victims to Victors*, pp. 82–3; see also E. Leoni (ed.), *Wolozin*, p. 32.
13. S. Spector, *The Holocaust of Volhynian Jews*, p. 186; *BA* R 58/220 EM 191, 10 April 1942 indicates that some 40 000 Jews had been killed in Volhynia-Podolia up to this date.
14. S. Cholawsky, *The Jews of Bielorussia*, pp. 70–5 and 150; the last Jews fled from Koldychevo camp on 7 March 1944.
15. *BA* R 19/121, p. 655 KdG Zhitomir strength on 15 June 1942: 3709 *Schutzmänner* and 766 Gendarmes; *BA* R 19/122 KdG Lutsk on 25 November 1942: 9553 *Schutzmänner* and 954 Gendarmes; S. Spector, *The Holocaust of Volhynian Jews*, p. 175.
16. C. Browning, *Ordinary Men*, p. 128.

Bibliography

Published Sources, Memorial Books and Memoirs

N. Alpert, *The Destruction of Slonim Jewry: The Story of the Jews of Slonim during the Holocaust* (New York: Holocaust Library, 1989).

M. Altshuler, *Distribution of the Jewish Population of the USSR 1939* (Jerusalem: Maccabi Press, 1993).

L. Berk, *Destined to Live: Memoirs of a Doctor with the Russian Partisans* (Melbourne: Paragon, 1992).

D. Budnik and Y. Kaper, *Nothing is Forgotten: Jewish Fates in Kiev 1941–43* (Konstanz: Hartung-Gorre, 1993).

S. Cholawski, *Soldiers from the Ghetto* (London: Tantivy Press, 1980).

The Dark Side of the Moon (London: Faber & Faber, 1946).

David-Horodoker Memorial Book (Manuscript source: translated by Norman Helman, 1981).

I. Ehrenburg and V. Grossman, *The Black Book: The Ruthless Murder of Jews by German-Fascist Invaders throughout the Temporarily-Occupied Regions of the Soviet Union and in the Death Camps of Poland during the War of 1941–1945*, translated from the Russian by J. Glad and J. S. Levine (New York: Holocaust Library, 1981).

I. Grudzinska-Gross and J. T. Gross (eds), *War through Children's Eyes: The Soviet Occupation of Poland and the Deportations, 1939–41* (Stanford, CA: Hoover Institution Press, 1981).

H. Guderian, *Panzer Leader* (Costa Mesa, CA: Noontide Press, 1990).

Justiz und NS-Verbrechen, vols XVI–XX (Amsterdam: UPA, 1978).

J. Kagan and D. Cohen, *Surviving the Holocaust with the Russian Jewish Partisans* (London: Vallentine Mitchell, 1998).

P. Klein (ed.), *Die Einsatzgruppen in der besetzten Sowjetunion 1941/42: Die Tätigkeits- und Lageberichte des Chefs der Sicherheitspolizei und des SD* (Berlin: Hentrich, 1997).

M. Lachowicki, *The Victims of Nesvizh* (Tel Aviv: Committee of Emigrants from Nesvizh, 1948).

W. Lammers (ed.), *'Fahrtberichte' aus der Zeit des Deutsch-Sowjetischen Krieges 1941: Protokolle des Begleitoffiziers des Kommandierenden Generals LIII. Armeekorps* (Boppard: Harald Boldt, 1988).

W. Leonhard, *Die Revolution entläßt ihre Kinder* (Cologne and Berlin: Kiepenheuer & Witsch, 1955).

E. Leoni (ed.), *Wolozin: The Book of the City and of the Etz Hayyim Yeshiva* (Tel Aviv: Wolozhin Landsleit, 1970).

Memorial Book of Glebokie, a translation into English of *Khurbn Glubok* by M. and Z. Rajak which was originally published in 1956 in Yiddish in Buenos Aires by the Former Residents' Association in Argentina, 1994.

Memorial Book of Kobrin: The Scroll of Life and Destruction, translated from the Hebrew by Nilli Avidan and Avner Perry; edited and printed by Joel Neuburg for the Holocaust Center of Northern California, February 1992.

N. Müller (ed.), *Die Faschistische Okkupationspolitik in den zeitweilig besetzten Gebieten der Sowjetunion (1941–44)* (Berlin: Deutscher Verlag der Wiss., 1991). Published in the documentary series *Europa unterm Hakenkreuz* edited by W. Schumann and L. Nestler.

J. Noakes and G. Pridham (eds), *Nazism 1919–45: Vol. 3 Foreign Policy, War and Racial Extermination* (Exeter: Exeter University Press, 1988).

'Opinion of Lord Milligan *in causa* Antony GECAS against Scottish Television PLC'.

H. Picker (ed.), *Hitlers Tischgespräche im Führerhauptquartier 1941–42*, 2nd edn (Stuttgart: Seewald, 1965).

Report of the Investigations of War Criminals in Australia, Attorney General's Department (Canberra: Australian Govt, 1993).

P. Silverman, D. Smuschkowitz and P. Smuschkowicz, *From Victims to Victors: The Incredible Saga of Armed Resistance Fighters that thwarted the Nazis' Goal in the Second World War. The Story of a Small Group of Brave Jews of Jody during the Holocaust* (Concord, Ontario: Canadian Society for Yad Vashem, 1992).

Sepher Lida: The Book of Lida, edited by A. Manor, I. Ganusovitch and A. Lando (Tel Aviv: United Lider Relief, 1970).

H. Smolar, *The Minsk Ghetto: Soviet-Jewish partisans against the Nazis*, translated from the Yiddish by Max Rosenfeld (New York: Holocaust Publications, 1989).

Unsere Ehre heißt Treue: Kriegstagebuch des Kommandostabes Reichsführer SS (Vienna: Europa Verlag, 1965).

A.F. Vysotsky *et al.*, *Nazi Crimes in Ukraine, 1941–44: Documents and Materials* (Kiev: Naukova Dumka, 1987).

War Crimes: Report of the War Crimes Inquiry (London: HMSO, 1989).

H. Werner, *Fighting Back: A Memoir of Jewish Resistance in World War II* (New York: Columbia University Press, 1992).

G. Zhukov, *Reminiscences and Reflections* (Moscow: Progress, 1985).

Books and Articles

R. Ainsztein, *Jewish Resistance in Nazi-Occupied Eastern Europe* (London: Paul Elek, 1974).

M. Altshuler, 'Escape and Evacuation of Soviet Jews at the Time of the Nazi Invasion: Policies and Realities', in L. Dobroszycki and J. S. Gurock (eds), *The Holocaust in the Soviet Union. Studies and Sources on the Destruction of the Jews in the Nazi-Occupied Territories of the USSR, 1941–45* (Armonk, New York: M.E. Sharpe, 1993) 77–104.

A. Angrick, '*Die Einsatzgruppe D*', in P. Klein (Hrsg.), *Die Einsatzgruppen in der besetzten Sowjetunion 1941/42* (Berlin: Hentrich, 1997).

A. Angrick, M. Voigt, S. Ammerschubert, P. Klein, C. Alheit and M. Tycher, '''*Da hätte man schon ein Tagebuch führen müssen.*'' *Das Polizeibataillon 322 und Judenmorde in Bereich des Heeresgruppe Mitte während des Sommer und Herbstes 1941*', in H. Grabitz, K. Bästlein and J. Tuchel, *Die Normalität des Verbrechens* (Berlin: Hentrich, 1994) 325–85.

Y. Arad, 'The Holocaust and Soviet Jewry in the Occupied Territories of the Soviet Union', *Yad Vashem Studies*, XXI (1991) 1–47.

Y. Arad, 'Peculiarities of the Holocaust in the Occupied Territories of the USSR', in *Shadow of the Holocaust: Second International Symposium "Lessons of the Holocaust and Contemporary Russia"*, Moscow, 4–7 May 1997 (Moscow: The Russian Holocaust Library, 1998) 254–62.

Y. Arad, S. Krakowski and S. Spector (eds), *The Einsatzgruppen Reports*. Translated by Stella Schossberger (New York: Holocaust Library, 1989).

J.A. Armstrong (ed.), *Soviet Partisans in WWII* (Madison: University of Wisconsin Press, 1964).

J.A. Armstrong, *Ukrainian Nationalism* (Eaglewood, Colorado: Ukrainian Academic Press, 1990).

I. Aron, *Fallen Leaves: Stories of the Holocaust and the Partisans* (New York: Shengold, 1981).

C. Ashman and R.J. Wagman, *The Nazi Hunters* (New York: Warner Books, 1988).

J. Barber, 'Popular reactions in Moscow to the German invasion of June 22, 1941', in J. L. Wieczynski (ed.), *Operation Barbarossa: The German Attack on the Soviet Union June 22, 1941* (Salt Lake City: Charles, Schlacks, Jr, 1993).

O. Bartov, *The Eastern Front, 1941–45. German Troops and the Barbarization of Warfare* (New York: St Martin's, 1986).

Z. Bauman, *Modernity and the Holocaust* (New York: Cornell University Press, 1989).

M. Beer, '*Die Entwicklung der Gaswagen beim Mord an den Juden*', *Vierteljahreshefte für Zeitgeschichte* 35 (1987) 403–17.

K.C. Berkhoff, 'Ukraine under Nazi Rule (1941–44): Sources and Finding Aids, Part II Published Materials', *Jahrbücher für Geschichte Osteuropas* 45 (1997) H.2, 273–309.

R.B. Birn, *Die Höheren SS- und Polizeiführer: Himmlers Vertreter im Reich und in den besetzten Gebieten* (Düsseldorf: Droste, 1986).

R.B. Birn, '*Zweierlei Wirklichkeit? Fallbeispiele zur Partisanenbekämpfung im Osten*', in B. Wegner (ed.), *Zwei Wege nach Moskau: Vom Hitler-Stalin-Pakt zum 'Unternehmen Barbarossa'* (Munich: R. Piper, 1991) 275–90.

R.B. Birn and V. Riess, 'Revising the Holocaust', *The Historical Journal*, Vol. 40/I (March 1997) 195–216.

J. Boyarin and J. Kugelmass (eds), *From a Ruined Garden: The Memorial Books of Polish Jewry* (New York: Schocken, 1983).

K.D. Bracher, *The German Dictatorship* (London: Peregrine, 1978).

R. Breitmann, *The Architect of Genocide: Himmler and the Final Solution* (New York: Knopf, 1991).

C. Browning, *Fateful Months: Essays on the Emergence of the Final Solution*, revised edn (New York: Holmes & Meier, 1991).

C. Browning, *Ordinary Men: Reserve Police Battalion 101 and the Final Solution in Poland* (New York: HarperCollins, 1992).

C. Browning, *The Path to Genocide: Essays on Launching the Final Solution*, Reprint (New York: Cambridge University Press, 1993).

C. Browning, 'Hitler and the euphoria of victory: the path to the Final Solution', in D. Cesarani (ed.), *The Final Solution: Origins and Implementation* (London and New York: Routledge, 1994) 137–47.

Y. Büchler, '*Kommandostab RFSS*: Himmler's Personal Murder Brigades in 1941', *Holocaust and Gendocide Studies, I/1* (1986) 11–26.

D. Cesarani, *Justice Delayed: How Britain became a Refuge for Nazi War Criminals* (London: Mandarin, 1992).

B. Chiari, '*Die Büchse der Pandora. Ein Dorf in Weißrußland 1939 bis 1944*', unpublished manuscript article.

B. Chiari, '*Deutsche Herrschaft in Weißrußland 1941–44*', Dissertation zur Erlangung des akademischen Grades Doktor der Philosophie in der Geschichtswissenschaftlichen Fakultät der Eberhard-Karls-Universität zu Tübingen vorgelegt, 1997.

B. Chiari, '*Deutsche Zivilverwaltung in Weißrußland 1941–44. Die lokale Perspektive der Besatzungsgeschichte*', *Militärgeschichtliche Mitteilungen*, 52 (1993), Heft 1.

S. Cholawsky, *The Jews of Bielorussia during World War II* (Amsterdam: Harwood Academic Publishers, 1998).

M. Cooper, *The Nazi War against Soviet Partisans, 1941–44* (New York: Stein & Day, 1979).

A. Dallin, *German Rule in Russia, 1941–45. A Study in Occupation Policies*, 2nd edn (London: Macmillan, 1981).

A. Dallin, 'Stalin and the German Invasion', in J. L. Wieczynski (ed.), *Operation Barbarossa: The German Attack on the Soviet Union June 22, 1941* (Salt Lake City: Charles, Schlacks, Jr, 1993).

M.C. Dean, 'The German *Gendarmerie*, the Ukrainian *Schutzmannschaft* and the "Second Wave" of Jewish Killings in Occupied Ukraine: German Policing at the Local Level in the Zhitomir Region, 1941–44', *German History*, Vol. 14, No. 2 (1996) 168–92.

L. Dinnerstein, *America and the Survivors of the Holocaust* (New York: Columbia University Press, 1982).

F. Dorn and K. Heuer (eds), *'Ich war immer gut zu meiner Russin': Zur Struktur und Praxis des Zwangsarbeitssystems im Zweiten Weltkrieg in der Region Südhessen* (Pfaffenweiler: Centaurus, 1991).

L. Eckmann and C. Lazar, *The Jewish Resistance. The History of the Jewish Partisans in Lithuania and White Russia during the Nazi Occupation 1940–45* (New York: Shengold, 1977).

Encyclopaedia Judaica (Jerusalem: Keter, 1972).

Encyclopaedia of the Holocaust (New York: Macmillan, 1990).

O. Figes, *A People's Tragedy: the Russian Revolution 1891–1924* (London: Jonathan Cape, 1996).

G. Fleming, *Hitler and the Final Solution* (Oxford: Oxford University Press, 1986).

J. Förster, *'Das Unternehmen "Barbarossa" als Eroberungs- und Vernichtungskrieg'*, in MGFA (ed.), *Das Deutsche Reich und der Zweite Weltkrieg. Bd. 4, Der Angriff auf die Sowjetunion* (Stuttgart: Deutsche Verlags-Anstalt, 1987) 413–47.

A. Galinski, 'The extermination of the Polish intelligentsia in the summer of 1942 in the Novogrodek area (problems of investigation)', pp. 185–98. Article in Polish received from Mr Galinski at the Lodz branch of the Polish Main Commission in 1993.

C. Gerlach, *'Die Einsatzgruppe B 1941/42'*, in P. Klein (ed.), *Die Einsatzgruppen in der besetzten Sowjetunion 1941/42* (Berlin: Hentrich, 1997).

C. Gerlach, *'Die Wannsee-Konferenz, das Schicksal der deutschen Juden und Hitlers politische Grundsatzentscheidung, alle Juden Europas zu ermorden'*, *Werkstattgeschichte* 18 (1997) 7–44.

C. Gerlach, *'Deutsche Wirtschaftsinteressen, Besatzungspolitik und der Mord an den Juden in Weißrußland 1941–43'*, in U. Herbert (ed.), *Nationalsozialistische Vernichtungspolitik 1939–1945: Neue Forschungen und Kontroversen* (Frankfurt am Main: Fischer, 1998).

M. Gilbert, *The Holocaust: The Jewish Tragedy* (Glasgow: Fontana/Collins, 1989).

M. Gilbert, *Israel: A History* (London: Transworld, 1998).

F. Golczewski, *'Entgegen dem Klischee: Die Rettung von verfolgten Juden im Zweiten Weltkrieg durch Ukrainer'*, in W. Benz and J. Wetzel (eds), *Solidarität und Hilfe für Juden während der NS-Zeit Bd. II* (Berlin, Metropol, 1998).

F. Golczewski, *'Organe der deutschen Besatzungsmacht: die ukrainischen Schutzmannschaften'*, in W. Benz, J. Houwink ten Cate and G. Otto (eds), *Die Bürokratie der Okkupation: Strukturen der Herrschaft und Verwaltung im besetzten Europa* (Berlin: Metropol, 1998).

D. J. Goldhagen, *Hitler's Willing Executioners: Ordinary Germans and the Holocaust* (New York: Alfred A. Knopf, 1996).

H. Grabitz, *'Iwan Demjanjuk zum Tode verurteilt. Anmerkungen zur strafrechtlichen Verantwortung der "Trawnikis"'*, *Tribüne* 27 H. 108 (1988) 176–82.

J. T. Gross, 'The Jewish Community in the Soviet-Annexed Territories on the Eve of the Holocaust', in L. Dobroszycki and J. S. Gurock (eds), *The Holocaust in the Soviet Union. Studies and Sources on the Destruction of the Jews in the Nazi-Occupied Territories of the USSR, 1941–45* (Armonk, New York: M. E. Sharpe, 1993).

J. T. Gross, *Polish Society under German Occupation. The Generalgouvernement, 1939– 44* (Princeton, NJ: Princeton University Press, 1979).

J. T. Gross, *Revolution from Abroad. The Soviet Conquest of Poland's Western Ukraine and Western Byelorussia* (Princeton, NJ: Princeton University Press, 1988).

J. T. Gross, 'Polish POW Camps in the Soviet-Occupied Western Ukraine', in K. Sword (ed.), *The Soviet Takeover of the Polish Eastern Provinces, 1939–41* (London: Macmillan, 1991).

R. Headland, *Messages of Murder. A Study of the Reports of the Einsatzgruppen of the Security Police and the Security Service, 1941* (London: Associated University Presses, 1992).

H. Heer, 'Killing Fields: *Die Wehrmacht und der Holocaust*', in H. Heer and K. Naumann (eds), *Vernichtungskrieg: Verbrechen der Wehrmacht 1941 bis 1944* (Hamburg: HIS Verlagsges., 1995) 57–77.

U. Herbert, *Fremdarbeiter: Politik und Praxis des 'Ausländer-Einsatzes' in der Kriegswirtschaft des Dritten Reiches* (Berlin: J. H. W. Dietz, 1986).

R. E. Herzstein, *The War that Hitler Won: The Most Infamous Propaganda Campaign in History* (New York: Putnam, 1978).

R. Hilberg, *The Destruction of the European Jews*, revised edn, 3 vols (New York: Holmes & Meier, 1985).

P. Hoffmann, *Hitler's Personal Security* (London: Macmillan, 1979).

E. M. Howell, *The Soviet Partisan Movement 1941–44* (Washington DC: US Army Dept 1956).

D. K. Huneke, *The Moses of Rovno* (New York: Dodd, Mead, 1985).

M. Iwanow, 'The Byelorussians of Eastern Poland under Soviet Occupation, 1939– 41', in K. Sword (ed.), *The Soviet Takeover of the Polish Eastern Provinces, 1939–41* (London: Macmillan, 1991).

G. Jukes, *Hitler's Stalingrad Decisions* (Berkeley: University of California, 1985).

J. Kipp, 'Barbarossa and the crisis of successive operations: the Smolensk engagements, July 10–August 7, 1941', in J. L. Wieczynski (ed.), *Operation Barbarossa: The German Attack on the Soviet Union June 22, 1941* (Salt Lake City: Charles, Schlacks, Jr, 1993).

P. Kohl, '*Ich wundere mich, daß ich noch lebe*' (Gütersloh: Gerd Mohn, 1990).

W. Kosyk, *The Third Reich and Ukraine* (New York: Peter Lang, 1993).

H. Krausnick and H.-H. Wilhelm, *Die Truppe des Weltanschauungskrieges. Die Einsatzgruppen der Sicherheitspolizei und des SD, 1938–42* (Frankfurt: Fischer, 1985).

G. A. Kumanev, 'The USSR's degree of readiness and the suddenness of the Nazi attack', in J. L. Wieczynski (ed.), *Operation Barbarossa: The German Attack on the Soviet Union June 22, 1941* (Salt Lake City: Charles, Schlacks, Jr, 1993).

D. Levin, 'The Fateful Decision: The Flight of the Jews into the Soviet Interior in the summer of 1941', *Yad Vashem Studies*, XX (1990) 115–42.

Y. Litvak, 'The plight of refugees from the German-occupied territories', in K. Sword (ed.), *The Soviet Takeover of the Polish Eastern Provinces, 1939–41* (London: Macmillan, 1991).

P. Longerich, '*Vom Massenmord zur Endlösung. Die Erschießungen von jüdischen Zivilisten in den ersten Monaten des Ostfeldzuges im Kontext des nationalsozialistischen Massenmordes*', in B. Wegner (ed.), *Zwei Wege nach Moskau* (Munich: Piper, 1991) 251–74.

C. Madajczyk, *Die Okkupationspolitik Nazideutschlands in Polen 1939–45* (Berlin: Akademie-Verlag, 1987).

D. R. Marples, 'The Ukrainians in Eastern Poland under Soviet Occupation, 1939–41: A study in Soviet rural policy', in K. Sword (ed.), *The Soviet Takeover of the Polish Eastern Provinces, 1939–41* (London: Macmillan, 1991).

J. Matthäus, ''*Reibungslos und planmäßig*'': *Die zweite Welle der Judenvernichtung im Generalkommissariat Weißruthenien (1942–44)'*, *Jahrbuch für Antisemitismusforschung* 4, 254–74.

MGFA (ed.), *Das Deutsche Reich und der zweite Weltkrieg*, Bd. *4 Der Angriff auf die Sowjetunion* (Stuttgart: Deutsche Verlags-Anstalt, 1987).

W. Moskoff, *The Bread of Affliction: The Food Supply in the USSR During World War II* (Cambridge: Cambridge University Press, 1990).

T. P. Mulligan, *The Politics of Illusion and Empire: German Occupation Policy in the Soviet Union, 1942–43* (New York: Praeger, 1988).

L. H. Nicholas, *The Rape of Europa: The Fate of Europe's Treasures in the Third Reich and the Second World War* (London: Macmillan, 1994).

R. Ogorreck, *Die Einsatzgruppen und die 'Genesis der Endlösung'* (Berlin: Metropol, 1996).

R. Overy, *Russia's War: Blood upon the Snow* (New York: TV Books, 1997).

A. Paul, *Katyn: The Untold Story of Stalin's Polish massacre* (New York: Macmillan, 1991).

B. Pinchuk, *Shtetl Jews under Soviet Rule: Eastern Poland on the Eve of the Holocaust* (Oxford: Basil Blackwell, 1990).

T. Piotrowski, *Poland's Holocaust: Ethnic Strife, Collaboration with Occupying Forces and Genocide in the Second Republic, 1918–47* (Jefferson, North Carolina: McFarland, 1998).

Z. Pivcova, '*Das Militärhistorische Archiv in Prag und seine deutschen Bestände*' in *Militärgeschichtliche Mitteilungen*, 52 (1993) Heft 2, 429–35.

D. Pohl, *Von der 'Judenpolitik' zum Judenmord: Der Distrikt Lublin des Generalgouvernements 1939–44* (Frankfurt am Main: Peter Lang, 1993).

D. Pohl, *Nationalsozialistische Judenverfolgung in Ostgalizien 1941–44* (Munich: Oldenbourg, 1996).

D. Pohl, '*Die Einsatzgruppe C 1941/42*', in P. Klein (ed.), *Die Einsatzgruppen in der besetzten Sowjetunion 1941/42* (Berlin: Hentrich, 1997).

T. Richmond, *Konin: A Quest* (London: Jonathan Cape, 1995).

G. Robel, '*Sowjetunion*', in W. Benz (ed.), *Dimension des Völkermords: Die Zahl der jüdischen Opfer des Nationalsozialismus* (Munich: Oldenbourg, 1991) 499–560.

D. Romanovsky, 'Nazi Occupation in Northeastern Belarus and Western Russia', in Z. Gitelman (ed.), *Bitter Legacy: Confronting the Holocaust in the USSR* (Bloomington and Indianapolis: Indiana University Press, 1997).

T. Sandkühler, '*Endlösung' in Galizien: Der Judenmord in Ostpolen und die Rettungsinitiativen von Berthold Beitz 1941–44* (Kempton: J. H. W. Dietz, 1996).

W. Scheffler, '*Die Einsatzgruppe A*', in P. Klein (ed.), *Die Einsatzgruppen in der besetzten Sowjetunion 1941/42* (Berlin: Hentrich, 1997).

J. Schlootz (ed.), *Deutsche Propaganda in Weißrußland: Eine Konfrontation von Propaganda und Wirklichkeit. Ausstellung in Berlin und Minsk* (Berlin: Freie Universität, 1996).

T. Schulte, *The German Army and Nazi Policies in Occupied Russia* (Oxford: Oxford University Press, 1989).

K. Segbers, *Die Sowjetunion im Zweiten Weltkrieg: Die Mobilisierung von Verwaltung, Wirtschaft und Gesellschaft im 'Großen Vaterländischen Krieg' 1941–43* (Munich: Oldenbourg, 1987).

W. A. Serczyk, '*Die sowjetische und die ''polnische'' Ukraine zwischen den Weltkriegen*' in F. Golczewski (ed.), *Geschichte der Ukraine* (Göttingen: Vandenhoeck & Ruprecht, 1993).

K.-J. Siegfried, *Das Leben der Zwangsarbeiter im Volkswagenwerk 1939–45* (New York: Campus, 1988).

Z. S. Siemaszko, 'The mass deportations of the Polish population to the USSR, 1940–1941', in K. Sword (ed.), *The Soviet Takeover of the Polish Eastern Provinces, 1939–41* (London: Macmillan, 1991) 217–35.

A. Skrzypek, '*Die polnische Minderheitenpolitik im Wilnagebiet (1916–1939)*', *Nordost-Archiv*, II (1993) H. 2.

L. Smilovitsky, 'Righteous Gentiles, the Partisans, and Jewish Survival in Belorussia, 1941–1944', *Holocaust and Genocide Studies*, Vol. 11, No. 3 (Winter 1997) 301–29.

B. V. Sokolov, 'The Cost of War: Human Losses for the USSR and Germany, 1939–45', *The Journal of Slavic Military Studies*, Vol. 9, No. 1 (March 1996) 152–93.

S. Spector, 'The Jews of Volhynia and the Reaction to Extermination', *Yad Vashem Studies* (1983) 159–86.

S. Spector, *The Holocaust of Volhynian Jews, 1941–44* (Jerusalem: Achva Press, 1990).

K. Stang, *Kollaboration und Massenmord: Die litauische Hilfspolizei, das Rollkommando Hamann und die Ermordung der litauischen Juden* (Frankfurt and Main: Peter Lang, 1996).

J. Steinberg, 'The Third Reich Reflected: German Civil Administration in the Occupied Soviet Union, 1941–4', *The English Historical Review*, CX, No. 437 (June 1995) 620–51.

C. Streit, *Keine Kameraden. Die Wehrmacht und die sowjetischen Kriegsgefangenen, 1941–45* (Stuttgart: Deutsche Verlags-Anstalt, 1978).

C. Streit, '*Die Behandlung der sowjetischen Kriegsgefangenen und völkerrechtliche Probleme des Kriegs gegen die Sowjetunion*', in W. Wette and G. R. Überschär (eds), *Der deutsche Überfall auf die Sowjetunion* (Frankfurt am Main: Fischer, 1991) 159–83.

C. Streit, 'Partisans – Resistance – Prisoners of War', in J. L. Wieczynski (ed.), *Operation Barbarossa: The German Attack on the Soviet Union June 22, 1941* (Salt Lake City: Charles, Schlacks, Jr, 1993) 260–75.

Y. Suhl (ed.), *They Fought Back: The Story of the Jewish Resistance in Nazi Europe* (New York: Schocken, 1975).

K. Sword, *Deportation and Exile: Poles in the Soviet Union, 1939–48* (London: Macmillan, 1994).

N. Tec, *Defiance: The Bielski Partisans, The Story of the Largest Armed Resistance by Jews during World War II* (Oxford: Oxford University Press, 1993).

N. Tec, *In the Lion's Den: The Life of Oswald Rufeisen* (Oxford: Oxford University Press, 1993).

M. Terles, *Ethnic Cleansing of Poles in Volhynia and Eastern Galicia, 1942–46* (Toronto: Alliance of the Polish Eastern Provinces, 1993).

I. Trunk, *Judenrat: the Jewish Councils in Eastern Europe, 1918–45* (New York: Stein & Day, 1977).

N. P. Vakar, *Belorussia: The Making of a Nation* (Cambridge, Mass.: Harvard University Press, 1956).

W. Wette and G. R. überschär (eds), *Der deutsche Überfall auf die Sowjetunion: 'Unternehmen Barbarossa' 1941* (Frankfurt am Main: Fischer, 1991).

S. Wiesenthal, *Every Day, Remembrance Day: A Chronicle of Jewish Martyrdom* (New York: Henry Holt, 1987).

W. Wilenchik, '*Die Partisanenbewegung im Weißrußland, 1941–44*', *Forschungen zur Osteuropäischen Geschichte*, 34 (1984) 129–297.

H.-H. Wilhelm, *Rassenpolitik und Kriegführung: Sicherheitspolizei und Wehrmacht in Polen und der Sowjetunion* (Passau: Wissenschaftsverl. Richard Rothe, 1991).

H.-H. Wilhelm, *Die Einsatzgruppe A der Sicherheitspolizei und des SD 1941/42* (Frankfurt am Main: Peter Lang, 1996).

H.-H. Wilhelm, 'Hitlers "Europäische Neuordnung" und deren "Lebende Objekte" auf dem Territorium der Sowjetunion 1941 bis 1944', in R. Bohn (ed.), *Die deutsche Herrschaft in den 'germanischen' Ländern 1944–45 HMRG-Beiheft* 26 (Stuttgart: Franz Steiner, 1997).

J. Winter and J-L. Robert (eds), *Capital Cities at War: London, Paris, Berlin, 1914–19* (Cambridge: Cambridge University Press, 1997).

D. Wolkogonow, *Stalin: Triumph und Tragödie* (Düsseldorf: Claassen, 1989).

M. Wyman, *DP: Europe's Displaced Persons, 1945–51* (Philadelphia: The Balch Institute Press, 1988).

O. A. Zarubinsky, 'The "Red" Partisan Movement in Ukraine during World War II: A Contemporary Assessment', *The Journal of Slavic Military Studies*, Vol. 9, No. 2 (June 1996) 399–416.

E. Ziemke, 'Composition and Morale of the Partisan Movement', in J. A. Armstrong (ed.), *Soviet Partisans in WWII* (Madison: University of Wisconsin Press, 1964).

Index